ANDRIA OWEN

CONNECTION OVER PERFECTION

The Power of Intentional Parenting with Love

Dedication

To Coach Robert Weiner, whose inspiration and generosity opened the doors to his exceptional football program, allowing me to serve and guide his athletes in mastering vital life skills over the past decade. You've helped me turn my passion into impact—my heartfelt thanks.

To my four incredible children, Tate, Reeves, Abby, and Scotty, whose boundless love and authentic "connection" have carried me through the peaks and valleys of parenthood, grounding me with humility and filling my days with joy. Your respect, love, and honesty have filled my life with purpose. You've taught me as much as I've ever hoped to teach you. Parenting you has been the greatest privilege and an ongoing lesson in growth, perseverance, and joy. I'm so grateful for all of you.

To my mom and dad—thank you for being the best parents I could have ever asked for. You led by example, with wisdom, grace, love, and forgiveness. Your steady presence and encouragement shaped the foundation of who I am. Without you, this book would not exist. I am forever grateful and thankful for you both.

And finally, to my wonderful husband, Dom, my unwavering rock, whose encouragement has fueled me to chase my dreams. Your patience is truly made of steel, and your support means everything to me. You've stood by me with quiet strength and constant love, even through the busiest and most trying seasons.

Table of Contents

INTRODUCTION

My Why

I was curious and maybe a bit apprehensive when I had a text from Head Coach Robert Weiner (winner of 4 State Championships), my three sons' football coach at Plant High School in Tampa, asking me to come to his office that afternoon after practice. Had one of my boys done something wrong? As it transpired, my sons weren't the reason for the coach wanting me to be there, but the meeting would change our lives in many ways.

The coach wanted my help for a boy on the team. His middle linebacker was a young man of tremendous talent but little interest in the classroom. James had said that he wanted to play in the NFL as his father had, but what he didn't realize was that to get to the NFL meant getting into college, and getting into college required that he had to graduate from high school first, and graduating from high school meant attending class and making good enough grades to graduate. Being the #1 top linebacker recruit in the nation, he certainly was college ball material, but he lacked the drive, vision, and self-discipline in the classroom needed to reach his goals. He had Division 1 football scholarship offers from most of the top schools, but he was academically ineligible for acceptance. All this Coach Weiner laid out before me.

"But what had I to do with this huge dilemma?" I wondered as I listened to Coach. I knew James well, as he was the middle linebacker on the team, with my boys flanking him on either side. He was fearless, engaging, easy to be around, and talented, of course, and my boys truly loved him like a brother. Seeing this camaraderie, Coach candidly asked if James could come home with my boys after practice each day in order that I could motivate him to take his academics seriously by attending class each day, doing his homework (and turning it in), and getting a vision of what it would take for him to realize his ultimate dream. And so, it began. James became a daily part of our household.

I have 4 children who are all very close in age, and adding James (and friend) to the mix that year, the ages of the kids in our household were 19, 18, 17, 16, 14, and 11. Although my immediate goal was to motivate James to WANT to take the initiative to be successful academically, it also made me take a close look at how my own children were performing. Were they using the life skills we had been teaching them to achieve their own success, or were they "flying by the seat of their pants," trying to make good grades and gain their much-sought-after sports positions? We all know that the latter would be short-lived until their competition became tougher, academically and athletically, as they grew older.

I realized that my kids needed to be more intentional about things like defining their values and what they were posting on social media. Believing that many teens may be in the same boat, I asked Coach Weiner if I could have a platform to teach the football team basic life skills. Fast-forward, for 10 years, every Monday, I taught them skills for success. The results were life-changing, and my desire grew to help as many kids as possible, so I developed 25 courses that over 500,000 youth have taken in schools across the country. TUF (Train Up First) Life Skills has been recognized as a "breakthrough" program by educators, and for the past few years, parents have requested access to my content through a book so they can give their children the same "toolkit" for success.

These courses have proven to have positively affected their relationships with their families and peers and have helped them make better choices in this ever-changing world. Through my book, I hope that you will have an opportunity to have open dialogue with your children at meaningful times: the dinner table, bedtime, or for those with a hectic schedule, in the car! I hope you will be inspired and that the outcome will be rewarding for both you and your children.

So, this is my "why." I love young people, and I want them to succeed by truly connecting with them and engaging their hearts, and as we all know, only true change can take place when the heart is engaged.

My inspiration for the title, "Connection Over Perfection":

If we prioritize connection over perfection, we raise young people who are confident, resilient, and willing to learn. They don't need to be perfect—they need to feel supported as they figure things out. And that's what truly prepares them for life.

While raising my four kids, I have found these incredible truths:

1. Trust Opens the Door to Learning

If my kids feel judged or pressured to be perfect, they'll shut down or resist. But when they feel understood and supported, they're more open to guidance. Connection with them builds trust, which makes them more likely to listen and engage.

2. Life Skills Are Learned Through Experience, Not Just Instruction

None of us masters communication, responsibility, or problem-solving overnight. Our kids need space to make mistakes and try again. When we have a strong connection with our children, it means they'll feel safe to fail, learn, and grow, without the fear of disappointing us. It's so important to let them fail when they are young. They will be confident knowing that they can overcome struggles and setbacks and have more "tools" in their life skills belt for the next time something doesn't go their way.

3. Perfection Creates Pressure, Connection Creates Confidence

When perfection is the goal, kids and teens feel like they can never measure up. That pressure leads to anxiety, avoidance, or, many times, dishonesty. Real life is messy! Life isn't perfect, so training kids for perfection sets them up for frustration and disappointment. Teaching them how to handle challenges, manage emotions, and keep going when things don't go as planned is far more valuable than making them "get it right" every time.

But when parents focus on connection, kids feel secure enough to take risks, ask questions, and keep trying. It's also important for our kids to see us make mistakes as well. Their little eyes are always watching how we handle things. Our actions (over words) can be very powerful.

4. Connected Kids Are More Motivated to Learn

Think about the teachers, coaches, or mentors who have impacted you the most. They probably weren't the ones who demanded perfection, but the ones who saw your potential and supported and encouraged you. Our kids will work more efficiently when they feel seen, heard, and valued. We live in a culture obsessed with productivity, where our worth is often measured by how much we can accomplish and how well we can accomplish things. It's easy to believe that our value is tied to what we do and how well we do it, but our value is actually who we are. We are not defined by our success. We are valued by God and created for a purpose.

5. Connection Keeps the Conversation Going

When our kids feel connected, they're more likely to come to us when they need help, rather than hiding struggles or pretending they have it all together. A connected relationship keeps the door open for ongoing learning and guidance. I used to tell my kids that we are all on the same team, supporting and encouraging each other. There has never been a team that wins 100% of the time. The good news is that we learn far more from our losses than our wins. This philosophy more or less "evens the playing field" for our kids to feel comfortable and confident, knowing we are all supporting each other through the good times and the hard times.

As you read through this book, you will see sample dialogues in each chapter showing real conversations as well as Table Talks at the end of each chapter.

Table Talk is a designated time for a parent and a child to connect while having discussions surrounding each topic covered. It's important to choose a time when your kids aren't rushed to have these conversations: at the breakfast table, in the car, at dinner time, before bed, etc. It's up to you! These questions can lead to great conversations and promote open communication where you can truly connect with your children. Let's go!

A great relationship with your kids is all about supporting, connecting, and guiding... not controlling.

Guide them to who they are meant to be!

PART 1

BUILDING YOUR BRAND

CHAPTER 1

You – The Brand

 **Goal: Define the term Brand as it relates to a company and then how Brand relates to a person; Introduce the concept that your personal brand is who you are, how people remember you, and what sets you apart from everyone else. Encourage your children to take a deep look at themselves and inspire them to be intentional about the decisions they make.**

Being Intentional About Your Child's Growth and Values

As parents of elementary-aged children, we are intentional about their playmates, diet, sleep habits, and daily routines. As they grow older, our focus shifts to their participation in sports, musical instruments, and extracurricular activities. However, in the busyness of life, we may overlook teaching them how to be intentional about who they want to become. How can we guide them to define their own values, enabling them to make good choices and achieve success in life?

When children understand their core values at a young age, decision-making becomes much easier. For instance, if children value hard work, they'll know how to prioritize when faced with the choice of skipping soccer practice to attend a friend's birthday party. Without clear values, they may waver, leading to stress and uncertainty. Knowing their values simplifies choices and reduces anxiety.

Through this book, you will be able to help your child discover their values, and at the same time, they will learn what you value as well. This mutual understanding can profoundly impact their lives—and yours.

Teaching Kids to Build Their Personal Brand

First of all, we all know that kids love talking about their favorite brands, whether it's their Jordans, Apple AirPods, or Chick-fil-A Restaurant, they are surrounded by brands 24/7. But they probably have never thought about themselves as a brand. Once they realize that they, too, can build their own brand, they think that's a pretty cool idea. It empowers them.

Teaching your child to be intentional about building their personal brand—or reputation—is an invaluable lesson. Their "personal brand" is the way others perceive them based on their actions, words, and attitudes. It shapes how they're treated, the opportunities they're offered, and the legacy they leave behind. Helping your child understand the importance of their personal brand will empower them to make choices that align with who they want to be.

Start by explaining that everyone has a reputation, whether they think about it or not. Their personal brand isn't about pretending to be someone they're not—it's about being their best self and letting their values shine through. Encourage them to think about how they want to be remembered. Are they someone who is kind, hardworking, and trustworthy? Or do they come across as careless, unreliable, or negative? Help them see that their actions, whether big or small, contribute to how others see them.

Teach them to be intentional with their choices. Remind them that words matter—whether spoken in person or shared online—and that how they treat others says a lot about their character. Encourage them to show respect, take responsibility for their mistakes, and follow through on their commitments. Even small acts, like helping a classmate, being on time, or showing gratitude, can build a positive personal brand over time.

Social media is another important area to address. Help your children understand that what they post online becomes part of their personal brand. Teach them to think before they share: Is this respectful? Does it align with who I want to be? Show them that a strong personal brand includes being mindful of how they represent themselves both in person and online.

Lastly, encourage your children to focus on consistency. Building a good reputation takes time and effort, but it's worth it. When they consistently act with integrity, kindness, and determination, people will know they can be trusted and relied on. Teach them that their personal brand is something they have the power to shape every day, and it will serve them well in school, friendships, and future opportunities.

This conversation is a win because it's less about the parent telling the teen what to do and more about guiding them to think for themselves. It's helping the teen build a foundation for self-awareness, responsibility, and intentionality—all while strengthening their bond with the parent. The teen walks away feeling motivated ("you've totally got this") rather than judged, which is a huge plus for their emotional and social growth.

The Power of First Impressions

 **Parent/Teen Dialogue Example:**

Parent: Hey, let's chat about something cool—brands. When you hear "brand," what pops into your head? Maybe a slick logo, a vibe-y name, or one of those ads you can't get out of your head? It's kind of hard to pin down because brands are literally everywhere. Those new Jordans you're rocking? Brand. Your AirPods blasting music? Brand. And here's the wild part—you're a brand too.

Teen: Wait, me? I don't have a logo or my own shoe line or anything!

Parent: Fair point! But think of it this way: your brand isn't about stuff—it's about *you*. It's who you are, what you care about, how people see you, and what makes you, well, *you*.

Teen: So, like... my reputation?

Parent: Boom, you nailed it! It's totally your reputation. Check this out—take Snapchat. You know that ghost logo? It's got a name: "Ghostface Chillah." Yeah, it's a nod to Ghostface Killah from Wu-Tang Clan.

Teen: No way, that's actually so cool you know that!

Parent: I know, right? But it's not just a cool ghost—it's about how snaps show up and then *poof*, they're gone. That's what a brand does—it tells a story. For you, your brand is your vibe, your actions, how you treat people, and what you stand for. It's awesome to build, but here's the catch: one messy move can mess it up fast.

Teen: Okay, so how do I even start making my brand?

Parent: Great question! Let's peek at social media—it's a huge piece of the puzzle. Pull up your Instagram real quick. Scroll through—every pic, comment, or story your friends post is them showing the world who they want to be. They're building their brands. But in real life? No filters, no edits. It's just you, in the moment, and that's what really shapes how people see you.

Teen: Yeah, real life hits different than Insta for sure.

Parent: Absolutely. That's why it's smart to pause before you hit "post." You can build a brand on purpose—one that pulls in the right friends, opens doors for college, or even impresses a future boss. Or you can just wing it, which can get dicey.

Teen: Yeah, I can see why thinking it through matters.

Parent: You're getting it! And it's not just online—everything counts. How you talk, how you treat people, how you handle the tough stuff—that's all your brand too.

Teen: Thanks for explaining it like that, Mom. I kinda wanna be more on purpose with how I come across.

Parent: Love that energy! It takes some work and sticking with it, but you've totally got this. You know I'm always here to back you up.

First impressions matter—they're difficult to change. When people observe your attitude, values, work ethic, and self-control, they decide whether they want to engage with you. As one actor famously said, "It's not what people say about you—it's what they whisper."

Teaching your child about the power of first impressions is an important life lesson that will help them succeed in relationships, school, and eventually their career. A first impression happens in just a few seconds, and during that time, people make judgments—fair or not—based on how someone looks, acts, and speaks. Helping your child understand how to make a positive first impression will give them the tools to start any interaction on the right foot.

Start by explaining that first impressions are like the opening scene of a movie. If the beginning catches your attention, you're more likely to stay engaged and interested. In the same way, when they meet someone new, their appearance, body language, and attitude all set the tone for how they'll be remembered. This doesn't mean they have to be perfect, but it does mean putting effort into how they present themselves.

Teach them a few simple ways to make a great first impression. A warm smile is one of the easiest ways to show kindness and confidence. Making eye contact shows they're paying attention and interested in the other person. Encourage them to practice a firm but friendly handshake (or greeting) and to introduce themselves clearly. These small gestures can go a long way in making others feel valued and respected.

It's also important to talk about the role of appearance. While true character matters most, people often judge based on what they see first. Help your child understand that dressing appropriately for the situation, keeping clean, and showing good posture communicate that they take themselves and others seriously.

Finally, remind your child that first impressions aren't just about looking good—they're about showing who they really are. A genuine attitude of respect, kindness, and confidence will leave a lasting positive impression far beyond that first moment. Encourage them to think about first impressions not as pressure but as an opportunity to make a great start. Whether they're meeting a teacher, coach, or new friend, these skills will help them stand out in the best way possible.

To Rebrand or Not to Rebrand?

Sometimes, we need to tweak our personal brand. Rebranding isn't about losing yourself or fixing something broken. It's about preserving the good, eliminating the bad, and enhancing the great.

Many famous people have rebranded:

- **Apple** transformed its image in the 1990s under Steve Jobs, creating innovative products and redefining its reputation.
- **Robert Downey Jr.** overcame personal struggles to become one of Hollywood's most respected actors.
- **Taylor Swift** shifted from country music to pop stardom, reaching new heights.
- **Derek Jeter** consistently refined his brand, maintaining his stellar reputation.

Rebranding requires effort, determination, and a desire to be better. The question is: Are you— and your kids—ready to embrace it?

The Bottom Line: Being intentional about building and refining your personal brand can lead to a more fulfilling, successful life. Encourage your children to start now—they have the power to shape how the world sees them, one thoughtful decision at a time.

Rebranding: A Fresh Start

In my experience writing 25 life skills courses for schools nationwide, one lesson consistently stood out: branding. Teachers often shared feedback about how impactful the lesson was, but they also noted a common question from students afterward: *"How do I rebrand myself?"*

Initially, I hadn't written a rebranding lesson, but the demand was clear. So, here it is—a guide to help kids change the way they are perceived, starting from the inside out.

Rebranding is for everyone. It isn't just about fixing a bad reputation. It's about keeping the good, letting go of the bad, and improving the rest. Even the most successful people and companies have rebranded to stay aligned with their values and goals.

The lesson here is clear: Rebranding is possible for anyone willing to work for it.

Encourage your child to take the first step in their rebranding journey by focusing on small, consistent changes. Whether it's building confidence, improving social skills, or excelling academically, remind them that the effort they put in today will shape how the world sees them tomorrow.

Rebranding isn't about perfection—it's about progress. With passion, motivation, and determination, they can create a brand they're proud of.

Ask the Big Question

Ask your child: *"Are you happy with your brand?"*

They may feel content with who they are and how they're perceived. But for others, they may feel dissatisfied—perhaps they have a reputation they'd like to leave behind or an image they're eager to improve. The thought of rebranding can feel overwhelming: *"How do I change how people see me?"*

Good news! Changing your personal brand is possible.

Rebranding from the Inside Out

Rebranding starts with a commitment to change and a realistic plan. It won't happen overnight, and it requires daily effort. Your encouragement as a parent is vital in helping them stay motivated.

Even companies that spend millions on rebranding face challenges, but with persistence, the results can be transformative. Here's how your child can begin rebranding themselves from the inside out:

1. Character Traits: Start with Self-Reflection

Take a "character inventory." Identify traits that define who you are and decide which ones you want to improve.

2. Friendships: Evaluate Relationships

Who are your friends? Are they supportive and aligned with the person you want to become?

3. Outward Appearance

What does the way you present yourself say about you?

Point #1: Character Traits and Practical Strategies

I had a student that I was working with who was extremely shy, and so she was portrayed by her peers as being unfriendly. She began to lack confidence in herself, and her grades started failing.

We sat down together to develop some strategies to help her "rebrand".

- **Confidence:**
  I am shy and want to build confidence:
  - ○ Join a club or volunteer for a cause I care about.
  - ○ Practice good posture.
  - ○ Spend time doing activities I excel in.
  - ○ Branch out of my comfort zone to meet new people.

- **Friendliness:**
  I want to be more approachable:
  - ○ Smile and maintain a positive attitude. Make eye contact.
  - ○ Compliment others and avoid gossip.
  - ○ Ask friends thoughtful questions and listen actively.

- **Academic Success:**
  I want to perform better in school:
  - ○ Complete my homework on time and don't be afraid to ask for help.
  - ○ Sit at the front of the classroom and participate.
  - ○ Communicate better with my teachers.

Her results were successful! Of course, this didn't happen overnight, but she was disciplined enough to practice these strategies consistently with encouragement and accountability from several of her mentors.

I encourage you to sit down with your child and go over the list below. There may be some specific strategies that really resonate, or please feel free to add your own!

Character Traits and Strategies

Sense of Humor

1. Use humor to laugh at yourself. Don't take yourself so seriously. This tells people that you're confident.
2. Use humor to build others up. Memorize a good joke so you can share when the time is right!
3. When teased, don't be too sensitive. Be a good sport and laugh it off.

Teamwork

1. There's no letter "I" in the word team. Realize that the project or game is not all about you. TEAM effort!
2. Put others first and be an encourager.
3. Understand that everyone has different roles that are equally important.

Self-Control

1. Commit to a good plan BEFORE you are in a tempting situation.
2. Use your MIND over your EMOTIONS.
3. Choose a trusted friend who will help you stay on track.

Forgiving

1. Don't hold a grudge! It's actually bad for your health! It can affect you physically and emotionally.
2. Think of the times when you hurt others, and you were forgiven.
3. Don't think about the situation over and over again. Move on!

Perseverance

1. Identify things that distract you and focus on giving your best from start to finish.
2. Challenge yourself to finish every task.
3. Learn that procrastinating is your enemy.

Compassion

1. Use kind words to encourage others when they are feeling down.
2. Be sensitive to other people's feelings and try to put yourself in their shoes.
3. Volunteer to help someone in need.

Gratitude

1. Before you go to bed, take time to think about the positive things that happened throughout your day.
2. Make a list of the things that you are grateful for and look at them regularly. Take a picture of them with your phone.
3. Make it a habit to ALWAYS thank others who have helped you.

Social Skills

1. Realize that most people aren't thinking about you. They are thinking about themselves, so you can relax.
2. Talk to people about things that THEY are interested in talking about. Ask them lots of questions and be a good listener.
3. Answer their questions with follow-up questions. Ex., *"Did you enjoy the new Star Wars movie?" "Yes, I thought it was great! What did YOU think about it?"*

Humility

1. Don't brag and talk about yourself.
2. Don't overrate your abilities and achievements.
3. Give other people compliments to lift them up and make them feel good.

Open-Mindedness

1. Take a deep breath and be willing to listen to others' opinions.
2. Understand that it's not being weak to change your mind.
3. Put yourself in someone else's shoes and challenge yourself to understand where they are coming from.

Once you have gone over this list with your child, I recommend printing the character trait(s) that he/she wants to work on and putting them in a place that will be seen on a regular basis as a reminder. This exercise could also be a good activity for the entire family, parents included!

Point #2: Friendships – Healthy or Toxic?

Friendships play a huge role in shaping who we are. Unfortunately, some friendships can drag us down instead of lifting us up. It's crucial for your kids to evaluate their friendships and determine which ones have a positive influence and which ones are negative. When rebranding themselves, they should ensure their friends align with the new identity and goals they're striving for.

Surrounding themselves with the right people is essential to reaching their full potential. There's a popular saying: *"You become like the five people you spend the most time with."* This is why choosing friends wisely is so important. While many kids believe they can handle toxic friendships without being affected, this is rarely true. Toxic relationships often have a subtle but powerful negative impact over time.

What Are Toxic Friendships?

Toxic friendships bring out negative behaviors and emotions, causing stress, frustration, and exhaustion. They can prevent kids from achieving their best. Let's explore the different types of toxic friends:

1. **Drama-Seekers**
   These friends thrive on constant drama. They're always in conflicts, stirring up trouble, or surrounded by chaotic situations.

2. **Bad Influences**

   These friends encourage poor choices. They might say things like, *"Don't be a wimp; no one will find out!"*

3. **Takers**

   These friends constantly ask for favors but rarely give back. They dominate conversations and focus only on their needs.

4. **The Downers**

   These friends never offer compliments or encouragement. Instead, they criticize, complain, and drag others down with their negativity.

5. **Competitors**

   These friends always want to outdo you. They dislike seeing you succeed and strive to have or do better than you in everything.

6. **Copycats**

   These friends mimic your behavior, style, or choices to an extreme degree, which can feel invasive and unsettling.

7. **The Needy**

   These friends demand excessive attention, calling or texting constantly, and not respecting boundaries.

8. **Jealous Friends**

   These friends are possessive and often badmouth others to monopolize your time and isolate you.

9. **Guilt-Trippers**

   These friends manipulate you with sob stories, making you feel responsible for their well-being and pressuring you to prioritize them.

10. **Backstabbers**

    These friends pretend to be supportive but talk behind your back and spread rumors.

11. **Arguers and Fighters**

    These friends constantly argue over small things, making it hard to get along.

Taking a "Friend Inventory"

Now, encourage your kids to reflect on their current friendships. You may need to assist with some questions that may help them identify any toxic relationships.

Questions About the Friend's Behavior

1. How does this friend make you feel when you spend time with them?
2. Does this friend support your goals, or do they try to distract you from things that matter to you?
3. Have you noticed this friend frequently lying, breaking promises, or acting differently around others?
4. Does this friend encourage or pressure you to do things you're uncomfortable with?

Questions About the Dynamics of the Friendship

1. Do you feel like the friendship is balanced, or does one of you put in most of the effort?
2. Can you trust this friend with personal information, or do you worry they might share it with others?
3. When you have a disagreement, does this friend respect your feelings, or do they get defensive or dismissive?
4. Do you feel like you can be yourself, or do you feel like you need to act a certain way to fit in?

Questions About Your Child's Feelings

1. Do you feel drained, anxious, or stressed after spending time with this friend?
2. Do you feel like you have to constantly prove your worth/value to this person?
3. Do you feel supported when you're upset, or does this friend make it about themselves?
4. Does this friend build your confidence or make you doubt yourself?

Encouraging Reflection

1. What would you say to someone else who was describing a friendship like this?
2. Do you feel like this friendship helps you grow into the person you want to be?
3. Are there other friends who make you feel safer, happier, or more understood?
4. How do you think this friendship might affect you in the long term?

These questions can gently guide your child to reflect on their relationships without feeling judged or pressured. Encourage open-ended discussions and remind them that it's okay to set boundaries or step away from a friendship that isn't healthy.

Once they have identified an unhealthy friendship, they might ask: *"How do I handle these negative influences?"*

Here are 3 approaches for your kids to consider:

OPTION 1:

If you think that there is a possibility of change, the best thing to do is...

TALK to your friend and be honest. He or she might not even realize how they're acting and how they're making you feel. Be truthful, and then give it some time. Maybe your friend is going through a difficult time and was just taking it out on you. But, if things don't change, you can slowly take a step back from the friendship, which means you might start spending less time with them...and hopefully, they'll come around.

OPTION 2:

If there's no hope for change and they're bringing you down fast, cut them off immediately and completely. This may seem hard to do, and it is, but use your self-control to be cool ...maintain radio silence... and limit yourself to one-word responses if communicating is necessary. Sometimes you may even have to unfollow or even block them from social media if it gets to that point.

OPTION 3:

Making new friends should always be an option! You can never have enough great people in your life who support you and have the same values as you do. Check out a new club at school, take up a new hobby, learn a new sport, or join a youth group where you can meet new people. It may seem awkward at first, but remember that most of the friends you have now were strangers at one point, right?

The bottom line is that you only control YOU... your attitude, work ethic, self-control, and values. You can't control or change the brand of others. And no one should be allowed to change or control your brand.

Hold on tight to the good friends in your life because they are truly valuable.

Toxic friends hold us back. Releasing them opens space for healthier relationships. Encourage your kids to seek out new, supportive friends. It may take time, but it's worth it.

What to Look for in Positive Friendships

Healthy friendships help your child become the best version of themselves. Great friends are:

1. **Positive** – Focus on the good in life.
2. **Supportive** – Stand by you through highs and lows.
3. **Encouraging** – Motivate you to make good choices.
4. **Trustworthy** – Keep your secrets safe.
5. **Unselfish** – Care about you without selfish motives.
6. **Moral** – Uphold strong values.
7. **Sincere** – Act honestly and genuinely.
8. **Reliable** – Show up and follow through.
9. **Considerate** – Respect your feelings and needs.
10. **A Good Influence** – Inspire you to grow and thrive.

Now is a good time for your kids to identify the positive/healthy relationships in their lives. A good reminder: *"You become like the people you surround yourself with.*" Choosing positive friends helps cultivate those qualities within oneself.

Ask your child: *"Now that you have identified both healthy and unhealthy friendships, what type of friend do you feel like you are? And what type of friend would your friends say you are?"*

Once again, this exercise is a great activity for all of us.

Point #3: Outward Appearance

While it's ideal not to judge a book by its cover, appearance often creates first impressions. Encourage your child to consider what their outward image conveys about them, including:

- Hairstyle
- Clothing style
- Piercings or tattoos
- Posture
- Cleanliness
- Grooming (e.g., nails, hygiene)
- Language and tone

This is a great opportunity to guide your children in intentionally shaping their personal brand. Help them set realistic goals for their appearance that align with their desired self-image. Remember, personal growth is an ongoing process, and they will continue rebranding throughout life.

Lastly, ask your kids how you can support them without overstepping. Being a source of encouragement while allowing them independence is key to their growth.

 **Action Steps:**

Action Step #1: List three changes you can make to improve your brand today.

Action Step #2: What obstacles might get in the way of achieving your goal, and how can you overcome them?

Action Step #3: Who can you ask for help in achieving your goal? It's very important to tell someone your goals to help keep you accountable.

Action Step #4: Spend time TODAY looking at your social media accounts to see what story they tell about you and your brand. Are they saying the right things about you? Think about the changes you may need to make, and then get after it! Today is ALWAYS a perfect day to start rebranding yourself.

Activity #1: Have the child complete the Snowflake "Values" Diagram and share.

Let's begin to define YOUR Brand

Look at the Snowflake Diagram. Be honest with yourself and fill in the shapes with words that describe who you are, the things you like, and the things you value.

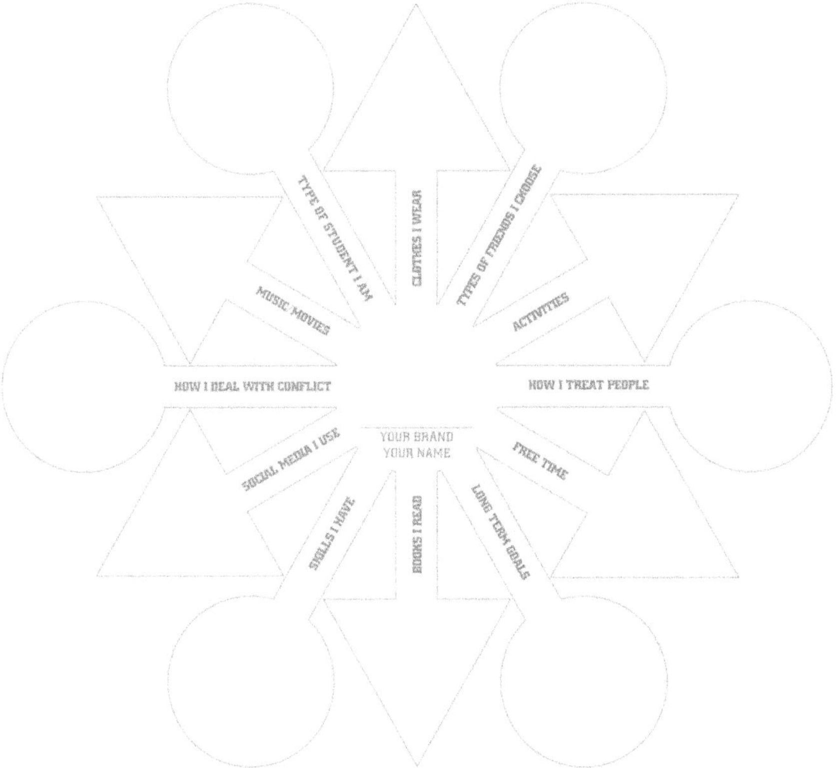

TYPE OF STUDENT I AM

CLOTHES I WEAR

TYPES OF FRIENDS I CHOOSE

MUSIC MOVIES

ACTIVITIES

HOW I DEAL WITH CONFLICT

HOW I TREAT PEOPLE

YOUR BRAND
YOUR NAME

FREE TIME

SOCIAL MEDIA I USE

SKILLS I HAVE

BOOKS I READ

LONG TERM GOALS

Activity #2: Have the child complete the Snowflake "Friends" Diagram and share

SNOWFLAKE FRIENDSHIP DIAGRAM

Look at the Snowflake Diagram below and fill in the shapes with the names of your friend/friends that display the specific character trait.

Table Talk 1: Understanding Brands

- What are some of your favorite brands?
- Why do you prefer those brands?
- What do you think makes a brand popular?
- Do you believe creative commercials make a brand more appealing? Why or why not?
- Does having celebrities promote a brand make it more desirable to you? Why or why not?

Table Talk 2: Exploring Personal Branding

- Have you ever thought of yourself as a brand? If so, in what way?
- Do you think your personal brand is similar to your reputation? Why or why not?
- Do you believe it's possible to change your personal brand (or reputation)? If so, how?
- Should you be intentional about building your personal brand, or should you let it develop naturally?
- What qualities or traits do you think should be part of your personal brand?

Table Talk 3: First Impressions and Social Media

- Can you share a time when you made a great first impression? How about a poor one? How did those experiences make you feel?
- Do you think your social media posts reflect the personal brand you want to convey? Why or why not?
- Are you intentional about what you post, or do you usually post based on how you're feeling at the moment?
- Did you know that colleges and employers often review social media profiles during the application process?

- How can you be more thoughtful about posting positive content so that your social media reflects the brand you're proud of?

Table Talk 4: Friendships and Their Impact

- How do you feel about your current friendships? Are they healthy?
- What do you think defines a toxic friendship?
- Are there any changes you think you need to make in your friendships? Why or why not?
- Do you consider yourself a good friend to others? Why or why not?
- Do you believe being a strong person makes you immune to the effects of toxic friendships? Why or why not?

CHAPTER 2

Positive Attitude

Goal: Teach that a positive attitude is built on gratitude, resilience, outward appearance, and a good support system. Equip your children with strategies that will cultivate a positive mindset when things go wrong. Teach them to understand that many times they can't control bad things that will happen in life, but what they can have is 100% control over their attitudes. They will learn that your attitude can be your most powerful tool. If you are POSITIVE, you will attract POSITIVE people and opportunities. Our learning goal is to recognize that our attitudes affect the outcomes in our lives.

Attitude

Teaching our kids why a positive attitude is important helps them build confidence, cope with challenges better, develop healthy relationships, and achieve their goals by fostering a mindset that focuses on the good, encourages resilience, and promotes healthy self-talk, allowing them to navigate life's ups and downs with greater optimism and determination.

Building a Positive Attitude

It couldn't be truer that our attitude can determine the success or failure of every day, every game, every grade, and every relationship in our lives. A positive attitude can eventually lead to positive results, and a negative one can eventually lead to negative results. It's that simple. A positive attitude is a philosophy of approaching life with optimism and confidence. Developing a positive attitude requires replacing negative thinking with positive thinking to create a successful outlook on life and experiences.

FACT:

If you can CHOOSE to SMILE and be POSITIVE, you can get past the annoying bumps in the road. However, if you trudge through your day with a grumpy attitude, those bumps in the road are going to control you and your day.

Having a negative attitude drains not only your energy, but it also drains the energy of everyone around you. This is not to say that you can't feel sad or angry when you're facing difficult situations. Acknowledge those feelings, think about why you feel that way, and figure out a way to spin it into something beneficial or a way to deal with it.

You are in the driver's seat when it comes to your attitude, no matter what's going on around you! BELIEVE IT!

 **Parent/Teen Dialogue example:**

Parent: Hey, Luke, can we hang out and chat for a sec? I've noticed you've been kind of frustrated lately—like stuff's been getting under your skin. Everything okay?

Teen: Yeah, I guess. It's just... ugh, sometimes everything feels so hard. Like, things never go my way, so why even bother trying to stay upbeat?

Parent: Oh, I totally get that. Life can be a lot, and it's okay to feel bummed sometimes. But let me throw this at you—does focusing on the bad stuff actually make it easier to deal with?

Teen: Not really. But when things go wrong, it's just way easier to vent or throw in the towel.

Parent: I hear you—it's super easy to go there. But here's something cool about attitude: it's one of the few things you've got total control over. Being positive doesn't mean pretending everything's perfect. It's more like saying, "Okay, this is rough, but I've got this."

Teen: But what if I don't? What if it just stays awful no matter what?

Parent: That's where your mindset can totally shift things. Picture this: two people hit the same problem. One's like, "This is a disaster, I'm toast." The other's like, "Yeah, this stinks, but I'll figure it out." Who do you think has a better shot at making it through—or at least coming out stronger?

Teen: Probably the second one.

Parent: Right. A positive vibe doesn't fix everything, but it helps you spot ways out—or at least ways to grow. Plus, it makes you tougher. Life's always going to throw curveballs, but how you swing at them? That's what builds who you'll become.

Teen: I don't know... it's hard to just *be* positive like that.

Parent: Oh, for sure—it's not like a magic button you press. It's more like a muscle you work out. Start small. Next time something flops, instead of "Why me?" try "What's this teaching me?" Or even just, "This isn't forever." Little shifts like that add up.

Teen: Yeah, okay, that kinda makes sense.

Parent: See? And you don't have to nail it every time. But here's the bonus: staying positive isn't just about feeling good right now. It can make you a better friend, help you crush it at school or later at a job, and—get this—even keep you healthier.

Teen: Healthier? Like how?

Parent: Yep! People who roll with a positive attitude handle stress better and even catch fewer colds. Your brain and body are like besties—they vibe off each other.

Teen: Huh, that's actually kinda cool.

Parent: Yes! So, what do you say? Wanna team up and try keeping our heads up, even when things aren't going our way or people are letting us down?

Teen: Yeah, I'll give it a shot. Just don't freak if I slip up sometimes.

Parent: (laughs) Promise—no freak-outs here. We all have our slip ups. It's all about trying, not being perfect. You're already killing it just thinking about it! Let's help each other.

This parent-teen dialogue is a win because it empowers the teen to take control of their mindset, building resilience and hope while deepening their trust in the parent as a supportive partner. By framing attitude as a choice and a skill they can develop, the parent helps the teen shift from feeling overwhelmed and defeated to seeing challenges as manageable and temporary, setting them up for emotional growth, better coping skills, and a stronger sense of self as they face life's ups and downs.

This conversation works because it meets the teen where they are—acknowledging their frustration—then gently guides them toward a practical, positive outlook without dismissing their struggles. It's a win for their confidence, their future relationships, and even their well-being, all while reinforcing a safe, open connection with the parent.

Three Ways to Teach Your Kids to Stay Positive

Teaching kids to embrace positivity is vital to helping them navigate life's challenges. Here's how to help them develop the mindset for success, resilience, and happiness.

1. Take Control

Life throws curveballs, but while we can't control the obstacles, we *can* control our reactions. A positive attitude transforms how we tackle tough times.

Your attitude is your mind's reaction to a situation or fact—and let's face it, we all have those *UGH!* moments.

Here's the good news: You control your attitude by managing your thoughts and how you present yourself.

For instance:

When your alarm buzzes in the morning, you can either:

- Decide to embrace the day with gratitude and excitement for the fresh 24 hours ahead.
- Or groan, shuffle out the door, and let the day drag you down.

See the difference?

A positive attitude starts with small decisions. Try this: Look in the mirror, smile, and say, *"Today is a great day to crush it! I'm grateful for the air in my lungs and the beat in my chest."* That simple act can shift your mindset and set the tone for your day.

Remember, you choose your thoughts, and therefore, you choose your attitude. You have 100% control.

Key Quote:

"The longer I live, the more I realize the impact of attitude on life.

Attitude, to me, is more important than facts. It is more important than the past, than education, than money, than circumstances, than failures, than successes, than what other people think or say or do. It is more important than appearance, giftedness, or skill. It will make or break a company...a church...a home. The remarkable thing is we have a choice every day regarding the attitude we will embrace for that day. We cannot change our past...we cannot change the fact that people will act in a certain way. We cannot change the inevitable. The only thing we can do is play on the one string we have, and that is our attitude...I am convinced that life is 10% what happens to me and 90% how I react to it. And so it is with you...we are in charge of our attitudes." ~ Charles R. Swindoll

This quote will help kids understand that positivity is a choice. By responding with optimism and determination, they will develop a mindset that turns setbacks into opportunities.

2. Gratitude

One of the most important things I have taught my four children is to practice gratitude. There are countless instances as our children grow up and the "comparison game" begins.

- *"Look what SHE got for Christmas."*
- *"Wow. I can't even begin to count how many football offers HE has received just this week!"*
- *"Why do I have to do chores all day Saturday when all of my friends are hanging out?"*
- *"I really wish I had long legs and could dance like her."*

Sound familiar?

Well, gratitude is like a superpower that can make your life better in so many ways. When you practice gratitude, you're training your mind to focus on the good things in your life instead of only seeing what's wrong or missing. It's easy to get caught up in comparing yourself to others, especially with social media showing everyone's highlight reels, but gratitude reminds you to appreciate what *you* have. Whether it's your family, friends, a favorite hobby, or even just a sunny day, noticing these things can make you feel happier and more content.

One of the coolest things about gratitude is how it changes your brain. Studies show that when you regularly practice gratitude, your brain starts to rewire itself to be more positive. This means you'll find it easier to see the good in situations and feel less stressed or overwhelmed when things don't go as planned. Plus, gratitude can help you build stronger relationships. When you take time to say "thank you" or show appreciation to the people in your life, they feel valued and are more likely to show kindness in return. It's a win-win.

Lastly, gratitude helps you stay grounded. Life can be tough sometimes—school pressure, drama with friends, or just feeling like you're not enough. But when you stop and think about the things you're grateful for, it's like hitting a reset button. It shifts your focus from what's wrong to what's right, which can give you the strength to keep going. Practicing gratitude doesn't mean you ignore the hard things; it just helps you balance them out with the good. So, start small—write down three things you're thankful for every day—and watch how it transforms your mood and mindset over time.

Gratitude is like a muscle. The more you use it, the stronger it becomes.

3. Find Your "Bounce"

Think about jumping on a trampoline—you defy gravity every time you bounce. That's exactly what having "bounce" in your attitude does.

Bouncing back from tough situations—whether your child is failing a test, losing a game, or dealing with drama in their life—is one of the most important skills they can learn. Life isn't always smooth, and everyone faces setbacks, even the most successful people you know. What separates those who thrive from those who get stuck is the ability to get back up and keep going. This skill, called resilience, will help them turn obstacles into opportunities to learn and grow.

Think about it like this: when you fall off a bike, you have two choices. You can sit on the ground and stay upset, or you can get back on and try again. Every time your child bounces back, they're learning that failure or setbacks aren't the end—they're just a part of the process. This mindset builds confidence because they start to believe that they can handle whatever comes their way. The more they bounce back, the stronger and more capable they'll feel.

Bouncing back also helps them avoid staying stuck in negative emotions like anger, frustration, or disappointment. It's okay to feel those things for a little while—they're natural—but if you let them take over, they can hold you back from moving forward. Resilience doesn't mean pretending everything is fine. It means accepting that things didn't go as planned, figuring out what you can learn from the experience, and taking the next step. Over time, your children will realize that even the toughest situations don't have to define them; it's how they respond to them that matters most.

So, next time something knocks them down, remember it's not about avoiding every challenge or failure—it's about bouncing back stronger each time. Resilience isn't just a skill for now; it's something they'll use for the rest of their lives.

Although it can be extremely painful, please allow your children to fail.

Letting your child experience failure can be tough as a parent, but it's one of the greatest gifts you can give them. When you step in to prevent failure or solve every problem for your child, you unintentionally rob them of the chance to develop resilience, problem-solving skills, and confidence. Failure, as difficult as it can be, is a powerful teacher that helps children learn how to navigate life's challenges and build independence.

When children fail, they learn firsthand the consequences of their choices and actions. This helps them develop critical thinking and decision-making skills as they reflect on what went wrong and how to improve next time. If parents always step in to rescue their children, they miss out on these valuable opportunities for growth. Over time, children who aren't allowed to face failure may grow up feeling helpless or dependent, struggling to handle challenges on their own.

Failure also builds resilience—the ability to bounce back from setbacks. Resilient children understand that failure isn't the end; it's just a step on the path to success. Allowing your child to experience failure teaches them that mistakes are normal and manageable, not something to fear or avoid at all costs. This mindset will serve them well in adulthood, where challenges and disappointments are inevitable.

Finally, letting your child fail shows them that you trust their ability to figure things out. It sends a powerful message: "I believe in you." While it's natural to want to shield your child from pain or struggle, stepping back and letting them face difficulties is an act of love that empowers them to grow into capable, confident, and self-reliant individuals. Of course, this doesn't mean abandoning them in tough times—be there to guide, support, and encourage them. But letting them experience the learning process, even when it involves failure, is essential for their long-term success and happiness.

A great example for your children:

Imagine you're about to set sail on an open ocean. You have two sailors to choose from: one has spent their whole life navigating calm, smooth waters, where everything goes as planned. The other has weathered fierce storms, handled unpredictable winds, and navigated treacherous currents. Who would you trust to guide you safely if a storm suddenly rolled in?

Most of us would choose the experienced sailor—the one who's been tested by challenges and knows how to stay calm and make smart decisions when things get rough. That's because it's not the smooth waters that teach you how to handle a crisis; it's the storms that build skill, courage, and resilience.

Life is a lot like the open ocean. Smooth days are great, but it's the tough moments—the "rough waters"—that prepare us for the challenges ahead. Just like the seasoned sailor, we grow stronger, smarter, and more capable every time we face and overcome difficulties. So, while calm waters might seem easier in the moment, it's the high winds and rough seas that truly prepare us for the journey ahead.

To wrap up, "bouncing back" adds value to their "personal "brand." It is a great example for others, creates solutions, and frees them from negativity.

4. Surround Yourself with Positive People: Your Vibe Attracts Your Tribe

There are few things in this world that you have the freedom to choose, but you can always choose your friends. The people we spend time with shape our outlook on life. As parents, one of the most important lessons you can teach your children is the power of the company they keep. The people they surround themselves with—friends, classmates, teammates—will have a huge impact on how they see the world, how they feel about themselves, and the choices they make.

Encouraging your child to seek out positive, uplifting relationships is key to helping them grow into confident, resilient, and happy individuals.

Positive people inspire and encourage your child to be their best self. When surrounded by friends who believe in them, cheer them on, and push them to work hard, your child is more likely to develop confidence and motivation. In contrast, negative influences can drag them down, whether through constant criticism, peer pressure, or toxic behaviors. Positive relationships create an environment where your child feels supported and valued, making it easier for them to tackle challenges and make healthy choices.

Another key reason to emphasize positive relationships is how they shape your child's mindset. Kids tend to mirror the attitudes and behaviors of those around them. If their peers are optimistic, kind, and hardworking, those qualities will rub off. On the other hand, if they're surrounded by negativity, complaining, or risky behavior, it can be hard for them to stay on the right path. By helping your child understand this, you're giving them the tools to choose friendships that lift them up instead of dragging them down.

Finally, surrounding themselves with positive people teaches your child what a healthy relationship looks like. These friendships set the standard for mutual respect, kindness, and trust—qualities they'll carry into their future relationships, whether it's with friends, colleagues, or even romantic partners. Encourage your child to reflect on how their friends make them feel and whether those relationships help them grow. Helping them prioritize positive connections is one of the greatest gifts you can give them as a parent.

Do your kids have Positive Influencers?

- Help them identify people in their lives who inspire or motivate them.
- Encourage them to seek support from friends, mentors, and family members when they feel down.

Remember this from Chapter 1? You are the average of the five people you spend the most time with, so choose wisely! Surround yourself with positive, uplifting people who support your goals and banish "stinkin' thinkin'."

Identify those who lift you up and keep them close. These people will help you stay strong when life gets tough.

"You can't hang out with negative people and expect to live a positive life."

Let's look at the 5 Characteristics of Positive People. This is a great exercise for your children to determine whether they are positive people.

- **Smile a Lot**
- **Like Themselves**

- **Find Their Passion**
- **Have a Great Sense of Humor**
- **Are Grateful**

Talk with your child about where they fall on the positivity scale in the 5 activities below.

#1 Positive people smile a lot.

A smile is a facial expression that expresses kindness, happiness, and approval.

How often do you smile?

Rate yourself, honestly, according to the scenarios listed below.

- What would your **friends** say that you do the most?
  ☐ Smile ☐ Frown ☐ "Whatever"
- What would your **family** say that you do the most?
  ☐ Smile ☐ Frown ☐ "Whatever"
- What would your **teachers** say that you do the most?
  ☐ Smile ☐ Frown ☐ "Whatever"
- What would your **coaches** say that you do the most?
  ☐ Smile ☐ Frown ☐ "Whatever"

#2 Positive people like themselves.

Liking yourself doesn't mean you're an egomaniac. It simply means that you accept who you are, both the positive and the negative. Do you like yourself?

Read the following statements and determine which ones are true and which ones are false.

- I like myself and believe I can succeed when I work hard and give my best.
- I like myself when others say I'm doing a good job and cheer me on.
- I don't feel very good about myself. I don't expect to succeed.
- When I describe myself, there are only good qualities on my list.

- When someone gives me a compliment, I am shocked and/or uncomfortable.

#3 Positive people are passionate.

Having passion means having strong emotions and beliefs about something or someone. Are you passionate about something?

Read the following statements and check the one that applies the most to you.

- I am not passionate about anything.
- I want to find something that I am passionate about.
- I am very passionate about something.

If you do have a particular passion, what is it?

If you want to find your passion, answer the following questions:

- What do you really love or love to do?
- What would you want to do 24/7 if you could?
- What are the things that you have dreamed about doing?
- What is the reason that you haven't tried these things?

#4 Positive people have a sense of humor.

Having a sense of humor involves not only the ability to laugh at things around you, but also the ability to laugh at yourself.

Answer the following questions:

- Do you have a sense of humor?
- Can you laugh at yourself when you make mistakes?
- Can you find humor in bad situations?
- Do you help others laugh when they are down?

#5 Positive people are grateful.

Being grateful means appreciating and being thankful for what you already have. Are you grateful?

Name five things that you are grateful for in your life right now.

1.

2.

3.

4.

5.

5. Your Attitude Shows on the Outside

A positive attitude isn't just about what's inside—it's about what you project outwardly. Your body language and expressions speak volumes. As parents, it's important to help your children understand that their outward appearance— how they carry themselves, dress, and express their emotions—can communicate a lot about their attitude.

People often form impressions based on what they see, and teaching your child how to project positivity on the outside can open doors, build stronger relationships, and boost their confidence. Start by explaining that their outward appearance is like a billboard for their attitude. For example, slouched posture, a scowling face, or messy clothing might unintentionally send a message that they're unapproachable or uninterested, even if that's not how they feel inside. On the other hand, standing tall, smiling, and dressing neatly can make them seem confident, friendly, and open. These simple changes in how they present themselves can shape how others treat them and how they feel about themselves.

Encourage your child to show positivity through small but meaningful actions. Teach them to smile often—it's a universal way to show kindness and approachability. Maintaining good posture not only conveys confidence but also boosts their mood and energy. Even their tone of voice can reflect their attitude. Speak calmly and clearly, and they'll notice that people respond more positively to them.

It's also important to talk about personal presentation, such as wearing clean and appropriate clothes. While what they wear doesn't define who they are, it does show that they respect themselves and the people they interact with. Dressing neatly and grooming well can boost their self-esteem and help them feel more prepared to tackle their day.

Finally, remind them that positivity starts from the inside. The more they practice gratitude, kindness, and self-respect, the easier it will be for their outward appearance to naturally reflect those qualities. Let them know that presenting themselves with care and positivity doesn't mean being fake—it's about being the best version of who they really are. By teaching them these lessons, you're setting them up for success in their personal, social, and professional lives. This is a great tool to put into their "Personal Brand" toolkit.

Wrap-Up: The Positivity Toolkit

1. **You Are in Control:** Attitude is a choice. Encourage your kids to consciously decide how they respond to challenges.
2. **Gratitude Changes Everything:** Focusing on the good in life enhances happiness and resilience.
3. **Bounce Back Stronger:** Teach them to face setbacks with humor, forgiveness, and resilience.
4. **Positive People Rule:** Surrounding themselves with optimistic, supportive people leads to better outcomes.
5. **Body Language and Smile:** Their outward appearance speaks volumes and influences how others perceive them.

Final Thought:

"A positive attitude is contagious and transformative. Be the reason others see the good in the world."

Action Steps:

Help kids set goals for positivity.

My 3 goals to stay positive:

1.

2.

3.

Activities

These activities will encourage your kids to actively practice positivity, helping them build the habit of focusing on the good even in difficult times.

1. Gratitude Journal

Encourage your child to keep a daily or weekly gratitude journal. Each day, they write down three things they're grateful for. These can be big or small—anything from a supportive friend to a beautiful sunset. This practice helps them focus on the positive aspects of their life, which can shift their mindset, especially during tough times.

How to get started:

"I want you to write three things you're grateful for every evening before bed. It could be anything that made your day better, even if it's something small. Let's see how the list grows over time."

2. Reframing Negative Thoughts

Kids can learn to identify negative self-talk and replace it with positive, constructive thoughts. This activity helps them become aware of their inner dialogue and practice turning frustration or failure into growth opportunities.

How to get started:

Have your child write down a negative thought they've had (e.g., "I'm bad at math").

Then, ask them to reframe it: "What could be a more positive way of thinking about this?" (e.g., "I haven't mastered math yet, but I can improve with practice.")

Discuss how reframing negative thoughts can help them approach challenges more positively.

3. Power of "Yet"

This activity centers on adding the word "yet" to any self-limiting belief or statement. Instead of saying, "I can't do this," encourage your child to say, "I can't do this yet." This simple shift can transform a fixed mindset into a growth mindset.

How to get started:

"Next time you're stuck or feel frustrated, try adding 'yet' to your thoughts. For example, instead of saying, 'I'm terrible at this,' try, 'I'm not good at this yet, but I can get better.' Let's see if it changes the way you feel about challenges."

4. Positive Self-Talk

Introduce your teen to the power of positive self-talk. These short, empowering statements can help improve self-confidence and encourage a positive outlook on life. Ask them to say these affirmations aloud each morning or when they feel discouraged.

How to get started:

Create a list of positive affirmations together (e.g., "I am capable of handling challenges" or "I am confident and strong").

Encourage them to say these out loud in front of a mirror or as part of their morning routine. This helps reinforce a positive self-image.

5. Acts of Kindness Challenge

Doing something kind for others can boost your child's mood and help them focus on the good in the world. Set up a weekly challenge where your child does at least one small act of kindness for someone else, whether it's a friend or family member.

How to get started:

"Each week, let's come up with at least one small act of kindness you can do. It can be anything from complimenting a friend to helping with chores around the house. How do you feel after doing something kind for someone else?"

6. Positivity Jar

Create a "positivity jar" where your child writes down good things that happen throughout the week, no matter how small. At the end of each week or month, they can read through the notes to reflect on how many positive moments they've had, shifting their focus toward the good.

How to get started:

"Every time something positive happens, write it down on a piece of paper and add it to the jar. At the end of the week, let's sit down and read them together to celebrate all the good things you experienced."

7. Vision Board

Creating a vision board helps kids visualize their goals and dreams, which can reinforce a positive outlook on the future. This activity encourages them to focus on what they want to achieve and how they can work toward those goals with optimism.

How to get started:

"Let's create a vision board with things you want to accomplish this year—whether it's personal goals, travel plans, or achievements. Every time you feel discouraged, look at your board and remember the bigger picture."

8. Compliment Swap

Get your teen involved in a compliment exchange with family members or friends. This encourages them to see the positive qualities in others and boosts their own self-esteem.

How to get started:

"This week, try complimenting at least three people—something real and meaningful. It could be about their skills, personality, or appearance. It's a great way to lift each other up and practice seeing the good in people."

9. The "Good Things" Reflection

After a tough day, help your child reflect on the positive aspects of their experience. They might feel frustrated about school or social struggles, but guiding them to identify at least one good thing from the day can foster a more positive perspective.

How to get started:

"At the end of each day, tell me about one good thing that happened. Even if it was a tough day, there's always something positive you can find."

10. Create a "Positivity Playlist"

Music can be a great mood booster. Help your teen create a playlist of upbeat, positive songs that they can listen to when they need a mental reset or to boost their spirits.

How to get started:

"Let's make a playlist of songs that make you feel good—songs that are energizing and uplifting. Whenever you feel down or need a quick attitude adjustment, hit play and let the music do its magic."

Table Talk 1:

What is one of the few things you have complete control over?

How can you brand your attitude to be positive from the inside out?

- You control your attitude
- You practice gratitude
- You practice "bounce"
- You smile and use big body language
- You keep a good support system

Table Talk 2:

- Do you think it's true that you are either a positive person or you aren't? Why or why not?
- How do you control your attitude?
- What are some strategies that you use when you are having a bad day to overcome negativity?

Table Talk 3:

Say: "Remember, gratitude is like a muscle, and when it's used every day, it becomes a habit. Let's talk about things we are grateful for …

(Here are some sentence stems you can use to guide your child:)

- Something I am grateful for...
- Today was special because...
- I appreciate (person), because...
- Something I accomplished today...
- Something that makes me smile...
- Something I'm looking forward to...
- Something I like about my family...
- Three friends whom I appreciate...
- My friend (name) is important to me because...

You can also start a "gratitude jar" with your family. Cut out some strips of paper and leave them with a pen by a glass jar. When a family member is grateful for something, they write it down and put it in the jar. Once a week at dinner, read things your family has been grateful for during the week!

Table Talk 4:

- What do we mean when we say that you can "bounce back" from a bad situation? (It's when you control your attitude when something goes wrong, or you make a mistake; when you take control of the situation, rather than letting the situation take control of you; not letting things get to you or ruin your mood.)
- Why is it important to be able to bounce? (Bounce impresses your friends; creates more options, lets you let go of grudges, lets you find humor in a difficult situation, it's more fun to bounce than to flop.)

Table Talk 5:

We know that we can control our attitude, but how can we control what people see on the outside? (*We can control our body language and facial expressions by using big body language, standing up straight, looking people in the eye, giving a firm handshake, and smiling; fake it until you make it.*)

- Do you feel like your attitude changes depending on what you are wearing?

- Do you feel like you can tell what a person's like by the way that they dress?
- Do you think it's important to dress in specific ways at specific times? (school, job interview, etc.) Why?

Table Talk 6:

- What kind of people do you surround yourself with? Think about the friends and family you are closest to.
- Do you have people in your life who can support you when you need it? Who are those people?
- What are you passionate about?
- What do you really love or love to do?
- What would you want to do 24/7 if you could?
- What are the things that you have dreamed about doing?
- What is the reason that you haven't tried these things?

CHAPTER 3

Work Ethic

 Goal: Teach your children that a strong work ethic is built on dedication, discipline, dependability, and the ability to "do work." Equip them with strategies that will build the habits they need to keep going, to not only get the job done but to get it done with excellence.

Teaching Kids the Value of Work Ethic

In a world filled with instant gratification, teaching kids the importance of work ethic has never been more critical. A strong work ethic isn't just about completing tasks—it's about shaping a mindset that values effort, responsibility, and persistence. It's a gift parents can give their children to help them succeed not only in their academic and professional lives but also in their relationships and personal growth.

So, how can parents guide their children to embrace qualities like dedication, discipline, dependability, and the ability to simply "do work"? It starts with modeling these traits and having intentional conversations about what they mean in everyday life. Let's look at these three characteristics of a good work ethic:

1. Dependability

Dependability is what builds trust. It's the habit of showing up, following through, and being reliable. Parents can teach this by giving kids responsibilities, no matter how small, and holding them accountable. Dependability isn't just a skill; it's a character trait that will set them apart in life.

What age do you think is appropriate to start giving your children responsibilities where they can be truly dependable? I have a good friend who has eight kids! Her kids dread their 7th birthday because they become PRODUCERS in their home with chores rather than merely CONSUMERS. I love this! I believe that between the ages of 6 and 8 is a good age to begin chores such as folding laundry, setting the table, etc.

 **Parent/Child Dialogue Example:**

Parent: Hey, can we chat about yesterday real quick? You mentioned you'd take out the trash before heading out, but it didn't happen.

Child: Oh, yeah... sorry. I totally spaced on it.

Parent: No biggie, it happens. But here's the thing—being dependable matters. When you say you'll do something, people start counting on you to make it happen.

Child: I mean, it's just trash. It's not *that* serious, right?

Parent: Fair point. It's not the end of the world. But think about it like this: little stuff builds up. What if I forgot to grab you from school or skipped paying your phone bill?

Child: Okay, yeah, I'd be pretty annoyed. I get it. Sorry about that—I'll try harder.

Parent: Love that attitude! So, how can we keep it on your radar next time? Maybe a quick phone reminder? That really helps me...

Child: Oh, yeah, that's smart! I'll set one for sure.

Parent: Awesome. Being someone people can count on is like stacking up trust points. It pays off down the road. You've got this!

This parent-child dialogue fosters accountability and problem-solving skills in the child while strengthening their sense of responsibility and trust within the family dynamic. By addressing a small lapse (forgetting the trash) in a calm, constructive way, the parent helps the child see how dependability in everyday tasks builds credibility and affects relationships, encouraging them to take commitments seriously without feeling attacked or overwhelmed.

This conversation shines because it turns a minor slip-up into a learning moment—linking small actions to bigger life lessons like reliability—while keeping the tone supportive and collaborative. The child walks away motivated to improve, equipped with a practical tool (a phone reminder), and feeling respected rather than nagged, which boosts their confidence and reinforces a positive, open relationship with the parent.

Teaching our kids to be dependable means:

- **Being committed.** Keep your promises. Do what you say you are going to do. Don't forget commitments. Write things down. No excuses. You will earn respect from others if you keep your promises and commitments.
- **Being on time.** Be where you say you are going to be exactly when you say you are going to be there. If you are constantly late, it is just plain selfish. It says to others, "My time is more valuable than your time," making them angry and disappointed in you.
- **Being trustworthy.** Being trustworthy is exactly what the word says... being worthy of someone's trust. The only way to be trustworthy is to be honest and reliable over and over and over again.

Questions to ask your child:

1. Are you dependable?
2. Can you list three situations or ways in which other people (parents, teachers, coaches, friends, etc.) would describe you as being dependable?
3. Can you list three tasks you often avoid or put off by making excuses? These tend to be things we are supposed to do but don't always enjoy. (For example, "I am usually late for my tutoring session.")

4. Look at the three tasks you just named. Now, list one strategy for each that you can use to be more dependable (more committed, more on time, more trustworthy, etc.). (For example, "I will set my alarm on my phone an hour ahead of my session.")

Remember: being dependable affects not only you but everyone around you. You must decide if you are going to be dependable or a "slacker." So, decide now:

- Are you going to show up or not?
- Are you going to give it your all or give a lame effort?
- Will you focus on the task at hand, or will you have your head in the clouds?

2. Dedication

Dedication is the foundation of any worthwhile pursuit. It's about commitment, perseverance, and staying the course even when the excitement fades. Parents can teach dedication by helping kids set goals, stick to them, and celebrate the milestones along the way. It's about showing them that meaningful achievements require effort and time.

 **Parent/Child Dialogue Example:**

Parent: "I noticed you've been practicing guitar a lot lately. How's it going?"

Child: "It's fine, but I don't feel like I'm improving as fast as I want."

Parent: "That's normal—it takes time. Remember when you started soccer? You didn't master dribbling overnight."

Child: "Yeah, but this feels way harder."

Parent: "Anything worth doing usually does feel that way. The key is sticking with it even when it feels tough. Think about how great it'll feel when you play that song perfectly in a few weeks."

> **Child:** "I hope so! It would feel really good to nail it."
>
> **Parent:** "Exactly! Let's set a small goal for this week, like practicing that tricky part every day for 10 minutes. You've got this!"

This dialogue nurtures the child's perseverance and self-confidence while teaching them the value of consistent effort toward a goal they care about, all within a supportive and encouraging relationship. By acknowledging the child's frustration with guitar practice and connecting it to a past success (soccer), the parent helps them reframe setbacks as part of the learning process, boosting their motivation and resilience.

This conversation excels because it validates the child's feelings, offers a practical strategy (small daily practice), and paints an inspiring picture of future success, making the challenge feel manageable and worthwhile. The child leaves the exchange feeling understood, empowered to keep going, and equipped with a clear next step, which strengthens their work ethic and deepens their trust in the parent as a cheerleader for their growth.

Teaching our kids to be dedicated means:

You are 100% committed to something, and that you are "all in!", no matter what.

Remember the 3 P's!

1. Practice, practice, practice: Put in more time than anyone else.
2. Plan: Have a specific plan of how you will be the best.
3. Persevere: Have grit. Gut it out. Stick through hard times.

Sometimes, it may seem that successful people have been born with extraordinary talent, have had great luck in life, or have happened to be in the right place at the right time. Chances are that those people also had to put in a lot of hard work. You won't go far in life if you only rely on talent, luck, or being in the right place at the right time.

Questions to ask your child:

1. Can you list three ways you can show your dedication in your OBLIGATIONS: school, job, training, etc. Think about how you can plan, practice, and persevere in your pursuit of knowledge!
2. Can you list three ways you can show your dedication in your INTERESTS: sports, musical instruments, hobbies, relationships... anything in which you REALLY want to excel? Think about how you can plan, practice, and persevere in your pursuit of the things you love!

Remember: What distinguishes the merely talented from the truly great is dedication—the willingness to get in earlier, stay later, set higher goals, and do more than everyone around them.

3. Doing the Work

Finally, teaching kids to simply "do the work" is essential. Whether it's completing chores, practicing for a recital, or preparing for a test, the ability to take action without excuses is what leads to growth. Parents can nurture this mindset by framing work as an opportunity rather than a burden and encouraging kids to tackle challenges head-on.

By focusing on these three pillars—dedication, dependability, and the ability to "do work"—parents can equip their children with the tools they need to navigate life with confidence and resilience. This is about more than building good habits; it's about shaping a lifelong attitude toward effort and success.

 **Parent/Child Dialogue Example:**

Child: "Ugh, I don't even know where to start with this history project. It's, like, way too much."

Parent: "Big projects can feel overwhelming. Let's break it down. What's the first thing you need to tackle?"

Child: "I guess... research the topic."

Parent: "Okay, so start there. Remember, progress is about doing the work one step at a time. You don't have to finish it all tonight. Take it one bite at a time. Start with the research and see where it goes. Sound good?"

Child: "But what if I mess it up?"

Parent: "That's okay. The important thing is starting. Doing the work doesn't mean it's perfect right away—it's about trying and learning as you go. Let's set a goal to get through the research today. You in?"

Child: "Yeah, I can do that."

Parent: "Great! I'm proud of you for jumping in. One step at a time, and you'll crush it—I've got your back!"

This parent-child dialogue builds the child's confidence and problem-solving skills by transforming an overwhelming task into manageable steps while reinforcing their sense of security and support from the parent. By breaking down the history project and normalizing imperfection, the parent helps the child overcome paralysis, embrace a growth mindset, and take action without fear of failure.

This conversation works because it meets the child's anxiety with empathy, offers a clear starting point (research), and emphasizes progress over perfection, making the task feel doable. The child emerges motivated to begin, reassured that mistakes are part of learning, and bolstered by the parent's encouragement, which fosters resilience, initiative, and a stronger parent-child bond.

Teaching Kids to Build Grit: The Backbone of a Strong Work Ethic

"Doing the work" is about grit. In today's fast-paced world, where challenges and distractions abound, grit stands out as a critical ingredient for success. Grit combines perseverance, passion, and resilience—the ability to push through obstacles and keep working toward long-term goals.

Teaching kids grit isn't about demanding perfection or pushing them to their limits. Instead, it's about helping them develop the mindset that setbacks are opportunities to grow and that effort, not talent alone, leads to achievement.

To instill grit, parents can start by emphasizing the value of persistence. Celebrate your child's efforts more than their results. For example, if they score well on a test, acknowledge the hours they spent studying rather than just praising the grade. This teaches them to value hard work as the pathway to success.

Likewise, encourage them to view mistakes as part of the learning process. A child who learns to say, "I didn't get it this time, but I'll try again," is building the grit that will carry them through life's inevitable challenges.

Parents can also model grit in their own behavior. Share stories about times when you faced difficulties but didn't give up. Whether it's completing a demanding project at work, fixing something around the house, or learning a new skill, let your kids see you demonstrate determination and resilience. When they witness your ability to stick with something hard, they'll be inspired to do the same.

Lastly, create opportunities for your kids to practice grit. Encourage them to commit to long-term activities like sports, music, or academic challenges that require regular effort and progress over time. Help them set small, achievable goals and celebrate their persistence along the way. Let them experience the satisfaction of overcoming obstacles, even when they initially wanted to quit. By fostering grit, you're giving your child the tools they need to develop a robust work ethic that will serve them for a lifetime.

Here are some practical examples of dialogue and activities parents can use to teach grit:

 ## Parent/Child Dialogue Examples:

1. When Your Child Wants to Quit

Child: "I'm over this calculus class. I'm just not smart enough for this."

Parent: "I get why you feel that way—it's a tough subject. But remember, grit isn't about being perfect; it's about putting in the effort to improve little by little. What part of it is tripping you up?"

Child: "The equations. I can't keep up with the steps."

Parent: "Let's figure out a plan. Maybe you can work with a tutor or study group. The important thing is not giving up on yourself."

2. When Your Child Faces Failure

Child: "I totally bombed my baseball tryouts. I'm not even going to bother next year."

Parent: "That must feel really discouraging. But not making the team doesn't mean you can't improve. Think about athletes like Michael Jordan— he didn't make his high school team, and look at what he accomplished."

Child: "I don't know... maybe I'm just not good enough."

Parent: "The only way to know your potential is to keep working at it. If this matters to you, let's figure out a training plan and make a stronger comeback next year."

3. When Your Child Procrastinates

Child: "Ugh, I'll do my science project later. I'm too tired now."

Parent: "I get it, but grit is about doing the work even when you're not in the mood. What's one small thing you could do now to get started?"

Child: "I guess I could outline the intro."

Parent: "Great idea. Once you get going, it won't feel so overwhelming. Let me know if you want me to look it over when you're done."

4. When Your Child Needs Encouragement

Child: "I don't see the point of all this—school, work, whatever. It's just so draining."

Parent: "I hear you. Sometimes, it feels like the effort isn't worth it. But grit isn't about today—it's about building a future you're proud of. What's one thing you're working on that you know will pay off later?"

> **Child:** "I guess saving up for my car."
>
> **Parent:** "Exactly. That same mindset—small steps now for big rewards later—applies to everything. It's hard, but you're tougher than you think."

There is one common character trait that embodies all 3 of these characteristics: Dependability, Dedication, and "Doing the Work," and that is DISCIPLINE.

Discipline is the daily practice of doing what needs to be done—even when it's hard or inconvenient. It's the backbone of progress and self-control. Parents can encourage discipline by setting clear expectations, reinforcing routines, and gently guiding kids to take responsibility for their actions.

 **Parent/Child Dialogue Example:**

Child: "Ugh, I really don't feel like doing my math homework right now."

Parent: "I hear you—it's not always fun. But skipping it isn't going to make it go away, right?"

Child: "I know, but I just don't feel motivated at all."

Parent: "I get that. Discipline isn't about feeling motivated; it's about doing what needs to be done, even when you don't feel like it. How about this? Let's set a timer for 25 minutes, and you tackle as much as you can. Then, take a break. Deal?"

Child: "Fine, I'll try."

Parent: "Good call. The more you stick to the habit of just starting, the easier it'll get over time."

This parent-child dialogue cultivates the child's sense of discipline and self-reliance by teaching them to push through resistance while strengthening their trust in the parent as a guide rather than an enforcer. By introducing the concept that discipline trumps motivation and offering a practical strategy (a 25-minute timer), the parent helps the child build a habit of taking action, even when enthusiasm is low, setting them up for long-term success in managing responsibilities.

This conversation succeeds because it validates the child's reluctance, reframes discipline as an empowering choice, and provides an achievable starting point, making the math homework less daunting. The child walks away with a small win, a budding understanding of perseverance, and reassurance from the parent's supportive approach, which enhances their work ethic and deepens their connection.

* * *

Discipline can sometimes feel like an uphill bike ride.

To reach your goal, which is the top, it's hard work... Your legs are burning, you're out of breath, your heart is pounding... But once you hit that peak? The other side of all your hard work is very exhilarating!

Being disciplined means resisting the urge to coast too early, knowing it's not over until it's over, and establishing rules for yourself to build good habits that line up with your goals!

We all have things we want to achieve, and that's great, but the key is being relentless about those actions over and over again until you reach them.

To be DISCIPLINED in your life...

#1 Set clear goals and expectations.
#2 Establish rules or steps to attain goals... and STICK TO THEM!
#3 No early coasting... because fun is for after the work is done!

 **Action Steps:**

Action Step #1: List one thing you will do to be more dependable.

Action Step #2: List one thing you will do to be more dedicated.

Action Step #3: List one thing you will do to be more "gritty" and "do work."

Activities to Build Grit

1. **"Hard Things" Journal**
    Encourage your child to keep a journal where they write down one challenge they faced each week and how they handled it. Over time, they'll see how they've grown and how persistence pays off.

2. **Set a Long-Term Goal with Milestones**
    Work with your child to identify a goal they're passionate about—like improving their grades, earning money for something they want, or training for a sport. Break it into milestones and check in periodically to celebrate progress and discuss challenges.

3. **Take on a Family "Challenge Series"**
    As a family, tackle something that requires grit, like running a 5K, completing a home project, or learning a new skill together. Discuss how persistence and teamwork make the challenge doable.

4. **Expose Them to Real Stories of Grit**
    Introduce your child to books, movies, or podcasts about people who overcame significant obstacles—like entrepreneurs, athletes, or activists. Afterward, discuss what lessons they took away and how they can apply those lessons to their own life.

5. **Teach Problem-Solving Skills**
    When your child feels stuck, guide them through brainstorming possible solutions instead of jumping in to solve the problem.

    For example:

    Parent: "Okay, so your project partner isn't pulling their weight. What are your options here?"

Child: "I guess I could talk to the teacher or try to cover more of the work myself."

Parent: "Both solid ideas. You could also talk to your project partner in a non-confrontational way to try to find out why she is slacking. Maybe something challenging is going on in her life that is affecting her work ethic. Which solution do you feel the most comfortable with trying?"

6. **Encourage Small Acts of Consistency**

    Challenge your child to commit to one habit that builds their grit, like working out regularly, reading a book for personal growth, or practicing a skill daily. Discuss how consistency builds discipline and resilience over time.

Table Talk:

- Is there a role model you know about that has overcome adversity with a strong work ethic?
- What are some ways that you show that you are dependable?
- What are some tasks that you often avoid or put off by making excuses? These tend to be things that you are supposed to do, but don't always enjoy.
- What are some specific strategies that you can use to become more dependable? (e.g., "I am often late, so I will set my alarm to leave the house at a certain time.")
- Have you ever heard the saying, "Hard work beats talent when talent doesn't work hard?" What do you think that means? How does that make you feel?

CHAPTER 4

Self-Control

 **Goal: Equip your children with the tools needed to avoid retaliating and understand the high cost of losing control.** Teach them that everything in their brand is created or destroyed through their ability to have self-control. Teach them to create good habits and give them strategies to use when temptations arise. Teach them how to avoid instant gratification.

"SELF-CONTROL is the quality that distinguishes the fittest to survive."
—*George Bernard Shaw*

Building Self-Control

Learning self-control is one of the most valuable skills for our children to learn at an early age because it forms the foundation for making thoughtful decisions, managing emotions, and achieving long-term success.

Teaching kids self-control early on sets them up for life in a way that's hard to replicate later. When kids learn to manage their impulses—whether it's not grabbing every cookie or waiting their turn—they're building a foundation for handling bigger challenges down the road. It's like giving them a mental muscle that gets stronger with practice. Studies show kids with solid self-control tend to do better in school, have healthier relationships, and even manage stress more effectively as adults. Think of the famous marshmallow test: kids who could wait for a second treat instead of eating the first one right away ended up with better outcomes years later.

For parents, it's not just about avoiding tantrums (though that's a perk). It's about helping kids learn to think before they act, which ties into emotional regulation and decision-making. If they don't get that early, it's tougher to catch up when the stakes are higher—like resisting peer pressure or sticking to goals. Plus, kids' brains are super malleable when they're young, so those lessons stick deeper and shape how they approach the world. It's less about control for control's sake and more about equipping them to navigate life without crashing and burning.

Let's dig deeper. Teaching self-control early is like planting a seed that grows into a whole tree of life skills. One main reason it's so crucial is that it ties directly into how kids develop executive function—those brain processes that help with planning, focusing, and resisting temptation. When parents guide kids through this at a young age, they're literally helping wire their brains for success. The prefrontal cortex, which handles self-regulation, is still forming in early childhood, so it's prime time to shape it. Miss that window, and it's not impossible to learn later, but it's like trying to train a stubborn old dog new tricks—doable, just harder.

Another angle is social. Kids without self-control struggle to play nicely with others. If they can't wait, share, or handle a no, they're more likely to clash with peers, which can snowball into bigger issues like isolation or acting out. Early lessons in patience and restraint teach them empathy and cooperation, too—skills that make them better friends, partners, and even coworkers later on. Parents who skip this part might find themselves dealing with a kid who's not just tough at home but also out in the world.

Then, there's the long-game payoff. Self-control isn't just about saying no to candy; it's about saying yes to bigger goals. Kids who master it early are more likely to stick with homework, save money, or chase a dream instead of chasing instant gratification. It's linked to lower rates of obesity, addiction, and even crime down the line—pretty wild how much it ripples. For parents, it's an investment: put in the work now, and you're not just raising a child who listens, but one who can steer their own ship through life's storms. And honestly, it's empowering for the kids, too—they feel in charge of themselves, not like the world's just yanking them around.

Why Is It So Important?

1. Promotes Emotional Regulation

Self-control helps children and teens manage their emotions in healthy ways. Instead of reacting impulsively—like lashing out in anger or shutting down when frustrated—they learn to pause, process their feelings, and respond constructively. This leads to better relationships and improved mental well-being.

2. Builds Resilience

We all know that life is full of challenges and temptations. Self-control equips them to handle setbacks without giving up, resist peer pressure, and stay focused on their goals. It teaches them how to persevere, which is a crucial trait for success in school, sports, and life.

3. Encourages Better Decision-Making

When kids learn to delay gratification—choosing what's best for their future over immediate satisfaction—they develop the ability to think critically and weigh consequences. This skill is essential for navigating everything from academics to friendships to career planning.

4. Improves Social Skills

Self-control helps kids develop empathy and patience. They learn to take turns, listen to others, and resist interrupting or acting out. These behaviors build trust and strengthen friendships, setting the stage for healthy social interactions throughout life.

5. Supports Academic and Personal Goals

From completing homework to practicing for a recital, success often requires resisting distractions and staying focused. Self-control helps kids prioritize tasks and develop discipline, which can lead to better academic performance and a stronger sense of accomplishment.

6. Reduces Risky Behaviors

Teens, in particular, face many opportunities to engage in risky behaviors, from experimenting with alcohol and drugs to engaging in unsafe online practices. Self-control empowers them to think through the consequences and make choices that align with their values and goals.

7. Fosters Independence and Responsibility

Kids who learn self-control are better equipped to take ownership of their actions. They understand the connection between their choices and outcomes, which helps them become more independent, responsible, and capable of handling challenges without relying on constant guidance.

8. Sets the Stage for Future Success

Research has shown that self-control in childhood is linked to greater success in adulthood, including higher educational attainment, better health, and improved financial stability. It's a skill that pays dividends for a lifetime.

So, how do we foster self-control in our kids?

- **Model It:** Kids learn from watching us! Demonstrate patience and thoughtful decision-making in your daily life.
- **Practice Mindfulness:** Teach them to pause and take a breath before reacting. I love the 10-second rule.
- **Set Achievable Goals:** Help them work on small tasks that require focus and discipline.
- **Encourage Delayed Gratification:** Games like waiting to eat a treat or saving allowance for a bigger purchase will build this muscle.
- **Celebrate Progress:** Acknowledge their effort often when they practice self-control, even in small ways.

By learning self-control, your kids will gain the tools to navigate the world with confidence, kindness, and resilience. It's a skill that helps them not just survive but thrive.

What's the Difference Between Willpower and Self-Control?

Ask your children:

What does the word self-control mean?
What does willpower mean?
Why are both important?

Self-control and willpower are like close cousins—they overlap a ton, but they're not quite identical. Self-control is the broader ability to manage your impulses, emotions, and actions, often in the moment. Willpower, though, is more like the fuel tank for that ability—it's the mental energy or resolve you tap into to make self-control happen, especially when it's tough. Think of self-control as the skill and willpower as the grit that powers it. When we keep ourselves from doing things that we know we shouldn't, we have used self-control. When we make ourselves do things that we should, we have used willpower.

Here's how they tie together: when your child learns self-control early, they're essentially training their willpower muscle, too. Every time they resist yelling in frustration or sneaking a snack before dinner, they're not just practicing restraint—they're building up that inner strength to push through resistance. Psychologists often call willpower a finite resource, like a battery that drains with use but recharges with rest. Kids who get good at self-control learn how to manage that battery better—knowing when to save it and how to refill it.

The connection gets clearer in tough spots. Let's say your child wants to finish a puzzle but keeps getting distracted. Self-control keeps them focused, but willpower is what keeps them going when they're tired or bored. Early lessons in self-control teach them to lean on willpower strategically—like breaking a big task into chunks or finding little rewards to keep going. Over time, this combo becomes second nature. Research backs this up: Studies like those from the American Psychological Association show that kids with stronger self-control (and the willpower behind it) tend to have higher resilience, better grades, and even improved health outcomes.

It's not all rosy, though—willpower can run dry, especially under stress. That's where self-control habits kick in. If children are used to pausing before acting, they don't need as much raw willpower to make good choices; it's baked into their routine. So, for parents, teaching self-control isn't just about building a skill—it's about boosting that willpower reserve, too, giving kids a double-edged tool to tackle life's curveballs.

Self-control keeps you out of trouble. Willpower helps you get ahead.

Activity:

Fill in the blank with either SC (for self-control) or WP (for willpower).

- When the alarm goes off early in the morning, so we can get a power run in before school, it takes ___ to get up and go.
- When the choice for lunch is between a delicious but greasy "sloppy joe" and a salad made of greens, chicken, and nuts, and we choose the salad, we have used our ___.
- When the guys are urging you to "hang out" after midnight, and you choose to go home to get eight hours of sleep, you are using ___.
- When an opponent on the field makes a nasty remark to you during a game, and you ignore it, you're using ___.
- When your coach makes you stay after practice and gives you a tongue-lashing, and you don't give him a dirty look, you're using ___.
- When your parents make what you consider "unfair" demands on you, and you accept them without saying what you are thinking about them, you're using ___.
- When a policeman stops you for speeding, and you treat him with respect, you're using ___.

 **Parent/Child Dialogue Example:**

Setting: *A mom and her child are on the couch after a blowup earlier. The child had fired off a snarky comment about a classmate on social media, and it blew up in her face.*

Parent: "Hey, let's unpack that post from earlier. What happened?"

Child: "I was just so mad! Clara was clowning me in the group chat, and I'd had it. So, I posted what I did."

Parent: "Yeah, I saw it... and the other 27 comments."

Child: "She had it coming! She struts around like she's the queen of everything. Why should I just sit there and take it?"

Parent: "I get it. I'd be mad, too. But how are you feeling now that it's out there?"

Child: "I don't know... kinda annoyed. It blew up way more than I thought. Now, people are acting like *I'm* the jerk."

Parent: "That one post painted a picture of you—like someone who snaps instead of keeping it cool. Probably not the vibe you were going for."

Child: "Yeah, it does make me look kinda lame now."

Parent: "Let's rewind it. What if you'd hit pause before posting? Thought about how it might play out. What else could you have done?"

Child: "Maybe skipped the post? Or just DM'd her instead?"

Parent: "Boom, you're onto it. That's self-control—taking a pause to figure out what's worth it. When you let the heat take over, it's like your emotions are running the show instead of you."

Child: "True, I didn't need to blast it everywhere. Ugh, what a mess."

Parent: "So, think of self-control like a secret weapon. It's not about bottling up how you feel—it's about picking how you want to roll with it."

Child: "Okay, you're right, Mom. I could've dodged this whole dumpster fire."

Parent: "Yes. But look—now you have learned something. We all trip up sometimes; it's what you do after that counts."

Child: "Got it. The lesson is locked in. Self-control mode on next time."

Parent: "That's my girl. Lesson learned."

Child: "Thanks, Mom. But, uh... what do I do now? This whole thing's still out there."

Parent: "Good question! You've got options to turn it around. First, how about pulling the post down? It's not erasing what happened, but it stops the fire from spreading more."

Child: "Yeah, I can delete it. That's easy."

Parent: "Great. Then, maybe think about smoothing things over with Clara. Doesn't have to be a big deal—just a quick message like, 'Hey, I was mad earlier, didn't mean to blow it up like that. I'm really sorry, and I hope you'll be able to forgive me.' Keeps it real without overdoing it."

Child: "Ugh, that feels weird. What if she's still a jerk about it?"

Parent: "Yes, it might feel awkward. If she's still salty, that's on her, not you. You're just doing the right thing and being the bigger person, so you need to feel good about that and move on."

Child: "Okay, I guess I could try that."

Parent: "Nice. And one more thing—maybe post something chill later, like a funny meme or a pic of something you're into. Nothing heavy, just a reset to show the real you, not the mad-you from earlier."

Child: "Really good idea."

Parent: "We all make mistakes, but when we learn from them... that's what makes all the difference."

Child: "You're so right. Thanks, Mom."

This exchange shows how self-control can prevent situations from escalating, and it frames the skill as empowering rather than restrictive. It also gives the teen a chance to reflect and take responsibility without feeling judged.

Self-control is what makes you behave responsibly, no matter what you are feeling inside. It also helps you to get through difficult situations without causing problems or pain to yourself or others who are involved.

More examples for children:

- When a teammate is driving you crazy and causing you FRUSTRATION, you tell yourself, *"Self, I'm not going to lose it. That is my teammate, and I'm going to support him for the good of the team."*
- When a friend is causing trouble by writing things about you on X and making you ANGRY, you tell yourself, *"Self, I am going to calm down first and get my thoughts together before I speak to her in a calm manner."*
- When you have a big game coming up and need to eat healthy food, but your friends are TEMPTING you with junk food, you tell yourself, *"Self, that stuff isn't good for me, and I will play my best if I stick to my own nutrition plan."*

You see, practicing self-control is critical to your success!

People who have great self-control are typically more successful in life.

People who lack self-control are often underachievers who may suffer from addictions, financial problems, or other painful consequences.

Activity:

What are some serious situations that you regularly find yourself in where not having self-control can lead to very severe consequences? Complete the chart below.

Example:

- Setting: Football game
- Common situation: Ref makes a bad call.
- Consequences without self-control: I go "nuts" on the ref and incur a penalty myself, putting my team in an even worse situation.

Sports Competitions and Games

- Setting:_____
- Common situation:_____
- Consequences without self-control:_____

Family

- Setting:_____
- Common situation:_____
- Consequences without self-control:_____

Girlfriend/Boyfriend

- Setting:_____
- Common situation:_____
- Consequences without self-control:_____

Alcohol/Drugs

- Setting:_____
- Common situation:_____
- Consequences without self-control:_____

Teachers

- Setting:_____
- Common situation:_____
- Consequences without self-control:_____

Coaches

- Setting:_____
- Common situation:_____
- Consequences without self-control:_____

You see, by not having self-control, your life can change dramatically because when you lose self-control, you will no longer be able to control the consequences of your actions.

For example, you may get angry and push someone. What if you only meant to push him with little force, but you end up pushing him harder than you anticipated, and he falls down, hits his head on the concrete, and you need to call 911? These types of scenarios happen too many times.

Think of the times you may have heard someone say:

- "But I didn't mean for that to happen!"
- "But I didn't think anyone would really get hurt!"
- "But I didn't mean for him to get in that much trouble."
- "But I was only going to have one drink."
- "But I only told one person, and somehow everyone knows now."

When you lose self-control, you cannot control the outcomes. Things often turn out differently from what you thought they would.

Below are some simple techniques for managing anger and frustration so that you will have a greater chance of having self-control.

- INVITE a friend or family member to help you stay focused in difficult situations.
- AVOID situations you expect to be particularly challenging.
- COUNT TO 10 before taking action.
- BREATHE DEEPLY to calm yourself.

- MAKE A LIST of the consequences you could face for giving in to temptations that confront you every day.

Retaliation. Who Gets Caught?

Because I have four very competitive children who are very close in age, teaching them about retaliation was a big one in our house! Whether they were angered by a sibling, friend, or teammate, this lesson came into play quite often.

When we are wronged, one of the most difficult things to do is to hold back from retaliating. We see it in sports games all the time.

For example, when you're watching a game and a fight breaks out, who usually gets the penalty? It's typically the one that retaliates, as many times you don't see the first "jab" or infraction. There are countless examples of pro athletes and celebrities losing self-control, which results in them getting kicked off the team, getting fined a lot of money, and losing endorsements. Sometimes, it ends up costing them their careers. Things never go the way you want them to go when you're out of control, and the costs are just way too high.

In the classroom, how many times does a student get called out for talking when it was their friend sitting next to them who whispered first?

It's important to note that self-control does NOT mean hiding or denying your true feelings, but it does mean controlling your feelings and NOT retaliating.

When you pause to think before reacting emotionally to a situation and are able to remain calm, you have just made a great decision!

Avoiding the urge to retaliate is a powerful tool. Every single person on earth has situations begging for retaliation, but the ones who have learned to exercise self-control have a greater advantage in achieving their goals.

Try Self-Talk to Avoid Retaliation

Having self-control when situations and people are poking at your nerves is not easy. You can only control yourself, and you can't control outside situations or other people.

In most cases, there's no victory in responding to conflict with more conflict. Think about that for a minute. When you say things or act in a way that causes pain or trouble for you and/or another person, you run the risk of:

- getting suspended or penalized
- looking crazy and irrational
- losing friends and ruining relationships

To be clear, no one is asking you to sit back and tolerate another person crossing your boundaries physically or emotionally, especially if you are in danger or feeling threatened. If that's the case, defend yourself and/or get help ASAP!

A good way to strengthen your self-control in times of stress is to engage in self-talk, which involves a positive affirmation of how you want to act.

Example for your child:

Your brother is making you insanely angry, and you really want to punch him in the face. Your self-talk might go something like this:

"Self, I will not let Jake's behavior cause me to get angry. He's my brother, I love him, and he usually makes me laugh."

Activity:

1. All of your friends get invited to a party, but you. How would you be tempted to retaliate? If you retaliate, what could possibly happen? What's the best way to respond to this situation?
2. Someone posts something horrible about you on social media. How would you be tempted to retaliate? If you retaliate, what could possibly happen? What's the best way to respond to this situation?
3. You're playing a game of basketball, and your team is behind by just a few goals. You start to go up for a 3-pointer, and your opponent elbows you intentionally, causing you to lose the ball. How would you

be tempted to retaliate? If you retaliate, what could possibly happen? What's the best way to respond to this situation?

4. You see someone flirting/texting with your girlfriend or boyfriend. You've told them to stop, and it doesn't seem to be working. You're angry, and you want to retaliate. How would you be tempted to retaliate? If you retaliate, what could possibly happen? What's the best way to respond to this situation?

Fight the Instant Gratification

Teaching your children delayed gratification is one of the most powerful ways to help them develop self-control and set them up for long-term success. In today's world of instant gratification—where likes, replies, and rewards are just a click away—it's easy for teens to prioritize short-term desires over long-term goals. However, learning to delay gratification teaches them to pause, consider the consequences, and make thoughtful choices that align with their values and aspirations. This skill is deeply tied to self-control because it trains them to manage impulses and resist immediate temptations, whether it's spending money impulsively, skipping homework for a video game, or posting something on social media in anger. Children who master delayed gratification are more likely to achieve their goals, build stronger relationships, and handle challenges with resilience. By helping your children understand the bigger picture and practice patience, you're equipping them with a critical tool for navigating life's complexities.

Good Habits Are Hard to Break, Too

Teaching your children that good habits are just as hard to break as bad habits is essential because it emphasizes the power of consistency and self-control in shaping their future. Once a positive habit—like regular exercise, saving money, or practicing kindness—becomes ingrained, it operates almost on autopilot, requiring less effort to maintain. This is why building good habits early is so valuable; they become part of your child's identity and routine, making it easier to stay on track even during challenging times. Highlighting this idea helps children see that the effort they put into developing positive behaviors today will pay off in the long run, creating a foundation of self-control that supports their goals. Just as bad habits can feel impossible to shake, good habits can become a strong guiding force in their lives. By fostering this perspective, you empower your child to intentionally create patterns that will benefit them for years to come.

Self-Control Tips

1. Recognize when your willpower muscle is weak. Avoid temptations at this time.
    Example: When you are trying to save money, don't go into your favorite store in the mall.

2. Commit to a plan BEFORE you are in a tempting situation.
    Example: You are trying to lose weight, and you have been invited to go to dinner with a friend at your favorite pizza place. Decide before you go that you are going to have only 1 slice of pizza or order a salad instead.

3. Reward yourself after using self-control. Dangle the carrot!
    Example: You make your goal of working out every day for a week. Reward yourself by going to a movie.

4. Penalize yourself for caving in. (This is tough to do, but it works.)
    Example: You didn't use self-control to focus on your schoolwork this week, so no Xbox all weekend.

 **Action Steps:**

Let's create some good habits!

Step 1: Decide exactly which habits you want to work on. List one good habit you want to create to reach a goal.

Step 2: Create some rewards and consequences. List one thing you will do to reward yourself if you stick to your new habit for a certain amount of time. Favorite meal? Massage? New outfit? Then, list one thing you will do if you break your new habit. Put a dollar in a jar? Give up your gaming system for a while?

Step 3: Figure out a way to track your habits and keep yourself accountable. List what method you will use to keep track of your new habit.

Extra credit: Build a super support team. List 2–3 people who will be your support team, and note specifically how they will support you and your new habit. Daily or weekly check-ins? Encouragement when you feel like giving up? Joining you in building the same good habit? Be creative and make this fun.

Activity:

Do you have strong willpower and self-control muscles?

Take this quiz to find out.

For each of the questions below, circle the answer closest to how you would NORMALLY react.

You were expecting to get a great position on a team, but instead, you were cut during tryouts. What do you do?

1. I ask the coach how I could improve my performance. (5 points)
2. I walk away feeling frustrated and upset. (3 points)
3. I yell at the coach and/or my teammates. (1 point)

You were out all day biking and swimming in the hot sun, and you were exhausted. When you get home, your mother reminds you to take out the trash right away. What do you do?

1. I take out the trash immediately. (5 points)
2. I take out the trash, but much later, once I have had time to rest. (3 points)
3. I tell my mom I'm exhausted and that someone else should take out the trash. (1 point)

Your teachers load you up with homework, your coach adds extra practice sessions, or your band adds extra rehearsals for a competition that's coming up. Now, your friend asks you to help her with her science project. What do you do?

1. I tell my friend I'm just too busy to help, but maybe I'll have time tomorrow. (5 points)
2. Try helping and then give up in frustration. (3 points)
3. Get angry with my friend and tell her she's driving me crazy. (1 point)

A friend invites you over when his parents are away, and it turns out he's having a party. He offers you a beer. What do you do?

1. I say "no thanks" and have a Coke. (5 points)
2. I say thanks, but have just a sip. (3 points)
3. I have a beer or two. (1 point)

RESULTS:

Add the numerical values of your answers above and add to determine your score below:

20 points: Congratulations! You seem to have very good self-control and willpower. Keep up the good work. If you also have strong values, a good work ethic, and a positive attitude, you have what it takes to succeed in life.

12–19 points: It looks like you have good self-control and willpower some of the time, but not all of the time. To improve these "muscles," you might want to keep a record of the kinds of situations in which you lose control, so you can avoid or manage those situations.

0–11 points: It looks like you have a tough time with self-control, and that's a problem that could land you in trouble. Before you lose control in the wrong situation, it's important to figure out why you're flying out of control and to learn methods that help you keep it together.

To wrap up, REMEMBER:

- **Self-control means behaving responsibly, no matter how you feel.**
- **The cost of losing your temper is too high.**
- **Instant gratification is only temporary.**
- **Good habits trump bad habits every time.**
- **Retaliation never EVER wins.**

Table Talk 1:

- Share about a time when you have "lost it." What happened next? What would you do differently next time?
- Share about a time when you have had self-control and had a good outcome.
- What's something that you want to have control over, but you feel like it has control over you?
- What are some things that you can do to have self-control regarding the situations you just named?
- How can you avoid retaliating when you see something you don't like on social media?
- How can you avoid retaliating in general?

Table Talk 2:

- Discuss ways to have self-control in the following situations:
    - o Trying to break bad habits
    - o Being lazy
    - o Bad language
    - o Too much Snapchatting
    - o Getting work done before fun
    - o Dealing with anger
    - o Keeping your mouth shut and avoiding retaliating
- Where do YOU need more self-control?

Table Talk 3:

Let's talk about some stories of consequences that you have had, or others have had, when making poor choices, and the lessons learned. Then ask these questions:

- What could happen when you choose to drive faster than the speed limit?
- What could happen when you choose to send a rage text in the heat of the moment to a friend or family member?
- What could happen when you choose to stay out past your curfew?
- What could happen when you lose your temper in a game?

Create a list of your "go-to" people who will help talk you out of making a poor decision, who will help you stay true to your word and your values, and who will help you have the self-control to stick to your goals when you are having a weak moment.

Table Talk 4:

Share a habit you want to work on, one thing you will do to reward yourself if accomplished, or the consequences if not. How will you keep yourself accountable? Who will be your support team, and how will they support? Have your child do the same.

CHAPTER 5

Values

 Goal: Teach your children that personal values are the core beliefs and philosophies that you hold about life. They will begin to define their personal values and learn how to respect the values of others. Introduce the concept that once you define your personal value system, it will be easier to make moral decisions. Encourage them to take a deep look at their personal value system.

Defining Their Values

As I mentioned, helping your children define their brand will also help them define their values. Their values are their core beliefs and philosophies about what's really important to them.

We all know that values determine how we judge things, right from wrong. When we were growing up, we probably used the values of the adults around us to make sense of the world, and we did this because it's what we knew. It was comfortable and easy that way.

As we became adults, we likely held on to some of our childhood values, rejected some, or may have even forgotten some. But have you ever really sat down with your kids and talked to them in a direct way about what YOUR values are? What standards do you use to guide your actions, judgments, and attitudes? And have you ever talked to them about what THEIR values are?

We may think we know based on how they spend their time and money and by what they are Snapchatting, but it's critical to have these conversations with them sooner or later before the tough decision-making begins!

In this chapter, you will learn to teach your child:

- Defining what their personal values are
- Understanding how values impact their brand
- Accepting other people's values, even if they're different from your own
- Knowing that their friends also reflect their values

 **Parent/Child Dialogue Example:**

Parent: "Hey, I noticed you didn't tell your coach the truth about why you missed practice yesterday."

Child: "I didn't think it really mattered. I mean, I didn't feel like dealing with it."

Parent: "I get that, but let's think about it. What's one of the values you really care about?"

Child: "I guess... being honest?"

Parent: "Right. So, when you decided not to tell the truth, how did that line up with your value of honesty?"

Child: "It didn't... but I didn't want to get in trouble."

Parent: "That's a tough spot. But if you let fear steer you instead of your values, it's easy to lose trust with people. Do you think it would feel better if you did what was right and own up to it now?"

Child: "Yeah, probably, but it's gonna be real hard to do that."

Parent: "I'm here to help and support. Let's figure out the best way to approach this situation with your coach."

Child: "Okay, what should I say? Can I just text him?"

Parent: "I think you would gain more of his respect if you spoke to him in person."

Child: "Ugh... I knew you were gonna say that. It's gonna be awful."

Parent: "It's the right way to handle it. Say something like this: "Hey Coach, I wasn't honest with you about why I missed practice. I was way behind on a project that was due, and I ran out of time. I let myself down by procrastinating, which also let you down, and I should have been honest with you. I'm really sorry, and I hope you'll forgive me."

Child: "Mom, this is gonna be so hard, and he's gonna be so mad."

Parent: "You can only control what you can control. Know that you are making the right choice, and you will feel much better. He may be mad at first, but I believe you will gain his respect for doing the right thing."

Child: "I hope you're right, Mom. But regardless, I already feel better with this approach. It doesn't feel good knowing that I lied."

This dialogue demonstrates a thoughtful approach to teaching the child about integrity, self-reflection, and accountability while highlighting the parent's role as a supportive guide in navigating moral dilemmas. It shows how the parent uses a real-life situation—lying to the coach—to prompt the child to examine their own values, recognize the disconnect between their actions and beliefs, and consider the consequences of their choices, all within a safe, nonjudgmental space.

The conversation reveals the parent's skill in fostering critical thinking by asking questions ("How did that line up with your value of honesty?") rather than lecturing, which empowers the child to connect their behavior to their identity. It also illustrates the tension between fear and doing what's right, showing the child that living by their values (honesty) can build trust and self-respect, even if it's uncomfortable. The parent's offer to help strategize a solution further shows a partnership approach, reinforcing the child's confidence to make amends and grow from the experience. Overall, it showcases a lesson in aligning actions with personal principles, supported by a strong, trusting parent-child relationship.

Knowing Your Values Matters

Knowing your values is like having a map for life. Think about it—when you don't know what you stand for, it's easy to get lost or make choices you regret later. Values help you figure out who you are and what's important to you, so when tough decisions come up, you're not just guessing or following the crowd.

Let's say your friend wants you to do something that feels wrong, but you know you value honesty and respect. Your values can give you the courage to say no and stick to what feels right for you.

Here's the good news: when you live by your values, you feel good about yourself because your actions match who you want to be. It's like being your own hero in the story of your life. But first, you have to know what those values are. They don't have to be perfect, and they might change as you grow, but knowing them now is the first step to building a life you're proud of.

Our child's values can be identified by reflecting on what matters most to them and how they want to live their lives. Here's a step-by-step guide they can follow:

1. What Makes You Feel Proud?

- Ask: *When was the last time I felt really proud of myself? What was I doing?*
- Example: If you felt proud after helping a friend, kindness or generosity might be one of your values.

2. What Upsets You?

- Ask: *What really frustrates or upsets me? Why does it bother me so much?*
- Example: If you get upset when someone is unfair, you might value justice or fairness.

3. Who Inspires You?

- Ask: *Who do I admire, and why? What qualities do they have that I respect?*

- Example: If you admire someone for standing up for others, courage or leadership might be a value.

4. What Feels Right?

- Ask: *When do I feel most like myself? What am I doing?*
- Example: If you feel happiest when you're creating something, creativity might be one of your values.

5. Try a Values List

- Make a list of common values, like honesty, friendship, care for others, family, etc.

6. Rank Your Top 3

- Narrow down your list by asking: *If I could only live by three values, which ones would they be?*

7. Check Your Choices

- Ask: *Do these values align with how I'm living my life? If not, what could I change to live closer to them?*

This process is about self-discovery, so encourage teens to take their time. Their values don't have to be perfect, and they can evolve as they grow and learn.

Your values decide everything.

Ask your child this:

- If you came across a one-hundred-dollar bill in the aisle of the grocery store, what would you do with it?
- Would you immediately take it to the customer service desk?
- Would you look around to see if anyone is searching for lost money?
- Or would you start thinking of ways to spend it right away?

EVERYTHING you do, including what you do with the $100 bill, defines your values. Your values are what's most important in your life and your guidelines for making ALL your decisions.

So, the good thing is… Once you define your values, your decisions are already made for you. Here's how they work. Values help you to decide how you spend your time and whom you build relationships with.

To determine if something falls into your values system, put it to the test. Ask these questions…

1 - Is this important?
2 - Does it feel right?
3 - Can it stand up to peer pressure?
4 - Does it fit my brand?

Live by the Platinum Rule

People value different things. In most cases, you can tell what someone's values are by the way they spend their time and the way they spend their money.

Your kids' classmates, teammates, friends, family members, and even random strangers will have a different perspective on values, and from time to time, their opinions may clash.

So, what should they do when that happens? The important thing to hold onto is this: Although their values may be different from someone else's, it's important to be accepting of others while also staying true to who they are.

Let me break it down to you "old school"…
As kids, we were always taught the Golden Rule:
Treat others the way that YOU want to be treated. Look at this example.

Golden Rule vs. Platinum Rule

Differences can make life interesting, but also challenging at the same time.

Sometimes, it is difficult to deal with someone who is completely different from you. I am sure you know what the Golden Rule is: Treat others the way that YOU want to be treated. However, let's look at the Platinum Rule: Treat others the way that THEY want to be treated.

What is the difference here?

The Platinum rule accommodates the feelings of others. Instead of giving others the same thing that you want, you learn what OTHERS want and give them what THEY want. Have you ever heard the phrase, "Put yourself in someone else's shoes?"

Look at this example.

A few months ago, one of my friends was having a tough time, and I wanted to do something nice for her. My favorite "food pick-me-up" is Oreo ice cream. So, I decided to take my friend Oreo ice cream. I was treating her the same way that I would want to be treated. But what if she isn't a big ice cream fan? Her favorite "feel-good" food is a hot glazed donut.

So, taking your friend what she likes best is the Platinum Rule. Even better! You are treating her like SHE wants to be treated.

See the difference?

The Platinum Rule accommodates the feelings of OTHERS and takes the focus from you.

Put yourself in someone else's shoes... that's the Platinum Rule!

Values and Friendships

We already looked at friendships in the first chapter, but here we are again because surrounding yourself with people who have the same values is important. I'll say it again: You are the average of the five people you spend the most time with. Seriously, think about that.

Ask your child the following questions:

- How do you feel about YOUR TOP 5 people?
- Relieved?
- Encouraged?
- Confident?
- Secure?

- Or does that make you feel insecure, scared, or panicked?
- How do your friends add or subtract from your brand?

It's up to you to surround yourself with the right people who hold similar values to yours. Choose the wrong people, and you're looking at some heavy damage to your reputation because your friends are your choices, and your friends are a direct reflection of your values. Hold on tight to the good friends in your life because they are truly valuable.

 **Action Steps:**

Look over the Snowflake diagram that you child filled out in the first lesson, Building Your Brand. Let's see if any changes have been made after working through this first section of the book.

ACTIVITY:

Let's begin to identify things you value in various aspects of your life. Circle below the things you value.

I value this person/these people in my life:
Friends
Mentor
Youth Minister
Coach
Family
Myself
Teammate
Girlfriend
Pet
Teacher

I value spending time at this place/these places:
Home
At church
At camp
Away from home
At a concert
At practice
At school
At a sporting event
At a party

I value doing this/these:
Exercising
Hanging out with friends
Shopping

Watching a movie
Chilling
Helping others
Cooking
Reading
Playing sports
Working
Listening to music
Playing video games

I feel valued when I'm:
Getting good grades
Overcoming an obstacle
Praised by my parents
Performing a talent well
Reaching a goal
Given a compliment
Wearing nice clothes
Being a good friend
Serving others
Making money
Standing up for what I believe in

Look at these examples below. Notice what each person in history valued.

Mother Teresa:
Faith and Service
She devoted her life to aiding sick and poor people around the world.

Martin Luther King Jr.:
Peace, Freedom, Justice
Leader of the civil rights movement of the 1960s.

Lou Gehrig
Bravery, Citizenship
A baseball hero who died bravely of a frightening disease.

Helen Keller
Education, Hard work
Inspirational blind and deaf author and speaker.

Now, let's try this with people you know. List three people in the boxes below that you value and write their names in the space provided. Then, list their occupation below the box and fill in the blanks with descriptive words of things you feel they value.

Name:
Occupation:

_____

_____

_____

Name:
Occupation:

_____

_____

_____

Name:
Occupation:

_____

_____

_____

"Your beliefs become your thoughts, your thoughts become your words,
your words become your actions, your actions become your habits,
your habits become your values, your values become your destiny."
—Mahatma Gandhi

"Values are like fingerprints. No one's are the same, but you leave
them all over everything you do."
—Elvis Presley

Table Talk 1:

Say: "Your values give you direction and help you to make good choices. They help you be a better you! But sometimes, when you're with other people, you make choices or actions that are different from your values. There may be other times when you disagree with the values of others, and it could cause conflicts. Our mission should be to find a way to be true to our values and learn to accept the values of others, even when we don't agree with them."

- Has it ever been hard for you to stay true to your values? Please explain.
- Has there ever been a time when you disagreed with a friend about a value, and it caused a problem in your relationship?
- Name three values that you believe to be typically American.
- Name three values that you believe would be important to a person in a third-world country.
- Name three values that you believe are important to your parents.

Table Talk 2:

- Did you know that you are the sum of the five friends or people that you spend the most time with?
- Do you think it's important to choose friends who have the same internal values that you have? Why or why not?
- Do you think it's important to choose friends who have the same external values that you have? Why or why not?

Sometimes in a weak moment, you may be tempted to compromise your values. For example, sometimes you may not have the self-control to make a good decision when faced with temptations, and that's why it's best to have friends who will be able to support you and encourage you to stay true to your values. So, to sum it up, in order to reach your greatest potential and be the best YOU that YOU can be, it is critical that you surround yourself with people who encourage you and help you stay true to your values.

CHAPTER 6

Smart Goals

 **Goal:** Teach your kids how to set both short-term and long-term goals. Learn that goals must be SMART (specific, measurable, attainable, realistic, time-bound). Learn that accountability is key to success. They will explore how to take a big life dream and turn it into an attainable goal, as well as learn how long-term and short-term goals are all part of achieving what they want from life.

Teaching Children to Set Goals Early in Life

Have you ever heard the saying that failing to plan is planning to fail? We all want to win in life and achieve our dreams. The difference between winning and losing is having a detailed, thought-out plan of how you are going to achieve your dreams.

Teaching children to set goals at an early age is one of the most important gifts parents can provide. This life skill shapes their ability to dream, plan, and achieve—setting a strong foundation for personal and professional success. Goal-setting fosters responsibility, resilience, and a growth mindset, all of which are crucial in navigating life's inevitable challenges.

Fostering Responsibility and Independence

When children set goals, they learn to take ownership of their actions and decisions. A child who aims to save money for a toy understands the value of effort and delayed gratification. (Remember the lesson on "instant gratification" from the Self-Control chapter.) This experience helps them connect the dots between actions and outcomes, instilling a sense of accountability. Over time, this practice encourages independence, as children realize they can influence their own future through planning and perseverance.

Building Confidence and Resilience

The process of striving toward a goal often involves overcoming obstacles, which builds resilience. When kids encounter setbacks—whether it's failing to master a skill or struggling to meet a deadline—they learn to adapt, persist, and try again. Achieving even small goals boosts their confidence, teaching them that effort leads to progress. This "can-do" attitude becomes a cornerstone for facing bigger challenges later in life.

Developing Focus and Motivation

Setting goals helps children prioritize their time and energy. In a world filled with distractions, this focus is invaluable. Whether aiming to improve their grades or make a sports team, goal setting keeps kids motivated by providing a clear sense of purpose. They also learn to break large aspirations into manageable steps, making daunting tasks feel achievable.

Encouraging a Growth Mindset

Early goal setting nurtures a growth mindset, the belief that abilities and intelligence can be developed through effort and practice. By celebrating the journey rather than just the outcome, parents can help children view challenges as opportunities to grow. This perspective promotes lifelong learning and adaptability, essential traits in an ever-changing world.

Practical Steps for Parents

We, as parents, can encourage goal setting by helping our children identify meaningful, age-appropriate objectives. A simple framework is to start with SMART goals—Specific, Measurable, Achievable, Relevant, and Time-

Bound. Celebrate progress and accomplishments together, no matter how small, to reinforce the value of hard work and perseverance. Equally important is modeling goal setting in your own life, showing children that the process is relevant and rewarding for everyone.

By teaching children to set goals, parents equip them with the tools to dream big and work hard. This practice not only prepares kids for success but also instills values that will serve them for a lifetime. It's not just about achieving milestones—it's about shaping a mindset that embraces challenges, celebrates growth, and fosters a belief in one's ability to make a difference.

Define SMART Goals

Let's break it down:

Specific: Goals should answer who, what, when, where, and why. They should be detailed.

For example: *"I want to get in shape and run the March Madness Marathon in California this year."* This answers what I want to do, why I want to do it, and where and when.

Measurable: Goals should be able to determine if you have hit your target.

For example: *"I want to finish all three seasons of my favorite Netflix series before exams start, so I won't have that distraction and be able to focus on studying."*

Attainable: Goals can't be far-fetched. They must be within your reach.

For example: *"I want to earn a college scholarship through hard work in the classroom."*

Realistic: Goals should be possible to reach within a certain amount of time.

For example: *"I want to lose 1 pound each week for 10 weeks."*

Time-Bound: Goals must have deadlines. Deadlines will keep you on track.

For example: *"I want to be able to purchase a car by graduation by saving my work money."*

So, to wrap up, when thinking about your goals, ask yourself these questions, and you will find that your goals are SMART!

Who: Who is involved?
What: What do I want to accomplish?
Where: Name a location.
When: Establish a time frame.
Why: Specific reasons why you want to accomplish the goal.

 **Parent/Child Dialogue Example:**

Scenario: Preparing for a Big School Presentation

Parent: "Hey, Claire, how's it going with your science presentation prep?"

Child: "Not good at all. I'm totally stressed out and anxious! It's due in two weeks, and I have no clue where to begin."

Parent: "I hear you—big tasks can definitely feel overwhelming. Have you considered splitting it into smaller, manageable pieces? Maybe setting a few targets to keep you moving forward?"

Child: "Targets? I don't even know what those pieces would look like."

Parent: "No worries, let's sort it out together. What's your endgame here? What would make this presentation a win for you?"

Child: "I'd love for my slides to look polished, to feel calm and ready when I present, and to score a solid grade."

Parent: "Those are fantastic goals! Let's tackle them one by one. What's the first thing you'd need for polished slides?"

Child: "I'd have to dig into my topic, grab some cool visuals and facts, and then put the slides together."

Parent: "Nice breakdown. How much time do you think the digging part will take?"

Child: "Probably three or four hours? But I can't do it all in one go—I'd lose it."

Parent: "That makes sense. How about aiming for an hour tonight and another tomorrow? You could wrap it up by Saturday."

Child: "Yeah, that sounds doable. What about the slide part?"

Parent: "Once your research is set, you could take an evening—like Sunday—to design them. Then next week, you'd have time to work on your speaking confidence. How do you feel about rehearsing with me or your friends?"

Child: "It's kind of weird, but I know it'll help. I could start with you, then maybe try my friends after?"

Parent: "Perfect plan! See how chopping it up into bite-size goals takes the pressure off?"

Child: "Totally—it doesn't feel like a monster anymore. I might jot down a list, so I stay on top of it."

Parent: "Smart move! Goals aren't just about the finish line—they're about mapping the path. You're gonna crush this, Claire. I'm excited to see it come together!"

Child: "Thanks, Mom. I'm actually feeling okay about it now."

This dialogue showcases a collaborative and empowering approach to helping a child manage stress and build planning skills while highlighting the parent's role as a calm, strategic partner in tackling a daunting task like a school presentation. It demonstrates how the parent guides Claire through her anxiety by breaking a large project into smaller, actionable steps, fostering her confidence and sense of control over the process.

Now, let's look at the difference between short-term and long-term goals.

Teaching the Difference Between Short-Term and Long-Term Goals

Helping your kids understand the difference between short-term and long-term goals equips them with essential life-planning skills. Parents can guide them to see how both types of goals work together to create a pathway to success while building habits of intentionality, focus, and resilience. Here's how to approach this lesson:

1. Explain the Concepts with Relatable Examples

- **Short-Term Goals:** These are objectives that can be achieved in a relatively short period, like a day, a week, or a few months. For example, completing homework, preparing for an upcoming test, or saving money for a new outfit.
  Examples:
    o I want to get an A on my math test on Tuesday
    o I want to make the cross-country team this year
    o I want to get that part in the play that I just auditioned for
- **Long-Term Goals:** These take more time to accomplish, often months or years, like graduating with honors, saving for college, or becoming a skilled athlete.
  Examples:
    o I want to be accepted to the college of my choice
    o I want to have my own business
    o I want to have a big family

Conversation Tip:

"Think of short-term goals like stepping stones. You use them to get closer to long-term goals. If your dream is to become a doctor, doing well on this week's biology test is a short-term goal that moves you toward that future."

2. Encourage Personal Reflection

Ask your teen what they want to achieve in the future (long-term goal) and discuss what smaller steps (short-term goals) could help them get there.

Example: A teen who wants to make the varsity soccer team next year could set short-term goals like attending extra practice sessions, improving their fitness, and studying game strategies.

3. Highlight the Importance of Balance

Teens may be tempted to focus only on long-term aspirations or get stuck in the immediate demands of short-term goals. Help them understand the need for both. For instance:

- Without short-term planning, long-term goals remain distant dreams.
- Without a long-term vision, short-term efforts can feel meaningless.

Example: *"Saving $20 this month may seem small, but if you do it consistently, you'll have $240 in a year. That's how short-term actions build up to long-term success."*

4. Model Goal Setting in Your Own Life

Show your teen how you balance short-term and long-term goals in your personal or professional life. This helps teens see that goal setting is a skill used throughout life.

Example: "I want to run a marathon next year (long-term), so I'm following a training plan where I increase my running distance each week (short-term)."

5. Celebrate Milestones Together

Acknowledging progress toward both short-term and long-term goals reinforces the value of persistence and hard work. Celebrating even small victories, like finishing a project or improving a grade, builds motivation to continue.

Example: *"You've been studying 30 minutes every night for your math quiz, and it paid off! That's how you build habits for bigger successes, like acing your final exams."*

6. Teach Adaptability

Life is unpredictable, and goals can shift. Encourage your children to review their progress regularly and adjust their short-term steps as needed. This flexibility prevents frustration and builds problem-solving skills.

Remember: It's okay to change your approach if things aren't working. The important thing is to keep moving toward what matters to you.

By teaching young people to differentiate between short-term and long-term goals, parents help them develop a roadmap for success. This skill not only prepares them for future challenges but also fosters a sense of purpose and confidence that will serve them throughout their lives.

Put a Plan in Place!

Once your kids have set their goals, they must have a plan in place to help them achieve them. Being intentional is always key! If the following things are in place, they have a great chance for success. If they don't, their goals are very likely to fall by the wayside.

1. **Accountability:** Tell someone they trust about their goals so that they'll have support from someone to help them stay focused.
2. **Obstacles:** Consider the potential obstacles that might get in their way, so they're prepared to face them.
3. **Passion:** How badly do they want to accomplish this goal?
4. **Take action:** Have the discipline and the persistence they need.
5. **Create a Habit:** Will they need to make this a part of their daily life?
6. **Rewards and Consequences:** Are there rewards or consequences for achieving or not achieving their goal? This should help with motivation!

 **Action Steps:**

1. Reflect on What Matters to You

- **Action Step:** Write down your interests, passions, and things that are important to you.
- **Why:** Understanding your values and aspirations helps identify goals that are meaningful and motivating.
- **Example:** "I love art and want to improve my skills."

2. Imagine Your Ideal Future

- **Action Step:** Picture where you want to be in 5–10 years and write it down.
- **Why:** This helps define your long-term goals.
- **Example:** "In 10 years, I want to be a graphic designer."

3. Use the SMART Framework

- **Action Step:** Ensure your goals are Specific, Measurable, Achievable, Relevant, and Time-Bound.
- **Why:** SMART goals are clear and actionable, which increases the likelihood of success.
- **Example:** Instead of "Get better at math," a better goal would be: "Study math for 30 minutes daily to improve my grade by one letter by the end of the semester."

By taking these steps, teens can define clear, achievable short-term and long-term goals, laying the groundwork for success and personal growth.

Activities:

1. SMART Goal Worksheet

- **Activity:** Provide a worksheet with sections for each SMART criterion. Teens write their goals and answer prompts:
    o **Specific:** What exactly do I want to achieve?
    o **Measurable:** How will I know I've succeeded?
    o **Achievable:** Is this realistic, given my time, skills, and resources?
    o **Relevant**: Why does this goal matter to me?
    o **Time-Bound:** What's my deadline?
- **Outcome:** Teens refine vague goals like "get better at sports" into SMART goals like "practice soccer drills for 30 minutes daily to improve my footwork by the next tryouts in April."

2. SMART Vision Boards

- **Activity:** Teens create a vision board with their goals written in SMART terms. Include timelines, measurable benchmarks, and visuals that represent their aspirations.
- **Outcome:** Visualizing their SMART goals reinforces clarity and motivation.

3. Goal-Tracking Journals

- **Activity:** Have teens maintain a journal where they record goals, measure progress, and reflect on results. Include prompts like:
    o "What's one measurable step I achieved this week?"
    o "Am I on track to meet my deadline?"
- **Outcome:** Teens build habits of self-monitoring and accountability.

4. Celebration Planner

- **Activity:** For each goal, teens plan a reward they'll earn upon completing it. Tie the reward to the timeline and measurable outcome.
    - **Example:** "If I work out 5 days a week for a month, I'll treat myself to a new workout outfit."
- **Outcome:** Teens learn to connect achievement with positive reinforcement, motivating them to set SMART goals.

These activities not only teach teens the SMART framework but also make goal-setting interactive, practical, and fun.

Table Talk 1:

- What do you think this means: "Dreams without goals just stay dreams"? *(A dream just stays a dream without making a plan to achieve it.)*
- How does setting goals give you purpose and direction? *(It helps you stay focused on not only what it is you want to achieve, but also the smaller steps to reach along the way. It's your game plan.)*
- At what age should you start setting goals? Why? *(When someone is old enough to set a goal and a plan for achievement.)*
- What are some goals that you can set on a daily basis?
- What do you think is the most challenging thing about reaching your goals?

Table Talk 2:

Discuss your child's goals and make sure that the goals are SMART.

Ask: *What makes your goal specific?*
Ask: *How is it measurable?*
Ask: *Is it attainable?*

Ask: *Is it realistic?*

Ask: *Does your goal have a deadline?*

Your child may want to set some short-term goals as well. Print more goal worksheets and hang them up on the fridge or somewhere in view.

Vision Board Space

Commit to the Goal

Long Term Goal:
_____
_____
_____

STEP 1:
_____

STEP 2:
_____

STEP 3:
_____

STEP 4:
_____

To whom will you be accountable?

What obstacles do you expect to encounter?

What is the deadline for your goal?

CHAPTER 7

Time Management

 **Goal: Teach your children how to budget their time and how to avoid distractions that can get them off track. They will also learn to prioritize, declutter, and create schedules.**

Giving Your Children the Gift of Time Management

Time management is critical for success! It is one of the most precious resources we have, and teaching our children to manage it wisely is a gift that will benefit them daily for the rest of their lives. Time management is not just about getting tasks completed—it's a fundamental skill that fosters responsibility, independence, and self-discipline. As parents, you have the unique opportunity to help your children master this essential skill, setting them up for success in all areas of their lives.

Building the Foundation for Success

Effective time management equips children with the ability to prioritize their responsibilities, meet deadlines, and achieve their goals. These skills are critical in school, where assignments, projects, and extracurricular activities compete for their attention. Learning to balance these demands early on helps kids feel less overwhelmed and more in control of their time. This foundation also prepares them for adulthood, where time management can determine professional success and personal well-being. Trust me, being on time can either be your greatest asset or your greatest detriment in the professional world!

 **Parent/Child Dialogue Example:**

Parent: "Hey, Eric! Rise and shine! You've hit snooze so many times you're practically late for *next* week's school!" (haha)

Child: "Ugh, Dad, I'm feeling like roadkill today. Can I please just stay home for once?"

Parent: "Wait, hold on. Last night, you were bouncing around like a caffeinated kangaroo. What's the real deal here?"

Child: "Okay, fine, truth bomb incoming…"

Parent: "Spill it. I'm all ears."

Child: "So, uh… my science project's due TODAY, and I totally spaced on it. I've been juggling a million things—football practice last night was brutal, and by the time I dragged myself home, I was too wiped to even think about volcanoes or whatever."

Parent: "Whoa, sounds like you're pretty overwhelmed—school, sports, and the quest for chill time. But forgetting your science project is not just 'busy'—that's a time-management issue. Agree?"

Child: "I dunno, maybe? I'm not *trying* to be in crisis mode—it just kinda… happens."

Parent: "Oh, I get it. But without a battle plan, you're basically begging for chaos. Want a pro tip from your wise ol' dad?"

Child: "Hit me."

Parent: "Step one: you need a command center—something like a planner or an app. Just get all your stuff in one spot so deadlines don't just sneak up on you."

Child: "I kinda use my phone calendar… sometimes."

Parent: "Boom! That's a good plan. But 'sometimes' won't cut it. You need to be religious about it—new project? Bam, it's in there. Practice? Pow, logged. Then you're not sprinting to the finish line like it's the Hunger Games."

Child: "But what if I'm already drowning? There's no *time* for all this!"

Parent: "That's the magic of planning, son. Picture this: game on Friday, project due Thursday. Instead of a Wednesday night panic-fest, you chop it up—research Monday, write Tuesday, polish Wednesday. Boom, stress is gone, and you're still a legend on the field."

Child: "Huh... okay, that's not terrible."

Parent: "Next level: priorities. If your crew's like, 'Yo, let's vibe,' but homework's glaring at you like an angry cat, it's okay to say, 'Catch you later.' Tough? Sure. But it's choosing the win over the whoops."

Child: "So, what, no fun ever again? "

Parent: "Of course not, fun is non-negotiable! But when you are able to manage your time, you'll actually have *more* time to kick back—without the guilt trip. Imagine no more 'oh dang' mornings like today. Doesn't that sound epic?"

Child: "Yeah, actually... that'd be clutch."

Parent: "Sweet! How about we team up and whip up a weekly master plan? We'll map out school and your gridiron greatness and still carve out some chill zones and fun times with friends. If it flops, we tweak it. Deal?"

Child: "Deal!"

Parent: "Awesome. Now, about that science project—show me what you've got so far.

Child: "Okay, but don't lose your mind when you see it's basically... nothing."

Parent: "Hey, Bud, we're in this together—let's get started. You can do this!"

This scenario is one of many that I have encountered with all four of my kids. All of them were student-athletes in high school, and my three boys all played college football. I must admit that my boys' high school football coach taught them time management from day one. He made it clear that it would never be a good idea to be late for practice. He would say, *"If you're on time, you're late!"* Running (instead of practicing) during the length of a 2-hour practice in 90-degree heat was terrifying to them. As young adults, my kids have all benefited from learning time management skills being student-athletes, as they have many more demands placed on them than the average student, and they need to have a great time management system in place.

Reducing Stress and Building Confidence

One of the most immediate benefits of time management is the reduction of stress. When kids know how to plan their days, they're less likely to scramble at the last minute to complete homework, study for tests, or get ready for a big event. This proactive approach fosters a sense of achievement as they begin to realize they can handle their responsibilities. The confidence that grows from successfully managing their time spills over into other aspects of their lives, encouraging them to take on challenges and explore new opportunities.

Instilling Responsibility and Accountability

Teaching kids to manage their time is so much more than just about keeping a schedule; it's about helping them understand the value of responsibility. When children learn to plan their days, prioritize tasks, and stick to commitments, they develop a sense of accountability for their actions. And not only that, but it also teaches them to value the time of others. This skill encourages them to think critically about how they use their time and how to be respectful of other people's time. Creating this good habit will serve them well as they navigate more complex responsibilities in adulthood.

Preparing for a Balanced Life

One of the most overlooked aspects of time management is its role in creating balance. Without it, children can easily find themselves overwhelmed by the demands of school, family, and social activities. By teaching your kids to allocate time for work, rest, and play, you're helping them cultivate a healthy lifestyle. They'll learn to value downtime as much as productivity, ensuring they avoid burnout and maintain their mental and physical health. Balance is key!

Leading by Example

It's up to us! Children learn best by observing the adults around them. As a parent, you can model effective time management by maintaining your own schedule, setting priorities, and showing how you handle unexpected changes. Share your strategies with your kids—whether it's creating to-do lists, using a calendar, or breaking big tasks into smaller steps. When they see you managing your time effectively, they'll be more inclined to adopt similar habits.

Identify "Time Suckers"

What are "time suckers"? They are "normal" activities that don't help you produce positive results, like watching videos on YouTube, playing video games, Snapchatting, lengthy chatter on the phone with friends, etc. These are the things that aid procrastination, and they must be identified and limited. We all have "time suckers," so take some time to share with your kids your list of "time suckers" and then ask them to share their list. Set a goal to help each other eliminate these things that aid procrastination.

Great Analogy!

Imagine packing for a trip. You have procrastinated, you are jammed for time, and now you must throw everything into your suitcase at the last minute. Chances are, by using this method to pack, you will not be able to get everything that you intended for the trip. However, if you had managed your time better, you would have had the time to carefully fold your clothes and get more in.

This is the same with the organization. If you are organized, then you can fit more into your life. Being organized will save you time and reduce your stress.

By being organized, doing homework at the last minute will never happen again! Also, you'll be able to find things that you put in an organized place and not spend hours looking for them or have your family members spend hours looking for them, which causes everyone frustration. Being organized will allow you to stay on top of what is most important to you.

Imagine that it's game time, and your team is about to execute everything you have been running in practice. You have the players, and you have the plays, but that's only half the battle. Everyone must know exactly what they are supposed to do at the exact time they are supposed to be doing it. Imagine if every player on the team attempted to execute the assignment of the same player at the same time. Everyone would run into each other, and the play would fail. The execution of the play is completely dependent on the organization.

Three Main Ways to Teach Your Kids Organization

#1 PRIORITIZE

Have them make a daily TASK list of the things they need to accomplish. Most people write down too many things, get overwhelmed, and give up. Their list should only include those things needed to accomplish TODAY and be limited to the five most important things.

#2 DECLUTTER

Clean up and throw away the junk... in their backpack, locker, bedroom, car, etc. This will improve their mental clarity and eliminate wasted time digging through piles of stuff looking for that one folder of notes they really need to study for their Chemistry test.

#3 SCHEDULE

Every Sunday, have them spend 15 minutes making a weekly calendar that sets aside blocks of time for individual activities, whether they're mandatory (school and practice), goal-oriented (study time and errands), social (outings with friends/family), or personal (just "you time"). If they knew that if you spent 15 minutes each Sunday doing an activity that saved you hours of time and reduced your stress, would they do it?

Helpful tip: Have them make a schedule of their upcoming week and put it in a place where they can see it. These questions may be useful in helping them plan.

- How much sleep do I need to have enough energy for the day?
- How long does it take me to get ready in the morning?
- How much time do I need for studying?
- How much leisure time can I expect to have?

Have them complete a weekly calendar. **Remember:** Keep things in 30-minute blocks.

- Start with the time you wake up: Is it the same every day?
- Fill in the school days. If it's from 7:30 a.m. to 3:00 p.m., then block that time out for school.
- Fill in your time for practices, training sessions, or any extracurricular activities that you have.
- Dinner time, family time, or anything else that you have going on that week for social commitments, come next.

Now that the things that they HAVE to do are filled in—all of their commitments—they will see what time is free for them to study or have free time.

- List tasks that you need to do immediately. (E.g., study for the quiz tomorrow.)
- List tasks that you will need to have done in the future. (E.g., have the closet organized by Friday.)
- List tasks for reaching short-term and long-term goals. (E.g., run three miles to get in shape.)
- Anything else? Haircuts, doctor's appointments, community service, etc.

This won't be too hard, right? Make sure you review your calendar for a few minutes each night before your tired body hits the pillow. Also, remember to make your daily TASK list. Chances are, it may help you remember an assignment that needs to be turned in, a form that is due, or the uniform you brought home to clean.

 **Action Steps:**

- **Start Early:** Begin with small tasks like organizing a study area, setting a bedtime routine, or scheduling homework time.

- **Use Visual Tools:** Calendars, planners, or apps can help kids see how their time is divided and encourage them to take ownership of their schedule.

- **Encourage Reflection:** Talk with your kids about what went well and what didn't. This helps them understand their strengths and identify areas for improvement.

- **Celebrate Progress:** Acknowledge their efforts and successes, no matter how small, to reinforce positive habits.

Conclusion

Time management is a skill that touches every part of life. By teaching your kids how to manage their time, you're empowering them with tools that will help them succeed in school, in their careers, and in their personal lives. It's an investment in their future and a legacy that will continue to shape their choices for years to come. So start today—guide them, encourage them, and watch them thrive as they learn to make the most of their most valuable resource: time.

ACTIVITIES: Have your children complete these worksheets.

	MONDAY	TUESDAY	WEDNESDAY	THURSDAY	FRIDAY	SATURDAY	SUNDAY
7:00 am							
7:30 am							
8:00 am							
8:30 am							
9:00 am							
9:30 am							
10:00 am							
10:30 am							
11:00 am							
11:30 am							
12:00 pm							
12:30 pm							
1:00 pm							
1:30 pm							
2:00 pm							
2:30 pm							
3:00 pm							
3:30 pm							
4:00 pm							
4:30 pm							
5:00 pm							
5:30 pm							
6:00 pm							
6:30 pm							
7:00 pm							
7:30 pm							
8:00 pm							
8:30 pm							
9:00 pm							
9:30 pm							
10:00 pm							
10:30 pm							
11:00 pm							
11:30 pm							

ACTIVITY

Let's do some math!

Think about your day since you woke up this morning, and then tomorrow, when you have to do it all again. Calculate how much time you have spent or will spend on the following activities. **BE HONEST**

- Time in school =   _____ hours
- Homework/Studying =   _____ hours
- Practice/Conditioning =   _____ hours
- Getting ready for school in the morning =   _____ hours
- Working/Job =   _____ hours
- Preparing/Eating food =   _____ hours
- Social media (Twitter/Instagram/Snapchat/etc.) =   _____ hours
- Gaming/Surfing the web/Shopping/YouTube videos =   _____ hours
- Socializing with friends/family/boyfriends/girlfriends =   _____ hours
- Sleeping =   _____ hours
- Me time (alone time) =   _____ hours
- Community service =   _____ hours
- Other (hobbies, clubs, activities, pets, etc.) =   _____ hours

   Total Hours = _____ hours out of 24 hours in a day

Do you have any time left over, or is it all used up? The answer to that question should give you even more insight into your **TIME MANAGEMENT SKILLS**

Table Talk:

- How do you feel when you procrastinate?
- How do you feel when you plan ahead and are organized?
- Go over the worksheets that your child filled out.

PART 2

GAMECHANGERS

CHAPTER 8

Dealing with Anger

Goal: Children will learn what triggers their anger and the sources of their anger, and develop healthy new responses to have more successful outcomes. Learn the "Retreat, Think, Act" method.

Of course, if you're human, you will get angry at times. It's just a part of life, right? But how we all deal with that anger can make us or break us. In this chapter, you will learn how to teach your kids healthy responses when they get angry so that they will have more successful outcomes.

Did you know that feeling angry can actually be useful at times? Anger can be used as a positive force when it gets our adrenaline going and motivates us to want to achieve.

We all know who Michael Jordan is. But I bet a lot of you didn't know that Michael Jordan got cut from his high school basketball team, and boy, was he angry! Obviously, he didn't let that stop him, and he used his anger to motivate himself and prove others wrong. His anger motivated him to achieve greatness, and as you know, he became one of the greatest players of all time! You see, he used his anger to make himself work harder to achieve his goals.

However, anger can also be destructive when it harms you and those around you. Your anger may have to do with something that is going on right now or something that has happened in the past. Either way, it can be very harmful.

More than likely, the way your family grew up dealing with anger will influence how you deal with it, too. For example, you may have been told that it's always OK to act out your anger, regardless of how destructive your ways of expressing it may be, or keep your angry thoughts inside. So, you can see that just because you were taught a certain way doesn't mean that it is the correct way to deal with anger. Even as adults, we sometimes have a hard time responding in the right way when we're angry and need to learn healthy responses. Just like in sports, or learning to play a musical instrument, learning new skills takes time and practice, so be patient because it won't happen overnight, but it will be worth it!

 **Parent/Child Dialogue Example:**

Parent: "Hey, James, I saw you got pretty heated out there during the game. What happened?"

Child: "Ugh, yeah. Thomas kept messing up! He missed every pass I sent him, and it cost us the game. I couldn't take it anymore, so I yelled at him."

Parent: "I get it—losing stinks, and it's frustrating when things don't go right. But blowing up at him—did that fix anything?"

Child: "No... it just made everyone stare at me, and Coach benched me. Thomas looked like he was gonna cry. Now, I feel kinda dumb."

Parent: "It's big that you can see that now. Anger's normal—it happens to all of us. What got you so fired up in the moment?"

Child: "I just wanted us to win, and it felt like he wasn't even trying. It's like all my hard work didn't matter."

Parent: "That makes sense—you put a lot into it. But here's the thing: you can't control what Thomas does, only how you react. Yelling might feel good for a second, but it didn't help, right?"

Child: "Yeah, it made it worse. But what am I supposed to do when I'm that mad?"

Parent: "Good question. Let's figure it out. First, how do you know when you're about to lose it? Any warning signs?"

Child: "I guess my chest gets tight, and I start clenching my fists. Then I just... explode."

Parent: "That's a great start—knowing your signals. Next time you feel that, try stepping back for a sec. Take a deep breath, like you're blowing out a candle, and count to five. It sounds simple, but it can give your brain a reset."

Child: "Okay, but what if I'm still mad after that?"

Parent: "Then, you've got options. You could focus on your own game—like, 'What can *I* do better here?' Or talk to Thomas later, calmly, like, 'Hey, let's work on those passes together.' Anger is energy. You can use it to push forward instead of blowing up."

Child: "I don't know if I can stay calm when it's happening. It just comes out so fast."

Parent: "That's why we practice. How about this: next time you're at practice and feel that tightness, try the breathing thing? See how it feels. You don't have to be perfect—just give it a shot."

Child: "I guess I could try. I don't want Coach benching me again."

Parent: "Exactly. And hey, if it happens again, we'll talk it through. You're not in this alone. What do you think you could say to Thomas next time you see him?"

Child: "Maybe... 'Sorry I yelled, man. Let's figure this out next game'?"

Parent: "That's solid. Shows you're owning it and moving on. Anger doesn't have to run the show—you can steer it. I'm proud of you for thinking it through, James."

Child: "Thanks, Mom. I'll try not to be such a hothead next time."

Parent: "You've got this. And I'll be cheering you on—hothead or not!"

The key takeaway here is that managing anger effectively involves recognizing its triggers, practicing self-control, and redirecting its energy into constructive actions, ultimately helping the child grow in emotional maturity and maintain stronger relationships. James learns that while frustration is natural, yelling at his teammate Thomas didn't solve the problem and instead damaged his standing with the team, but through reflection and practical strategies—like breathing to reset and offering an apology—he can handle similar situations better in the future.

This exchange emphasizes personal accountability and emotional intelligence, showing James how to identify his physical warning signs (tight chest, clenched fists) and use a simple technique to pause before reacting. It also highlights the parent's role in guiding him to shift focus from what he can't control (Thomas's performance) to what he can (his own response), fostering resilience and teamwork. The takeaway is a blend of self-awareness and actionable steps, reinforced by the parent's supportive encouragement, equipping James to navigate anger in a way that aligns with his goals—like staying in the game and being a good teammate—rather than letting it derail him.

Where Does Anger Come From?

The first thing our kids need to think about is where their anger comes from. This is important so that they can take the right steps to start dealing with it. There are essentially seven basic things that cause us to get angry:

1. **Unfairness:** Is someone mistreating you?
2. **Impatience:** Is there something you want right now that you can't have right away?
3. **Unmet Need:** Is someone letting you down? Is there a need that should be met that hasn't been?
4. **Jealousy:** Are you jealous of someone or something?
5. **Abuse:** Is someone abusing you physically, verbally, or emotionally?
6. **Feeling Controlled:** Is someone trying to control you, always telling you what to do?
7. **Animosity:** Do you constantly feel like you have hidden anger inside you?

Talk to your children about these seven things and have them rank in order which things are the greatest cause of their anger. Once identified, discuss the following strategies to help them deal with these issues in a healthy and productive way.

1. When Your Child Is Treated Unfairly

- Validate their feelings: Acknowledge their experience with empathy ("I can see why that would feel unfair").
- Help them identify what's in their control: Guide them in deciding whether to address the situation or let it go.
- Teach assertive communication: Role-play how to express their feelings calmly and clearly.
- Model fairness: Show them through your actions how to handle unfair situations constructively.
- Encourage perspective: Ask questions like, "Why do you think this might have happened?" to build understanding.

2. When Your Child Is Feeling Impatient

- Name the feeling: Teach them to recognize and verbalize their impatience.
- Practice mindfulness: Introduce techniques like deep breathing or counting to ten.
- Set realistic expectations: Help them understand what's causing the wait and how long it might be.
- Distraction tactics: Suggest an engaging activity to pass the time.
- Praise patience: Highlight moments when they do wait calmly to reinforce the behavior.

3. When a Need Is Not Being Met

- Teach self-advocacy: Encourage them to communicate their needs clearly to the appropriate person.
- Explore alternatives: Brainstorm other ways to meet the need or find compromises.

- Empathize and strategize: Validate their frustration and work together on solutions.
- Model delayed gratification: Explain situations where patience or compromise is necessary.
- Check for misunderstandings: Ensure they accurately perceive the situation or others' intentions.

4. When They Are Jealous of Others

- Shift focus to gratitude: Encourage them to list things they are grateful for.
- Celebrate their uniqueness: Reinforce their strengths and what makes them special.
- Teach the value of effort: Highlight that achievements often come from hard work rather than comparison.
- Encourage collaboration: Help them see others' successes as inspiration or opportunities for teamwork.

5. When They Are Physically, Verbally, or Emotionally Abused

- Ensure safety first: Remove them from the harmful situation and provide immediate comfort.
- Listen without judgment: Let them share what happened in their own words.
- Reinforce their worth: Assure them it's not their fault, and they deserve respect.
- Teach boundaries: Explain what is and isn't acceptable behavior from others.
- Seek professional help: Connect with counselors or trusted authorities for support.
- Empower them: Role-play ways to seek help or assert themselves in the future.

6. When They Feel Controlled

- Acknowledge their need for autonomy: Validate their feelings and discuss their perspective.
- Offer choices: Give them opportunities to make decisions, even in small ways.
- Collaborate on rules: Involve them in creating boundaries or routines to increase their sense of ownership.
- Explain intentions: Share why certain rules or decisions are in place to foster understanding.
- Respect their individuality: Encourage them to express themselves in ways that align with their values.

7. When They Have Animosity/Anger Inside

- Encourage physical release: Suggest activities like running, dancing, or punching a pillow.
- Teach emotional expression: Provide safe outlets like journaling or drawing.
- Practice calming techniques: Guide them through deep breathing, meditation, or grounding exercises.
- Explore the root cause: Help them unpack what's triggering their anger and how to address it.
- Model healthy responses: Show them how you handle anger constructively.
- Set boundaries for behavior: Explain that while feelings are valid, harmful actions are not acceptable.

Teaching Kids To: Retreat. Think. Act.

You can't control all of the events of the day, but you **CAN** control how you respond to them. How are you going to react when they happen again? Here are the three critical steps to take next time you're angry.

Step 1: RETREAT

I've got a great analogy for this. When a coach has worked long and hard on a game plan and strategy, yet the other team is still winning, and his team is getting angry and frustrated, what is the first thing the coach will do? He'll call a time-out! The coach pulls the team into a huddle formation to slow things down, adjust the game plan, regroup the players, and refocus on the strengths of the game plan. So, when you are angry, retreating is calling your own needed time-out. Taking a time-out for yourself is the No. 1 play strategy when you're angry and fear that you will say or do something that you'll only regret later. It's not a magic pill that will cure everything, but it is a crucial step and skill to have that will force you to stop and think. This takes practice. The ultimate goal in taking a T.O. is to slow things down, think more clearly, be realistic, and gain control. Imagine if you had slowed down and taken a much-needed time out the last time you were really angry. Hurt feelings, holes in walls, and hurt loved ones would've been saved for sure! Just as it's the coach's responsibility in a game to call for a time-out, it's your responsibility to call your own time-out and to know what to do next. Now, the most common forms of "time-outs" are:

- **Exercising:** Take a walk, go for a run, or work out.
- **Listening to Music:** Music can change your mood quickly.
- **Taking a Shower:** Showering can immediately calm you down.
- **Counting to 10:** You might have learned this at a very young age, but it works for adults, too! And did you know that the way that your brain is wired, it is almost impossible to do math and be angry at the same time? Hence, the reason is that people began counting to ten when they were mad.
- **Taking a Deep Breath:** Slow breaths slow your heart rate down, so this one is actually good for your health!
- **Writing:** Writing your thoughts down helps you not to react. But remember, NEVER text or email when you are angry. You will likely say things that are hurtful and that you may not mean, and once they are out there, it's too late to take them back.

- **And last but not least, distracting yourself:** Take your mind off the problem temporarily by watching TV, playing a video game, reading a book, or watching a movie.

Step 2: THINK

Once you've retreated and your anger no longer has a grip on you: THINK!

- **THINK** through what caused the anger.
- **THINK** through if there is something you need to say or do.
- **THINK** through what your response should be to get the outcome you want.
- Now, **THINK** through these next few things:
    - Ask yourself: Why has this situation made me so angry?
    - List the reasons you feel you were wronged, or WHY the situation was unfair.
    - Is it enough for you just to be heard and explain why you're so angry?
    - Do you want something to change? If so, what and why?

Step 3: ACT

Express yourself in a calm manner. Once you've gained your composure and have thought through your desired outcome, you will be ready to **ACT** and express yourself in a calm manner. Blowing up is bad, but bottling up your anger can be just as negative. Over time, you will erupt, and this will only hurt you. Not expressing your anger can damage your health as well as your relationships. Don't stuff it; express it calmly!

Here are eight important steps your child should take when they're ready to talk to the person they are angry at in a calm manner:

1. Remind yourself of the desired outcome.
2. Choose and practice with words that are specific but respectful when you address the issue.
3. Don't start the conversation with "You" because the other person will feel like you are pointing fingers and blaming.

4. Don't generalize with the words "always" or "never."
5. Don't bring up past conflicts.
6. Be prepared to listen with an open mind.
7. Be prepared for the person to not agree with you.
8. Don't get angry all over again. Take another T.O. if you need to!

This is great advice when they are angry with someone, but sometimes the root of their anger is actually... them! We all get angry with ourselves at some time or another, right? Maybe your child forgot to do an assignment, or maybe he hit the snooze too many times and is now late for school, or maybe he forgot to charge his phone all night, and he wakes up, and his battery is on ZERO. I hate it when that happens! You can say and do destructive things to yourself just as easily as you can to someone else. Unfortunately, this self-defeating practice can become a habit, and action is needed!

So, here are a few tips when your child is angry with himself:

1. **STOP** thinking about yourself and replaying the tape in your head of why you are so mad at yourself.
2. **START** being positive and thinking of how you can make the situation better.
3. **TAKE ACTION** and overcome your situation. (Just like Michael Jordan did!)

So, let's wrap it up. Dealing with anger is tough. It's a raw emotion that can build up. The "rage monster" will only cause your kids emotional and physical harm. Huddle up and regroup. There's nothing that can be solved or defeated positively with explosive actions or words. Remember, you only have so much energy, just like a car only has so much gas in its tank. Once it runs out, you are on empty. Don't waste your mental, emotional, or physical energy. In other words, don't waste your "fuel" on being angry. Use your "fuel" for something positive!

And remember those three words: THINK. RETREAT. ACT. This strategy will help your kids WIN against their anger. And practice, practice, practice. Chances are that they will become better at it each time.

Now, this is important. If you see that your child simply can't calm down, ask him:

- Are you more angry than not angry most of the time?
- Do you want to hurt yourself or others?
- Do you argue or fight most of the time?

If his answer is yes to any of these questions, he may have a situation in his life that is causing him to be continually angry. When a child is continually angry, it's important to address both the underlying cause of their anger and help them develop healthy ways to process and express it. Here's a step-by-step approach:

1. Create a Safe Space for Communication

- **Show Empathy:** Let your child know you're there to listen without judgment.
  Example: "I can see you're upset a lot lately. Do you want to talk about what's going on?"
- **Stay Calm:** Don't match their anger with your own. Your calmness sets a tone.

2. Understand the Root Cause

- **Ask Open-Ended Questions:** Help them articulate what's happening.
  Example: "What's been the hardest thing for you lately?"
- **Look for Patterns:** Are their outbursts connected to school, friendships, family changes, or other stressors?
- **Be Patient:** Sometimes, kids don't open up immediately. Keep the door open for when they're ready.

3. Problem-Solve Together

Help them brainstorm solutions to what's causing their anger.

Example: "Let's think about what we can do to make this situation better. What do you think might help?"

Seek Additional Support If Needed

If the anger persists or escalates, it might be helpful to involve a counselor, therapist, or trusted mentor. Ongoing anger can sometimes signal deeper issues, like anxiety, depression, or trauma.

Reminder: Kids often use anger to mask other emotions, like fear, sadness, or insecurity. By staying patient and supportive, you can help them uncover and address what's really going on.

ACTION STEPS:

- **Describe a time when you made a mistake and acted badly.**

  _____

  _____

  _____

- **What could you have done differently?**

  _____

  _____

  _____

- **Describe a time when you were able to control your anger.**

  _____

  _____

  _____

- **What was the outcome?**

_____

_____

_____

ACTIVITY:

Read the following scenario. Then, have your child answer the questions below.

SCENARIO:

Texting during class is not allowed, and a friend of yours sitting close to you starts texting, but then she quickly puts her phone away. Your phone is sitting on your desk but is turned off. The teacher sees your phone sitting out, accuses you, and takes your phone. Your friend says nothing and lets the teacher think it was you who was texting, not her. After all, she doesn't want her phone to be taken away. What do you do next?

1. What is your desired outcome?
2. How do you plan to accomplish your desired outcome?
3. What will you say to your friend once you've calmed down?
4. What will you do if you get angry during the confrontation?
5. What will you do if your friend sees your point of view and apologizes?
6. What will you do if the conversation doesn't go so well and your friend won't listen?

Remember: "Holding on to anger is like grasping a hot coal with the intent of throwing it at someone else; you are the one who gets burned."

Table Talk 1:

Ask your child when they have encountered some of these seven "rage-makers."

- Unfairness
- Jealousy
- Impatience
- Unmet need
- Abuse
- Feeling controlled
- Animosity

Table Talk 2:

Ask your child to share his/her "game plans" when angry.

CHAPTER 9

Disappointments to Opportunities

🎯 **Goal: Children will learn how to turn disappointments into opportunities and how to keep disappointment in perspective and change their mindset.**

Guiding Kids Through Overcoming Disappointments

Disappointment is an inevitable part of life, yet it can feel overwhelming to a child who lacks the tools to process and move past it. Teaching children how to manage disappointment not only equips them with resilience but also fosters emotional intelligence and problem-solving skills. As parents, guiding children through these moments requires a balance of empathy, perspective, and actionable strategies. How can parents teach their children the importance of overcoming disappointments and know how to navigate these experiences?

Disappointment

So, what is a disappointment? A disappointment is something you expected that was not as good as you thought it would be or didn't even happen at all, which caused you to feel sad, unhappy, or maybe even angry. Everyone who is living and breathing has been disappointed, so how we handle our disappointments can really either set us up for success or set us up for failure. An unknown author once said this: "Some people get sad, others pout, some get angry and lash out, some get bitter and keep it inside, others deny and run and hide." So, how about you? How do YOU handle your disappointment? Chances are, the way we handle life's disappointments may be the same way our kids handle disappointments.

 **Parent/Child Dialogue Example (Mother and Daughter):**

Child: "I didn't make the dance team. I feel awful, and my best friend made it."

Parent: "Oh, honey, I'm so sorry. I know how excited you were about this. It's totally okay to feel bummed out right now—disappointment's a big deal."

Child: "It's so unfair. I practiced so much, and now I don't even get to dance."

Parent: "It really does sting when things don't line up, right? You put in all that effort, and it's tough when it doesn't pay off like you pictured. That's a hard spot to be in."

Child: "Yeah, and now my best friend's on the team, and I'm not."

Parent: "I can see why that twists the knife a little. You're thrilled for her, but it's rough not being in it together. That's a lot to deal with. Want to unpack how you're feeling, or maybe brainstorm what's next?"

Child: "I don't know... I just feel super down right now."

Parent: "That's perfectly fine. Sadness hits hard when something you care about falls through. How about we let it sit for a bit, and then we can figure out what you want to do—maybe gear up for next year or try something different? I've got your back either way."

Child: "Maybe I could work on my moves more. I want to give it another shot next time."

Parent: "That's awesome! Let's map out some 'SMART goals' to get you feeling strong and ready for the next tryout. I love that you're already looking ahead—it takes guts to bounce back like that. I'm so proud of you for keeping at it."

Child: "Thanks so much, Mom, you always help me so much."

The key takeaway is that setbacks, like not making the dance team, are opportunities to process disappointment, build resilience, and set new goals, with the support of a caring parent helping the child turn sadness into motivation for future growth. The parent validates the child's feelings of unfairness and loss—especially with her best friend succeeding—while gently guiding her toward proactive steps, like improving her skills for next time, showing that failure isn't the end but a chance to regroup and try again.

This exchange underscores the importance of emotional validation ("It's totally okay to feel bummed out") and the power of shifting focus from what's lost to what's possible, introducing the idea of "SMART goals" to channel the child's determination. It highlights how a supportive parent can help a child navigate complex emotions—disappointment mixed with jealousy—and emerge with renewed purpose, reinforcing her inner strength and the security of their bond. The takeaway is about embracing feelings and then using them as fuel to keep pursuing what matters, with a plan and a cheerleader in her corner.

 **Parent/Child Dialogue Example (Father and Son):**

Parent: "Hey, champ, you seem a bit off. What's up?"

Child: "I didn't make the soccer team... I worked so hard, but I still didn't get in."

Parent: "Oh, man, I'm really sorry to hear that. It's tough when you give it your all, and it doesn't pan out. What's running through your head right now?"

Child: "I just feel like I'm not good enough. Everyone else got picked, but not me, even after all that practice. I'm kinda embarrassed, too."

Parent: "It's totally normal to feel let down when something you want slips away—especially after pouring your heart into it. That's a rough hit to take."

Child: "But I really wanted to be on the team. I wanted to play with my friends."

Parent: "I bet they were hoping to have you out there, too. It stinks to miss out, no question. How do you feel about giving it another go down the line? No pressure to decide now—just something to chew on. I bombed my All-Star baseball tryout in middle school—felt like the world ended. But you know how that turned out: college ball. Sometimes a 'no' isn't about your talent—it's just about timing or luck. Other chances will come."

Child: "You think I could make it next time?"

Parent: "Absolutely, I believe in you. If soccer's still your thing, we can team up to keep sharpening your skills. Setbacks can be fuel to get better or try something fresh. What do you think you'd want to focus on for the next tryouts?"

Child: "Maybe my shots need work. And I could get faster, too."

Parent: "That's a solid game plan! We can carve out some practice time if you're up for it. And hey, it's okay to feel crummy about this—it happens to everyone. Doesn't mean you're done; it's just a bump in the road. What matters is you don't quit."

Child: "Yeah... okay. I think I'll try again next year."

Parent: "That's my boy! I'm proud of you for sticking with it—that's real guts. I've got your back at every step. It might feel heavy now, but you're tougher than this. Need a hug?"

Child: "Yeah. Thanks, Dad."

Parent: "Anytime. We'll tackle this together! Thanks for confiding in me."

The key takeaway from this dialogue is that rejection, like not making the soccer team, is a chance to build resilience and determination by reframing failure as a temporary setback rather than a reflection of worth. You, as the parent, are there to provide emotional comfort and a path forward. You are also able to help the child process feelings of inadequacy and embarrassment, using personal stories to show that setbacks are common and surmountable, inspiring the child to keep going with a renewed focus on improvement.

This exchange emphasizes the power of empathy ("It's tough when you give it your all and it doesn't pan out") and perspective, showing the child that a "no" doesn't define their ability but can actually fuel future success. It highlights how the parent can bolster the child's confidence by believing in their potential and offering practical teamwork ("We can carve out some practice time"), turning disappointment into a motivator. The takeaway is about embracing vulnerability, leaning on support, and channeling effort toward a comeback, with the child gaining both emotional strength and a concrete plan from a trusting, uplifting bond with the parent.

Disappointment Is Key

Teach your children how to adjust their mindset so that they can accept the REALITY of what has happened, acknowledge how they really feel about what has happened, and be honest with themselves. Denial is not an honest way of dealing with disappointment, because instead of expressing their feelings, they're keeping them inside, which means that they will eventually have to deal with them later on. Trust me, those feelings will pop back up if they don't let them out, so give them space to experience the emotions needed to process. You don't want their sadness to turn into bitterness and anger by keeping their emotions inside.

Keeping Perspective

Next, help them to keep perspective. Ask them: "Will this really matter in a week from now, a month from now, or even a year from now?" For instance, a little fender bender can be fixed, a failed quiz can be redeemed with a good test grade, and an injury may set them back in their sport but will heal over time. Teach children to view disappointments in the context of the bigger picture.

Share examples of setbacks that ultimately led to positive outcomes, such as missed opportunities that opened doors to something better. Also, encourage them to recognize their strengths and past achievements, reminding them that one disappointment doesn't define their overall abilities or worth.

Expectations

Did you know that many times we can cause our own disappointments? Sometimes, we have expectations that just aren't realistic and that can really set us up for a lot of disappointments. Sometimes, we expect more from ourselves and others than can be realistically fulfilled.

Let's use this scenario as an example for your kids: Hannah is the class president at her school this year. Her dad just got transferred, and she will be moving to a new school in a different state. Her goal is to run for class president at her new school and win. Now, do you think she has realistic expectations, or is she setting herself up for a big disappointment? Ask these questions:

- What does Hannah believe about this situation? (She believes that she will be voted Class President even though she's "the new kid" in town, and she has not had the chance to make any friends at her new school yet.)
- What will she expect? (She expects to win.)
- Is it reasonable to expect this will happen? (Probably not.)
- What set of expectations would be more realistic? (Probably for Hannah to make new friends and get acclimated to the school and run for Class President the FOLLOWING year, once people have gotten to know her and like her.)

So, you get the point, right? Setting the right expectations can lead to fewer disappointments

Count Your Blessings

One of the best things you can do when facing disappointment is to be GRATEFUL! Yes, you heard me right! Count your blessings! Once you start making a list of the things you DO have, chances are that you will soon see that life is now a little bit better than it was just five minutes ago. Turn those lemons into lemonade! Allow your defeat to build character and a positive learning experience by following these steps:

1. Make a new plan. Make a list of things that you can do to accomplish your goals that are realistic.
2. If you're stuck trying to create a new plan, seek advice from a trusted adult or mentor.
3. Look for new opportunities. For instance, if a friend keeps letting you down, finding a new friend can be a new opportunity. Don't limit your circle of friends. Choose friends who are positive influences and avoid people who are not! If you have experienced the disappointment of not making a sports team, not getting the part in the play you wanted, or not getting accepted into the club you wanted, there are always other activities to get involved in. Again, one day you may look back and be grateful that you weren't chosen because it opened the door to something else that was even better than you could have ever imagined. On that note, let's take a look at a few examples of this: people who were disappointed, who refocused, and then were grateful for their initial disappointment.

Share with your kids these two examples of people who have turned disappointments into opportunities:

1) Bethany Hamilton

Have you ever heard of the movie *Unstoppable*? (Great title, by the way...) *Unstoppable* is based on a true story about Hawaiian surfer Bethany Hamilton, who lost her left arm to a 1,500-pound shark. Her positive, upbeat response to this tragedy left everyone speechless. Just three months after the shark attack, Bethany was back surfing competitively, now just with one arm! She looks at her tragedy as a way to inspire others! She is actually grateful that she has such an opportunity! WOW. Talk about overcoming disappointment and refocusing on inspiring others. What an impact she has made!

2) W. Mitchell

Mitchell experienced two huge disasters in quick succession: a motorcycle accident that left his skin burned and shredded, and a plane crash that paralyzed him. Many people facing such disasters would become bitter and angry. Mitchell was neither. Instead, he used his life experience to show that even seemingly impossible setbacks can't keep somebody from success if he is truly determined.

Over the years, he founded a $65 million company and has been a two-term mayor, a congressional nominee, a radio host and television personality, a published author, and a Speaker Hall of Fame inductee.

Mitchell went so far beyond the "lemonade" concept that it's not on the same scale at all. He's become a truly transformational role model. I defy anyone who hears him speak to leave the auditorium believing in insurmountable obstacles.

James, G. (July 10, 2012). www.Inc.com. 3 Who Turned Tragedy Into Success. Retrieved June 12, 2014, from the World Wide Web

I'm sure you've heard the saying, "We learn more from our losses than from our wins."

This is why.

1. **We can learn to build resilience:** Life is full of ups and downs, and the ability to recover from setbacks is essential for long-term success and emotional well-being. Children who learn to manage disappointments early on develop the mental fortitude to handle future challenges.
2. **We can develop problem-solving skills:** As mentioned before, disappointments often arise from unmet expectations. Teaching kids to assess the situation and find alternative solutions encourages creativity and critical thinking.
3. **We can strengthen our emotional regulation:** Understanding and managing feelings of frustration, sadness, or anger helps children navigate their emotions constructively. This skill fosters healthier relationships and better decision-making.
4. **We can develop our growth mindset:** Overcoming disappointment teaches children that failures or setbacks are opportunities to learn and grow rather than definitive roadblocks.

5. **We can build confidence:** Successfully handling disappointment empowers children, reinforcing the belief that they can overcome obstacles and thrive despite challenges.

How to Help Children Overcome Disappointments

1. **Validate Their Feelings:**
   - When a child faces disappointment, the first step is to acknowledge their emotions. Phrases like "I can see that you're upset," or "It's okay to feel this way," show empathy and help the child feel understood.
   - Avoid dismissing their feelings with phrases like, "It's not a big deal." Instead, encourage open communication by asking, "Can you tell me what happened?"

2. **Normalize Disappointment:**
   - Explain that everyone experiences disappointment at some point. Share age-appropriate examples from your own life to show that it's a common human experience.
   - Teach them that disappointment is a temporary feeling and not a reflection of their worth or abilities.

3. **Reframe the Situation:**
   - Encourage your child to see setbacks as opportunities for growth. Ask questions like, "What can we learn from this?" or "Is there another way to approach this?"
   - Help them focus on what they can control rather than dwelling on what went wrong.

4. **Model Resilience:**
   - Children learn by observing their parents. Show them how you handle disappointments in your own life. For example, if you didn't get a promotion, express your feelings and then share how you plan to move forward.
   - Avoid overreacting to your own setbacks, as this can influence how they perceive disappointment.

5. **Teach Problem-Solving:**
   - Guide your child through brainstorming potential solutions. For instance, if they didn't make the soccer team, explore other activities they might enjoy or ways to improve their skills for next time.
   - Help them set realistic goals and break them into manageable steps.

6. **Encourage a Growth Mindset:**
   - Reinforce the idea that skills and abilities can be developed through effort and practice. Use phrases like, "You didn't get it this time, but if you keep practicing, you'll improve."
   - Celebrate their effort and progress rather than focusing solely on the outcome.

7. **Practice Gratitude:**
   - Help your child shift their focus by encouraging them to recognize the positives in their life. Ask them to name three things they're grateful for, even in disappointing moments.
   - Emphasize the importance of appreciating opportunities and experiences rather than dwelling on what didn't go as planned.

8. **Encourage Patience and Perseverance:**
   - Teach your child that success often requires time and persistence. Use examples from stories, historical figures, or family anecdotes to illustrate how persistence pays off.
   - Remind them that overcoming disappointment is part of achieving meaningful goals.

What Parents Should Avoid

1. **Shielding from Disappointment:** This is a hard one because often, our first response is to protect our children from disappointment. Unfortunately, this can hinder their ability to develop coping skills. As hard as it is, let them experience setbacks as you support them and encourage them.

2. **Minimizing Their Feelings:** Avoid saying things like, "It's not that bad," or "You'll get over it." These statements can make your child feel unheard and invalidated.

3. **Fixing Everything for Them:** Again, resist the urge to jump in and immediately solve their problems. Instead, guide them to think through the situation and find their own solutions. This will give them the confidence they need when a future disappointment arises.

4. **Overemphasizing Success:** We all know that placing too much importance on winning or achieving can create unnecessary pressure. Teach them to value effort and growth, and remind them it's about the journey over the outcome.

Wrap-Up

Teaching children to overcome disappointment is one of the most valuable life lessons a parent can impart. It builds resilience, fosters emotional intelligence, and prepares them to handle life's inevitable challenges with grace, courage, and determination. By validating their feelings, modeling resilience, and providing tools to navigate setbacks, we can empower our children to view disappointments not as failures, but as opportunities for growth. These skills will not only benefit them in childhood but will also serve as a foundation for them to become confident and capable adults.

 **Action Steps:**

Write down some disappointments that you have had in your life, how you handled them, and then share them with your child. They may be positive or negative. Both can be learning experiences, and our children will likely feel secure knowing that we have experienced disappointments just as they have and have managed to navigate through them.

ACTIVITY with your child:

"When One Door Closes, Another One Opens."

Below is a list of some of life's disappointments. Maybe you've experienced one or more of these, or maybe you've had different ones.

Choose two scenarios from either the list below or write two new ones of your own. If you had to go through these again, what would be your new plan or strategy for dealing with the disappointments they caused?

- **Not getting the starting position I wanted**
- **Not getting invited to a party**
- **Getting injured**
- **Fun plans getting canceled**
- **Not making it to the playoffs**
- **The girl/guy I like doesn't feel the same way**
- **A friend not including me**
- **Poor SAT scores**
- **Not being selected for a club at school**
- **Not getting the grade I wanted**
- **Having a bad game**
- **Losing a game**
- **Someone breaking a promise**
- **My project not winning the competition**
- **Not getting into my top college choice**
- **Not working to my best potential**

SITUATION #1:

How can I turn this disappointment into an opportunity or a new plan?

_____

_____

_____

SITUATION #2:

How can I turn this disappointment into an opportunity or a new plan?

_____

_____

_____

Table Talk 1:

- What big disappointments have you had?
- How did you deal with each?
- Can you see any good that's come from any of them? Often, when one door closes, another one opens. Can you think of anyone who has had a big disappointment, but it turned out to be a blessing in disguise?

Table Talk 2:

Ask your child to share the activity about expectations with you. What are their expectations for school? Their friends? Job? Career? Family? Sport or extracurricular activity?

Table Talk 3:

Ask your child to share the completed activity about the different scenarios with you.

It's a great idea to go over these possible scenarios with your child before a disappointment happens, so he/she will feel confident and equipped to deal with the disappointment. Talk about the possible ways of dealing with each.

CHAPTER 10

Privilege vs. Entitlement

Goal: Children will learn the difference between privilege and entitlement, which teaches that they aren't "owed" anything but gain happiness through hard work and gratitude.

Combating Entitlement: Raising Grounded, Grateful Kids

In today's world, entitlement has become a growing challenge among children and teens. Many kids grow up believing they deserve certain privileges without effort, hard work, or gratitude. This mindset can hinder their emotional growth, damage their relationships, and leave them ill-prepared for the realities of adulthood.

Entitlement often stems from well-meaning parents who want to give their children the best—whether it's material things, constant praise, or shielding them from disappointment. We have all been there, right? But when kids grow up believing that life should be easy or that they're owed success, they struggle to develop resilience, gratitude, and a strong work ethic.

Teaching kids that entitlement is harmful isn't about withholding love or opportunities—it's about helping them understand the value of effort, appreciation, and humility. It's about showing them that success is earned, not given, and that gratitude leads to greater happiness and fulfillment.

So how do we prevent entitlement?

1. **Teach Gratitude:** Encourage your kids to regularly express thanks—not just for big moments but for everyday things. Whether it's writing thank-you notes, acknowledging a friend's kindness, or appreciating family meals, gratitude grounds children and shifts their focus from "what I want" to "what I have."

2. **Set Boundaries and Say No:** It's okay—essential, even—to say no sometimes. Kids who get everything they want rarely learn patience or self-control. Boundaries teach them that life includes limits and that not every desire needs to be fulfilled immediately.

3. **Encourage Hard Work and Responsibility:** Chores, part-time jobs, and earning rewards rather than receiving them by default are powerful lessons. When kids work for something—whether it's a new bike, a spot on the team, or an allowance—they develop pride in their achievements and respect for effort.

4. **Model Humility and Generosity:** Kids are always watching. When they see their parents serve others, speak kindly, and approach life with humility, they're more likely to adopt those values themselves.

5. **Emphasize Effort Over Outcome:** Celebrate hard work, persistence, and growth—not just wins and achievements. When kids understand that effort is as important as results, they become more resilient and less focused on instant gratification.

Ultimately, the goal isn't to raise kids who never want more—it's to raise kids who appreciate what they have, work for what they want, and approach life with gratitude and humility. Teaching these lessons early helps kids grow into adults who are grounded, capable, and empathetic—qualities our world desperately needs.

Now, let's look at "privileged"...

We've all heard these words used before, but what exactly do they mean? Privileged means **"Through hard work, I have EARNED a special right to do something."**

A good example of privileged is this: "I got all of my homework done, so I have earned the privilege of going to hang out with my friends." Or "I have worked hard at being a leader on my team, and I have earned the privilege of being made Team Captain."

Wanting something and deserving something are two very different things. Unfortunately, when we feel like we deserve something, we focus on ourselves and what we are owed, not on others and how we can help them. It's a "one-way street" mindset. People who feel grateful and less entitled seem to have better relationships and greater self-esteem than people who think they're better than everyone else. Being unselfish and thinking of others leads to genuine, satisfying relationships.

The truth is this: It's basic human nature to feel entitled at times, but the hard truth is that we are not entitled to anything. Life does not **OWE** us, ever! It is perfectly fine to **WORK HARD** for what we want. For example:

- We aren't owed that high-paying job just because we may have graduated from an outstanding university, but it **IS** okay to **WORK HARD** for one.
- We aren't owed a starting position on a team or the lead role in a musical, but it **IS** okay if we **WORK HARD** for one.

WORKING HARD for your goals and your dreams with the right attitude starts with a grateful heart. This means feeling blessed and honored when you have the opportunity to do certain things, and throwing away that "I am owed" attitude.

 **Parent/Child Dialogue Example: Privilege**

Parent: "Hey, can we talk for a second about what happened earlier when you got so upset about not getting that new Xbox game?"

Child: "Yeah, but it's not fair! All my friends have it, and I *deserve* it!"

Parent: "I get that it's frustrating to see your friends with something you want. But let's talk about what it means to *deserve* something. Why do you think you deserve it?"

Child: "I don't know... because I want it?"

Parent: "Wanting something is okay, but just wanting it doesn't mean you automatically get it. Imagine if I acted like that at work—what do you think would happen if I expected to get paid without doing my job?"

Child: "You'd get fired."

Parent: "Exactly. We earn things through effort, kindness, or sometimes just by being patient. An entitled attitude can hurt us because it makes us expect things without putting in the work or appreciating what we have. That's why it's important to focus on being grateful and working toward our goals."

Child: "So, if I want the game, I should earn it?"

Parent: "That's right! How do you think you could do that?"

Child: "Maybe I could help more around the house or save my allowance."

Parent: "Great idea! And while you're working toward it, remember how awesome it will feel knowing you earned it yourself."

The parent here is trying to cultivate a mindset of gratitude and effort, rather than an entitled mindset, helping the child understand that rewards come from action and patience, not just desire, which fosters a sense of responsibility and appreciation. The parent gently challenges the child's belief that they "deserve" the game simply because they want it, using a relatable analogy (work and pay) to show how earning something through effort leads to greater satisfaction and personal growth.

Can you see how this example shows empathy while guiding the child to reflect on their feelings, reconsider entitlement, and take ownership of their actions?

Now, let's look at an example of privilege.

 **Parent/Child Dialogue Example: Privilege**

Child: "Mom, can I stay up late tonight to watch a movie?"

Parent: "Hmm, staying up late is a privilege. What do you think you need to do to earn it?"

Child: "I don't know... be good?"

Parent: "Being good is a start, but earning a privilege usually takes more than that. Privileges are rewards for effort, responsibility, or following through on a goal."

Child: "Like what?"

Parent: "Well, remember how you've been working on keeping your room clean? What if you showed me you could keep it tidy all week without reminders?"

Child: "So, if I keep it clean, I get to stay up late?"

Parent: "Yes! If you can show responsibility for a whole week, you've earned the trust that comes with extra freedom. Hard work builds trust—and trust earns more privileges."

Child: "Okay, I'll try. I'll keep my room clean so I can stay up late next weekend!"

Parent: "Perfect! I'm excited to see how it goes. And when you stick with it, you'll feel great knowing you earned it!"

This dialogue helps connect hard work, responsibility, and trust with the rewards of earned privileges. It encourages effort and reinforces the concept of working toward goals.

Be Grateful

One of the most successful ways you can change your attitude is to replace entitlement with gratitude. Studies have shown that having a grateful attitude can lead to better health, less anxiety, and being kinder to others. Feeling grateful can also make you less likely to become angry when you are provoked.

But did you know that people aren't wired naturally to be grateful? It requires practice, like many other things.

So then, how do we practice gratitude? Although these are critical points to teach our children, we, as parents, can learn something from these points as well!

- Think of gratitude as an emotional muscle. Use it and strengthen it by looking for things to be grateful for every single day.
- Notice the little things in life—the things you may take for granted: the sunshine, your pet, your family, your health, food on the table, clean clothes, etc.
- Don't complain or criticize. No one likes hanging out with a downer. Put your energy into positive things.
- Appreciate what you DO have. Don't focus on the things that you don't have.
- Keep a gratitude journal. Keep track of all the good things in your life.
- Tell others why you are grateful for them! Everyone likes to hear when they do things that make other people happy.

The benefits of gratitude are endless! Here are just a few:

- Gratitude makes people happier
- Gratitude strengthens relationships
- Gratitude improves health
- Gratitude reduces stress

Below is a great poem about thankfulness. Put it somewhere close by where you can read it every day.

"Be thankful that you don't already have everything you desire. If you did, what would there be to look forward to?
Be thankful when you don't know something,
for it gives you the opportunity to learn.
Be thankful for the difficult times.
During those times you grow.
Be thankful for your limitations,
because they give you opportunities for improvement. Be thankful for each new challenge,
because it will build your strength and character. Be thankful for your mistakes. They will teach you valuable lessons.
Be thankful when you're tired and weary, because it means you've made a difference.
It is easy to be thankful for the good things.
A life of rich fulfillment comes to those who are also thankful for the setbacks.
GRATITUDE can turn a negative into a positive. Find a way to be thankful for your troubles, and they can become your blessings."

—Author Unknown

A life of rich fulfillment comes to those who are also thankful for the setbacks.

GRATITUDE can turn a negative into a positive. Find a way to be thankful for your troubles, and they can become your blessings.

I would suggest both you and your child take a photo of this poem and save it on your phones to pull up and read when you are upset about something and need to count your blessings. **Now comes the most important part of this lesson.**

You need to spread your gratitude and thankfulness around to others so that you don't take them for granted or feel entitled to the wonderful things they bring to your life. TRY IT! And maybe you can also help them eliminate some entitlement from their own lives at the same time

Here are some practical strategies for teaching parents to help eliminate entitlement in their children:

1. Model Gratitude and Effort

Explanation: Kids learn by watching their parents. Demonstrate appreciation for what you have and show that rewards come from effort, not expectations.

Example: Instead of saying, "I deserve a break," say, "I worked hard all day, and now it's time for some rest."

Tip for Parents: Verbally express gratitude regularly, like, "I'm so thankful we have food on the table." It sets a tone of appreciation.

2. Shift from "Deserving" to "Earning"

Explanation: Reframe conversations about rewards and privileges from "You deserve this" to "You've earned this."

Example:

- *Child:* "Can I get a new bike?"
- *Parent:* "Sure, let's create a plan together. What can you do to earn it?"

Tip for Parents: Make a family "earn it" chart where kids track progress toward earning special rewards through specific tasks or behaviors.

3. Set Clear Expectations with Privileges

Explanation: Define what's required to earn privileges. Entitlement thrives when kids receive things without effort or responsibility.

Example:

- **Privilege:** Extra screen time.
- **Requirement:** Completing all homework and chores without complaints.

Tip for Parents: Clearly state, "In our family, privileges are earned, not given just because we want them."

4. Teach Empathy and Gratitude

Explanation: Encouraging children to think about others helps shift focus away from their own wants.

Example: Ask kids to donate toys or write thank-you notes to express gratitude.

Tip for Parents: Make gratitude a daily habit by sharing one thing you're thankful for at dinner or bedtime.

5. Encourage Problem-Solving Instead of Complaining

Explanation: Kids often feel entitled when they expect problems to be solved for them.

Example:

- *Child:* "I don't have any good snacks!"
- *Parent:* "What can you do to solve that? Could you help me choose better options for next week's grocery list?"

Tip for Parents: Replace complaints with a problem-solving mindset. Ask, "What's a way you could earn that?" or "How could you fix that yourself?"

6. Praise Effort and Responsibility, Not Results Alone

Explanation: Focusing only on outcomes can lead to entitlement. Celebrate hard work and responsibility, regardless of results.

Example: "I'm proud of how much effort you put into your project, even though it didn't win."

Tip for Parents: Use phrases like "You earned this because you kept trying" rather than "You're so talented."

7. Teach Patience and Delayed Gratification

Explanation: Entitlement grows when children are used to immediate rewards. Teach them to wait for things they want.

Example: Create a "save for it" jar where they put aside money or points to earn a toy or experience.

Tip for Parents: Use a visual tracker to show progress toward a goal, reinforcing patience.

8. Use Natural Consequences

Explanation: Allow kids to experience the results of their choices.

Example: If a child refuses to do their chores, they don't get their allowance or privileges tied to responsibility.

Tip for Parents: Stay consistent. Follow through on consequences to reinforce the connection between actions and outcomes.

These approaches encourage responsibility, gratitude, and effort while eliminating entitlement by reframing privileges as earned rewards rather than automatic rights. Consistency and positive reinforcement help parents guide children toward healthier, more balanced attitudes.

 **Action Steps:**

Here are three action steps kids can take to cultivate gratitude:

1. Keep a Gratitude Journal

Action: Write down or draw three things they are thankful for each day.

Benefit: Helps them focus on the positive aspects of their life and develop a habit of reflection.

Example: "I'm thankful for my best friend, my favorite snack, and playing soccer today."

2. Express Thankfulness Regularly

Action: Say "thank you" sincerely and often to family members, teachers, and friends.

Benefit: Builds a habit of acknowledging others' efforts and kindness.

Example: "Thank you for helping me with my homework" or "Thanks for making dinner."

3. Give to Others

Action: Donate toys, clothes, or time to help others in need.

Benefit: Shifts focus from "what I want" to "what I can give," fostering empathy and gratitude for what they have.

Example: Participating in a toy drive or helping a neighbor with a small chore.

These simple, consistent practices help children build a lifelong attitude of gratitude.

A few different activities for your kids to complete:

Activity 1: Feeling Owed

Complete the following statements based on a time you felt a sense of entitlement. Be honest. Everyone has had at least one moment when they felt they've been owed something.

- A time when things didn't go my way, and I **BLAMED** someone else was:

_____

- Things that I think are **OWED** to me or I have previously thought were **OWED** to me were:

  _____

- A time when feeling **ENTITLED** affected me emotionally, and I acted badly was:

  _____

- A time when someone did something nice for me or helped me, and I forgot to **THANK** him/her was:

  _____

- A time when feeling **ENTITLED** has affected an important relationship negatively was:

  _____

- A time when feeling **ENTITLED** has affected my performance in my sport was:

  _____

Activity 2: Gratitude Bank

The first activity asked you to list times you've felt or given in to entitlement. Now, it's time to build your gratitude bank. Create a listing of memories and experiences that have made you forget about entitlement and have made you grateful for what you **DO** have in your life.

Complete the following questions.

- How have I been blessed?

  _____

  _____

- What talents do I have that I am grateful for? Explain the talents and why they make you feel grateful.

  _____

  _____

- What experiences have I had that make me feel appreciative? Describe at least one experience and why you appreciated it.

  _____

  _____

- What are some things I have taken for granted, for which I feel grateful now that I have stopped and reflected on what they mean to me? List at least 3 things.

  _____

  _____

  _____

- What challenge or difficulty have I had to face or overcome that makes me a better person? Explain at least one difficulty and why you are grateful for the struggle.

  _____

  _____

Activity 3: Thankfulness Inventory

There are many people and things to be thankful for. This activity will help you keep your feelings of entitlement in check. Complete the following phrases with people, things, and memories for which you are **THANKFUL**.

- **Person with Great Qualities** ~ Person's Name:_____
- Why are you thankful for this person?

  _____

- **Person & Memories** ~ Person's Name:_____
- What awesome, funny, fond, or sentimental memory do you have of this person?

  _____

- **Person Who Does Nice Things** ~ Person's Name:_____
- What nice, generous, or thoughtful thing has this person done for you or someone else?

  _____

- **Meaningful Person in Your Life** ~ Person's Name:_____
- Why is this person important to you? What does it mean to have this person in your life?

  _____

- **Favorite Event** ~ List the Event (birthday, particular game, holiday, etc.):_____
- Why does the memory of this event make you thankful? How has it made you or your life better?

  _____

- **Important Life Lesson** ~ Who Taught You the Lesson:_____
- What is the lesson you learned, and how is it important?

_____

Activity 4: Gratitude Jar Activity

What You'll Need:

- A jar, box, or container
- Strips of paper or small notecards
- Pens or markers

Instructions:

- **Decorate the Jar Together:** Let the child decorate the jar with stickers, paint, or drawings to make it personal and fun.
- **Daily or Weekly Gratitude Notes:** Each day (or once a week), both the parent and child write down one thing they're thankful for and place it in the jar.
- **Read the Notes Regularly:** Choose a special time, such as at the end of each month or on holidays, to read the gratitude notes together and reflect on the positive moments.
- **Benefit:** This activity helps both parent and child develop a habit of recognizing the good in their lives, strengthens their bond, and creates a tangible collection of gratitude memories they can revisit.

I'll wrap it up with a great quote from Oprah:

"Be thankful for what you have; you'll end up having more. If you concentrate on what you don't have, you will never, ever have enough."

Table Talk:

1. Do you ever feel like you deserve something just because you want it? Why or why not?
2. How do you feel when someone gives you something without you having to work for it? How does that compare to when you earn it?
3. Can you think of times when you've been really grateful for something? What made it feel special?
4. Do you think everyone has the same opportunities and resources? Why is it important to recognize differences in privilege?
5. When you face challenges or don't get what you want right away, how does that make you feel? What do you think you can learn from those moments?

CHAPTER 11

Dealing with Distractions

 **Goal: Children will learn to identify both their internal and external distractions in the classroom and in life, and then be given the tools needed to deal with those distractions.**

Distractions, distractions, distractions!

Being distracted is one of the hardest things to overcome in life. It's also one of those things that can bring you down the fastest! More than ever before, our kids today are faced with distractions in the classroom and in life.

What Is a Distraction?

A distraction is anything begging for your **ATTENTION** that is not connected to the outcome you desire. *Example: If you just can't keep from Snapchatting every 10 seconds, that's a distraction that's going to interfere with doing your homework.*

Think about a dog being FOCUSED on catching a squirrel. It is almost impossible to distract him. Imagine having that kind of laser focus!

A study shows that it takes a person an average of 15 minutes to regain focus after being distracted. That's a lot of time wasted, especially in a classroom or a game situation.

How can we help our kids deal with their own distractions? First, we need to help them identify what things are distracting them.

 Parent/Child Dialogue Example:

Parent: "Hey, kiddo, can we chat for a sec? I've noticed your homework's been taking a little longer lately."

Child: "Yeah, I know. My phone keeps pulling me away, and then there's other stuff, too."

Parent: "Totally get it—distractions sneak up on everyone. Want to try a couple of tricks to keep them in check?"

Child: "I guess. What do you have in mind?"

Parent: "Let's start by figuring out the main culprit. What's grabbing your attention the most?"

Child: "My phone. I keep checking messages and scrolling."

Parent: "Makes sense—it's hard to resist. What's one thing you could do to keep it from stealing your focus?"

Child: "Maybe put it on silent or leave it somewhere else?"

Parent: "Nice one! How about this: set a timer for 25 minutes of work, then give yourself a 5-minute phone break as a reward?"

Child: "That could work."

Parent: "Cool! Oh, and breaking big tasks into smaller bits helps too. What's next on your list?"

Child: "My science worksheet."

Parent: "Alright, try the timer for 25 minutes on that and see how it goes. Then you can check your phone for a bit."

Child: "Okay, I'll give it a shot."

Parent: "Awesome! It takes a little practice to manage distractions, but you're already on the right track. I'm proud of you for trying it out."

The takeaway from this chat is all about taming distractions to get stuff done. The parent and child figured out that the phone was the big attention-thief, and they came up with a simple plan: put it on silent or stash it elsewhere, work in focused 25-minute bursts, and reward those efforts with 5-minute phone breaks. Plus, breaking tasks into smaller pieces makes them less overwhelming. It's a practical, doable way to stay on track—proof that little tweaks can make a big difference!

There are two types of distractions: EXTERNAL and INTERNAL.

1. **External distractions** are outside events that take your attention away.
2. **Internal distractions** are your own thoughts and feelings or physical aches and pains that take your attention away.

EXTERNAL DISTRACTIONS

Distractions in the Classroom

During any given classroom period, there are **External** distractions that come into play that are either within your control or out of your control. These distractions can cause your child to miss something important: an assignment, material that is being covered, or an immediate task. Even worse, distractions can cause them to look irresponsible or uninterested to their teacher.

Activity 1: An activity for your child to complete

Rate the following situations. Check the box if the situation is a distraction for you or if it's not a distraction for you.

- I just got an "URGENT" text message from my best friend.
  ☐ **Distraction** ☐ **Not a Distraction**

- That guy/girl sitting next to me is so hot.
  ☐ **Distraction** ☐ **Not a Distraction**

- The two girls next to you keep gossiping and whispering back and forth to each other.
  ☐ **Distraction** ☐ **Not a Distraction**

- It's SO cold in this room. I might die of frostbite.
  ☐ **Distraction** ☐ **Not a Distraction**

- The girl sitting in front of me always has too much perfume on or not enough deodorant on. Ugh!
  ☐ **Distraction** ☐ **Not a Distraction**

- The obnoxious kid next to me burped so loudly I could feel the vibrations.
  ☐ **Distraction** ☐ **Not a Distraction**

- That guy in class just asked ANOTHER stupid question.
  ☐ **Distraction** ☐ **Not a Distraction**

- The girl who comes in late all the time doesn't have a pen AGAIN.
  ☐ **Distraction** ☐ **Not a Distraction**

- That girl chews her gum SO loud, it's annoying.
  ☐ **Distraction** ☐ **Not a Distraction**

- That guy just interrupted our discussion once again to talk about his argument with his girlfriend.
  ☐ **Distraction** ☐ **Not a Distraction**

- Someone sitting behind me keeps clicking his pen.
  ☐ **Distraction** ☐ **Not a Distraction**

Hopefully, your children have just identified things that distract them. It's important for them to know that there are things they CAN control, but there are also things they CAN'T control. Once they identify the things they CAN control, they can start following these strategies:

- If a person assigned to sit near you is a constant distraction, ask the teacher to move your seat or the distractor's seat.
- Keep your eyes focused on the teacher and what she is saying. This will require extreme effort.
- Be prepared. If you know a certain classroom is super cold or hot, prepare accordingly.
- Turn off your phone or put it in your backpack during instruction time. If you don't feel it vibrating, you won't be tempted to use it.
- **STOP FOCUSING ON THE DISTRACTION!**
  For the things you CAN'T control, try the following:
  - Respectfully discuss this situation with your teacher, hoping that she/he will be able to eliminate it.
  - If nothing changes, accept the situation and realize that you will have to put supreme effort into focusing on the teacher. DON'T LET YOUR FRUSTRATION WITH THIS BECOME ANOTHER DISTRACTION. ACCEPT IT AND MOVE ON!

Distractions for the Athlete

Life in the classroom is just one warzone where distractions can get your kids off track. Student-athletes have even more distractions they need to deal with during their sporting events and practices. The problem is that most of these distractions are **External**, so it's crucial to know which ones get their head out of the game.

Athletes at all levels have to contend with external factors unless they want to play in a bubble with no spectators or opponents. What fun is that? These distractions can cause them to miss a call from their coach, can cause them to make a mental error, or, worse than that, can cause them to look like they're not a team player and not doing or playing their best.

Activity 2:

Rate the following situations. Check the box if the situation is a distraction for you or if it's not a distraction for you.

- Our opponent's fans are loud and mean.
  ☐ **Distraction** ☐ **Not a Distraction**

- Our band's drum line is very loud.
  ☐ **Distraction** ☐ **Not a Distraction**

- Our own fans are so loud that I can hear every word and feel the vibrations from the stands.
  ☐ **Distraction** ☐ **Not a Distraction**

- An athlete from the other team posted a cocky remark on Twitter.
  ☐ **Distraction** ☐ **Not a Distraction**

- My new boyfriend/girlfriend is watching.
  ☐ **Distraction** ☐ **Not a Distraction**

- Holy Moly! Our game is going to be televised.
  ☐ **Distraction** ☐ **Not a Distraction**

- A college scout is at the game.
  ☐ **Distraction** ☐ **Not a Distraction**

- We are losing... by a lot!
  ☐ **Distraction** ☐ **Not a Distraction**

- That player from the other team just way overdid her celebration after she scored.

  ☐ **Distraction** ☐ **Not a Distraction**

- The official just made a bad call.

  ☐ **Distraction** ☐ **Not a Distraction**

Many of these are things you cannot control, so again, you will need to identify your distractions and recognize that you need to tune these distractions out. No one knows you better than you do. If you know what situations cause you to lose focus, do something about it.

INTERNAL DISTRACTIONS

Distractions in the Classroom

Of course, there are also **Internal** distractions. Internal distractions are your own thoughts and feelings or physical aches and pains that come into play. Aches and pains are rarely in your control, yet thoughts and feelings can be controlled. Just like external distractions, they can also cause you to miss something important that the teacher has said.

Activity 3:

Rate the following situations as to whether or not they are distractions for you.

- I'm thirsty, and my water bottle is empty.

  ☐ **Distraction** ☐ **Not a Distraction**

- I really don't like this teacher.

  ☐ **Distraction** ☐ **Not a Distraction**

- I have no idea what this teacher is talking about.

  ☐ **Distraction** ☐ **Not a Distraction**

- I'm exhausted from staying up too late last night.

  ☐ **Distraction** ☐ **Not a Distraction**

- I'm feeling super hyper, and this class is boring me!
  ☐ **Distraction** ☐ **Not a Distraction**

- I want to text something funny I just thought of to my friend.
  ☐ **Distraction** ☐ **Not a Distraction**

- I'm HUNGRY!!!
  ☐ **Distraction** ☐ **Not a Distraction**

- We have a HUGE game tonight. I'm so pumped!!!
  ☐ **Distraction** ☐ **Not a Distraction**

- I have another assignment due in my next class that I didn't finish/forgot about.
  ☐ **Distraction** ☐ **Not a Distraction**

- This assignment seems pointless.
  ☐ **Distraction** ☐ **Not a Distraction**

"I've trained all my life not to be distracted by distractions." —Nik Wallenda

---

Distractions for the Athlete

Getting your head in the game is a personal quest and task. It's up to you to psych yourself up and apply the focus that you need. That includes dealing with your very own **Internal** distractions. Again, these inner distractions will cause you to miss calls from the coach, cause you to make mental errors, and cause you to look like you don't belong out there. The worst part about these distractions is that no one else can see them or feel them but you.

Activity 4:

Rate the following situations. Check the box if the situation is a distraction for you or if it's not a distraction for you.

- This is the exact same game situation where I made a mistake earlier in the season.
  ☐ **Distraction** ☐ **Not a Distraction**

- I'm focused on the scoreboard, and we're losing.
  ☐ **Distraction** ☐ **Not a Distraction**

- Something in my body hurts, but it's not injured.
  ☐ **Distraction** ☐ **Not a Distraction**

- I'm so angry at a teammate because she botched that last play.
  ☐ **Distraction** ☐ **Not a Distraction**

- I just collided with another player and got the wind knocked out of me.
  ☐ **Distraction** ☐ **Not a Distraction**

- The kid I'm playing against is bigger than me.
  ☐ **Distraction** ☐ **Not a Distraction**

- This is the team we lost to last year.
  ☐ **Distraction** ☐ **Not a Distraction**

- We beat this team every time we face them, so I'm not even worried.
  ☐ **Distraction** ☐ **Not a Distraction**

- That official called so many penalties on me earlier this season.
  ☐ **Distraction** ☐ **Not a Distraction**

- My coach just yelled at me, and I'm embarrassed.
  ☐ **Distraction** ☐ **Not a Distraction**

- I just made a mental error, and I can't let it go.
  ☐ **Distraction** ☐ **Not a Distraction**

*"One way to boost our will power and focus is to manage
our distractions instead of letting them manage us."*
—Daniel Goleman

Only you can stop **Internal** distractions. Get a game plan together before you self-destruct. Look at your weak areas again. What are the things that get your head out of the game?

Start fixing them with the following strategies:

- **FOCUS** on the present, don't think about the last season, the last game, or even the last play.
- **FOCUS** on the specific job that you have to do.
- **FOCUS** on your coach's game plan and strategy.

The time to deal with your mental errors and losses is **AFTER** the game, not **DURING** the game. *Five-second memory is essential in sporting competitions.*

Don't think about the bruise you're going to have. Don't think about your teammate's error. Don't think about the other team's players. Do your job to the best of your ability. Give your teammate an encouraging pat on the back or a quick word. Look the other player in the eye and give it your all. Leave it all out on the field, no matter whom you're playing, how much time is left, or what the scoreboard says.

OTHER LIFE DISTRACTIONS

But wait, there's more. There are other types of distractions that our kids have outside the classroom and sporting events. Once again, they need to know what they are and have a game plan **BEFORE** they get their head out of the game.

1. SOCIAL MEDIA: Social media can be an enormous distraction. In fact, many coaches ban social media the week before a big game. Some college coaches enforce fines on their players if they are caught using social media during the season. They know what a big distraction social media can be to their players.

Although social media can be a good way to promote "your brand" as well as connect with friends, it can also be very distracting.

DON'T:

- Post negative comments or criticize your opponents, your own teammates, officials, coaches, or fans.
- Post anything on social media directly before games or competitions.
- Spend hours on social media looking to see what people are saying about your upcoming game, match, or competition.

DO:

- Best choice: Stay away from social media 24 hours before and 24 hours after your completion.
- Next best choice: If you just can't keep yourself away, try to keep posts positive (not arrogant) about the game. REMEMBER THIS: Your talent should speak for itself... You don't need to talk about it. Show it—don't speak it.

2. HATERS: People will try to bring you down.

DON'T:

- Interact with haters!
- Pay attention to the media, watch the news, or read the paper before a competition. Focus on yourself, not what others are saying about you.

DO:

- Best Choice: Ignore them! Focus on yourself, not what others are saying about you. They will want you to fight back, so don't! Be silent.
- Next best choice: If you just have to know what they are saying about you, try to find some humor in it.

3. CLIQUES: Cliques are exclusive and are run by "control freaks."

DON'T:

- Don't befriend people who like to exclude others.
- Don't "sell yourself to the devil" to be in a group just to be popular. (Meaning: don't let your friends pressure you to be in a group where you have to give up the things that you are interested in and love to do, just to be in the popular group.)
- Don't surround yourself with friends who don't have the same values as you do.

DO:

- Best Choice: Run as far as you can from cliques. Be confident in yourself and make friends from different social circles and groups.
- Next best choice if you are already stuck in one: Have a mind of your own. You are the only one who should be in control of how you act and the choices that you make. If they are your true friends, they should respect your choices.

4. JEALOUSY: Jealous people make life difficult for you.

DON'T:

- When you know that someone is jealous of you, it means that you have something that they don't have and want. OR, it could also mean that they are fearful of losing something to you, like a friend, a boyfriend, a starting position on a team, etc. Don't say bad things about those who are jealous of you, because they are already insecure to begin with, and that will only increase their jealousy toward you.
- Don't brag! This only feeds more jealousy.
- Don't spend too much time with them, because they may not be trustworthy. Watch your back. When someone acts jealous of you, it does not mean that they care about you.

DO:

- Best Choice: Put yourself in their shoes and try to understand where they are coming from. Then, give that person extra attention, and it is likely that some of that jealousy may melt away.
- Next best choice if you are not there yet: Ignore their remarks and jabs against you and keep focusing on your goals and successes.

5. PARTYING: Partying is an "energy-sucker".

DON'T:

- Become distracted by excessive celebrating of your successes, especially before your next competition.
- Resort to partying when you don't feel good about yourself and want to "dull the pain." People will try to entice you to "party."

DO:

- Best Choice: Stay away from parties during your season. Hang out with friends in a controlled environment: movies, friends home, etc.
- Next best choice if you just can't stay away: give yourself an early curfew and set boundaries for yourself BEFORE you go.

6. RELATIONSHIPS: Relationship drama can get in the way of your game-time focus.

DON'T:

- Get into any serious relationship conversations during the time of a big competition. Emotionally, it requires too much of your time and focus. "Table it" until afterward. Significant others can tempt you to be distracted.

DO:

- Best choice: "Table" any potential emotional conversations with your boyfriend/girlfriend until AFTER your competition. Discuss your boundaries if this happens AHEAD of time.

- Next best choice if you just have to try to fix it: Communicate with them through text, email, or note, letting them know that you will be able to respond after you have had time to think about the situation, AFTER your competition.

7. GOSSIP: Gossip hurts!

DON'T:

- Don't say bad things about people or spread rumors.
- If someone is gossiping about you, don't show the "gossip queen/bully" that you are angry or upset. Keep your cool!
- Don't tell the "gossip queen/bully" to mind her/his own business. This will add fuel to the fire.

DO:

- Best choice: Be polite to those who are gossiping about you. Be confident and humble. Be the better person!
- Next best choice if you just can't keep it in any longer: Cover your mouth with duct tape! No, but seriously, walk away from the person or group if you are being tempted to gossip or if you are tempted to say anything to the person who is gossiping about you.

Activity 5:

Rate from greatest (1) to least (7) the things you are most distracted by.

- Gossip: _____
- Jealousy: _____
- Cliques: _____
- Social Media: _____
- Haters: _____
- Partying: _____
- Relationships: _____

Write about a time when you had one of these distractions and how you dealt with it. _____

_____

_____

What was the outcome?

_____

_____

_____

Would you have changed the way you dealt with it?

_____

_____

_____

If yes, what would you do differently now?

_____

_____

_____

Remember: A distraction is anyone or anything begging for your attention that is not connected to the outcomes you desire.

Keep your eye on the prize and what you want to achieve.

Identify any **External** and **Internal** distractions for what they are.

Ask yourself, "Is this particular person, action, or thing going to help me achieve my goals? Is he, she, or it a part of the solution or part of the distraction?" Don't focus on the distraction. Keep your head in the game!

 **Action Steps:**

What three things distract you the most in class?

1) _____

Solution:_____

2) _____

Solution:_____

3) _____

Solution:_____

What three things distract you the most in a game?

1) _____

Solution:_____

2) _____

Solution:_____

3) _____

Solution:_____

What three things distract you the most outside of school and sports?

1) _____

Solution:_____

2) _____

Solution:

3) _____

Solution:_____

Table Talk:

Talk to your child about his/her answers on the activities.

PART 3

LOVE, LIMITS, AND LIFELINE

CHAPTER 12

Bullying

 **Goal: When young people are bullied by their peers, they're at a much higher risk for low self-esteem, anxiety, stress, depression, and even suicidal thoughts. The bullies don't fare very well either. This chapter takes an in-depth look at both bullies and their victims, bullying prevention strategies, bullying intervention, cyberbullying, bullying and disabilities, and why we must take action.**

Chances are, one of your children has either been bullied, has bullied someone, or has been a bystander. Believe it or not, approximately 160,000 students a day—not a year—a DAY stay home from school due to fear of bullying. Good grief! That's a lot of kids, and that's why this chapter is so important. So, how long do you think that bullying has been around? I'll give you a little hint. Take a look at animals. Aggressive behavior is a way for pack animals to be dominant over other animals, so bullying has been around since animals have been around. I'm sure most of you have seen *The Lion King*, right? Remember when Pumbaa says, *"I will not be made to feel ashamed of who I am. I may run from hyenas, but I will always fight A BULLY!"* Pumbaa showed us to never let anyone make you feel ashamed of yourself and to never tolerate a bully. Well, just like animals, people have been bullying since the beginning of time, too. So, in this chapter, I'll cover the different characteristics of a bully, the effects and consequences of bullying, and what to do when you or someone you know is being bullied.

What Is Bullying?

As I just mentioned, bullying has been around for a long time, and the overall goal of pack animals is to dominate other animals. Well, what do you think the overall goal of a bully is? It's to try to make people feel bad about themselves by attacking their self-esteem. So, how do they do this? They use power to intimidate. They try to dominate by picking on those they think are weak. They plan to harm. They act in anger. They use hateful words. They want their own way. They rely on the strength of an audience. So, to sum it up, do you think bullies are happy people? We really don't know the answer to that, but what we DO know is that it isn't right to feel happy when you are intentionally hurting others and making them suffer. So now that you know the characteristics of a bully, what exactly IS bullying? Bullying is when someone is picked on by a person or a group, but not just once. Bullies bully over and over and over again, and they want to control you or harm you. Bullies make threats, spread rumors, and attack you with their words. They actually may even attack you physically, and they purposely like to exclude people from a group. Bullies make fun of others for many things, like their appearance (how someone looks), their behavior (how someone acts), their beliefs (their race or religion), their social status (whether someone is popular or not), and maybe even their sexual identity, like being gay, lesbian, or transgender.

 **Parent/Child Dialogue Example (When Your Child Is Bullying):**

Parent: "Hey, I need to talk to you about something serious. I got a call from one of your teachers today. She said that Jake's mom reached out because some mean texts were sent to Jake... from your phone."

Child: "Oh."

Parent: "What happened?"

Child: "We were just messing around. It's not a big deal."

Parent: "Hmm. Can we unpack that? Imagine for a minute that someone was saying those things to *you*. How would you feel?"

Child: "I guess... I'd be upset."

Parent: "Exactly. Words—especially in texts—can be powerful. When you write something hurtful, even if you think it's a joke, it sticks. Jake's mom says he's been really sad since reading those messages."

Child: "I didn't think it would hurt him *that much*."

Parent: "I get that. And I know you didn't mean for things to get out of control. But bullying is when you use words or actions to hurt someone over and over. Texts make it worse because they're permanent—he can read them again and again, even when you're not there."

Child: "So now, what? What do I do?"

Parent: "Well, you need to make this right. First, I want you to think about why you sent those texts. Were you trying to be funny? Cool? Were other kids pressuring you?"

Child: "Kind of both. Everyone else was teasing him, and I didn't want to be left out."

Parent: "That makes sense. Peer pressure is real, and it's tough to stand up for what's right when it feels like everyone's going along with something. But being a good friend and a good person means doing the hard thing— the right thing."

Child: "So... I guess I should say sorry?"

Parent: "Yes, but it needs to be more than that. Apologizing is a good first step, but real change happens when we *show* we're sorry. What can you do to be kind to Jake moving forward?"

Child: "Maybe I could sit with him at lunch or be nicer to him in the group chat."

Parent: "I like that. Let's also talk about how to avoid this in the future. What will you do if people start teasing someone again?"

Child: "I could just not join in. Or tell them it's not cool."

Parent: "Those are great ideas. You have a lot of influence with your friends—if you speak up, others might follow your lead."

Child: "Yeah, I guess."

Parent: "This is all part of figuring out who you want to be. You're a good person, and this is a chance to show it. Everyone makes mistakes—what matters is how we learn from them."

Child: "OK, Mom, I'll apologize tomorrow."

Parent: "I'm proud of you for stepping up. We'll get through this together, and hopefully you will be a good example to your friends."

Child: "You're right. Thank you, Mom."

This dialogue demonstrates empathy, active listening, and teaching without shaming, while helping the child understand the real impact of their behavior.

 **Parent/Child Dialogue Example (When Your Child Is Being Bullied):**

Parent: "Hey, I noticed you've been quieter than usual lately. You don't seem yourself. Is something bothering you?"

Child: "It's nothing."

Parent: "You know you can tell me anything, right?"

Child: "Well... There's this kid, Brad. He keeps making fun of me in front of everyone. He says I'm weird, and some of the other kids laugh."

Parent: "I'm really sorry to hear that. That sounds hurtful. How does it make you feel?"

Child: "I feel... embarrassed. Like, I want to hide."

Parent: "That's understandable. Being treated like that can feel awful. Thank you for trusting me enough to share it. Let's talk about some ways we can handle this together."

Child: "Like what?"

Parent: "First, remember this—it's not your fault. Bullying is about the other person's behavior, not about you. It says more about them than it does about who you are."

Child: "But why does he pick on me?"

Parent: "People bully for different reasons. Sometimes, they're trying to feel powerful or get attention. Other times, they might be dealing with their own hurt feelings and taking it out on others. But that still doesn't make it okay."

Child: "So, what should I do?"

Parent: "Let's start with staying calm. Bullies want a reaction, so if you stay cool, it takes away their power. Practice saying something simple like, *'Whatever, I'm not going to listen to that,'* and then walk away."

Child: "What if he keeps going?"

Parent: "If walking away doesn't stop it, tell a trusted adult—your teacher, school counselor, or me. Asking for help is not tattling; it's standing up for yourself."

Child: "But won't that make me look weak?"

Parent: "Actually, it shows you're strong. It takes courage to speak up and protect yourself. You're setting a boundary and showing that you deserve respect."

Child: "I guess that makes sense."

Parent: "Also, think about who your real friends are—the people who lift you up, not tear you down. Spend time with them and build each other up. Bullies thrive when they isolate people, but good friends can make you feel stronger."

Child: "I have a couple of good friends."

Parent: "That's great. Keep close to them. And if you ever feel overwhelmed, I'm here. We'll handle this together, step by step."

Child: "Thanks, Mom. I feel a bit better now."

Parent: "You're welcome. I'm proud of you for talking to me. You're smart, kind, and brave—don't ever forget that."

The key takeaway from this dialogue is that handling bullying requires staying calm, setting boundaries, and seeking support. The parent helps the child understand that bullies act out for their own reasons, but their behavior is never okay. The child learns practical strategies—like not reacting, walking away, and asking a trusted adult for help when needed. The conversation also reinforces the importance of surrounding oneself with positive friends and knowing that seeking help is a sign of strength, not weakness. Ultimately, the dialogue emphasizes open communication and parental support, showing the child that they are not alone in facing challenges.

Good Explanations for Your Children on the Three Different Types of Bullying

First, there is *verbal* bullying, which is when the bully tries to insult you and calls you names. Now, don't get this confused with joking. Here's the difference. Joking is saying funny things or playing tricks on your friends to make them laugh. Key word here is FRIENDS... Joking is done among friends. It isn't meant to be mean or unkind, and it doesn't make people feel bad about themselves. Joking stops before someone gets upset. On the other hand, bullying is NOT done among friends. It can include name-calling, insulting, gossiping, leaving people out, kicking, hitting, making someone look silly on purpose, spreading rumors, and sending mean text messages.

The second type of bullying is *physical*. Physical bullying is when bullies hurt others physically. This includes shoving, tripping, pushing, hitting, spitting, taking or destroying someone's things, and making mean or rude hand gestures. Also, any form of touching that a person does not want can be bullying.

The third type of bullying is *cyberbullying*. Yikes. Cyberbullying is when bullies use the internet and social media to say things to you that they might not say in person. They may send mean texts, post insults and horrible things about someone on social media, or make rude comments on their Instagram pictures. Cyberbullies may also post personal information, pictures, or videos of you, intending to hurt or embarrass you. Unlike traditional bullying, cyberbullying means that you don't have to have face-to-face contact. It also doesn't require the physical power or the audience that bullies typically want.

Anyone who has access to the internet or a cell phone can cyberbully someone else, and many times, they don't have to even reveal who they are. They can cyberbully in secret. This empowers cyberbullies, and they will go much further to harass you or make fun of you than they would if they were face-to-face with you. Unfortunately, cyberbullies can torment you 24 hours a day, seven days a week, and the bullying can follow you anywhere, so that no place, not even your own home or bedroom, feels safe. With just a few clicks, they can humiliate you in front of hundreds or even thousands of people on social media. The methods young people use to cyberbully can range from sending threatening or taunting messages through email, text, social media, or IM, to breaking into your email account or stealing your online identity to hurt you. Some cyberbullies may even create a social media page to target you. Did you know that both boys and girls are equally guilty of cyberbullying? Boys tend to cyberbully by sending messages that threaten physical harm. Girls cyberbully by spreading lies and rumors about you, sharing your secrets, or by excluding you from social media groups and friend lists.

The Circle of Bullying: Bullies, Assistants, Reinforcers, Outsiders, Defenders

Did you know that bullying usually doesn't consist of just the bully and the one being bullied? There are usually others that take part, too, and that's why it's called the circle of bullying. There are five different roles that people play in this circle: the bullies, the assistants, the reinforcers, the outsiders, and the defenders. Chances are that almost everyone has played a part in this circle during their lifetime. Let's take a look.

First, there are the *bullies* themselves. Let's look at a few different types of bullies.

> Bully #1: Derrick. He is outgoing and aggressive. He might make fun of you to your face or physically hurt you.

> Bully #2: Taylor. She is quiet and sneaky. She might try to manipulate you very secretly. She might anonymously start a terrible rumor about you just to see what happens.

Bully #3: Jordan. She is friendly and fake. She might pretend to be your friend so that you tell her your secrets, but then she does hurtful things and talks badly about you behind your back.

Unfortunately, I bet most of us have seen these kinds of bullies in action.

Moving on to the next group within the circle are the *assistants*. Assistants may not start the bullying, but they serve as assistants to the bully. They may egg the bully on and join in the bullying.

Then, there are the *reinforcers*. The Reinforcers aren't involved in the bullying behavior, but they are there to give the bully an audience. They will laugh and provide support for the kids who are bullying and encourage the bullying to continue.

The next group is the *outsiders*. The Outsiders separate themselves from the bullying situation. They will watch, but they won't choose sides because they won't want to egg on the bully. But they also won't defend the person being bullied. Often, these "outsiders" want to help, but they don't know how.

And last, but not least, there are the *defenders*. The Defenders provide comfort to the person being bullied and may come to the rescue of the one being bullied.

As I mentioned earlier, most kids play more than one role in bullying. In some cases, they may be directly involved in bullying as the one bullying others, or they may witness bullying and play an assisting or defending role. Every situation is different.

How Can Our Kids Deal with Bullies and Cyberbullies?

Please go over this Top 10 list with your child when they are confronted with VERBAL bullying.

Number 1. Have a winner's body language! That means stand up tall, pull your shoulders back, open your chest, hold your head high, and chin up! Having great posture will not only make you look taller, but it will also immediately boost your confidence. The best way to gain confidence is to physically take up more space. If you are standing, use a wider stance than usual and put your arms on your hips. If you are sitting at a desk, use your arms on the desk to take up space. This will make you feel more powerful and give you more confidence.

And one more thing. Look at the bully straight in the eye. If you have to practice this winning posture in the mirror at home, it will be worth it!

Number 2. Don't retaliate. This means don't fight back, verbally or physically. Although extremely tempting, you don't want to give a bully exactly what he wants. It will do you no good. The best thing you can do is to show the bully that their words have ZERO impact on you. Think about this. If someone is chasing you, they want you to run so they can catch you, but if you stand still, the chase is over. You have eliminated them from chasing you. So, the same is true when you "stand still" with your words. If you don't respond, the fun is over for the bully. Try to keep that visual in your mind. It will be very useful.

Number 3. Use humor. If you're the type that really needs to say something and strategy #2 is not for you, then add humor. For example, if the bully says to you, "You are so ugly with that huge zit on your face." Your response could be "Oh! I only have one? Last time I counted, I had five! Wow, things are really looking up! You made my day!" *(Say this with a chuckle.)*

Number 4. Don't blame yourself. It's not your fault. No matter what a bully says or does, don't be ashamed of who you are. Remember, it's the bully who has the problem, not you! There are many wonderful things about you, so be proud of who you are. Focus on all the positive things in your life.

Number 5. Boost your confidence. A great way to boost your self-esteem and reduce stress at the same time is to exercise. Try to get into a daily routine of getting some form of exercise. Go for a run, or even better, take up kickboxing or martial arts to really boost your confidence and work off some of your stress or anger in a healthy way.

Number 6. Try to view the bully from a different perspective. The bully may not look like it on the outside, but deep down is probably an unhappy, frustrated person who has very low self-esteem and wants to have control over you so that you feel as badly as he or she does. He or she may not be as strong as you think.

Number 7. Spend time with your friends. The time you spend hanging out with your friends and doing the things you enjoy will be a distraction from the bullying.

Number 8: Try not to be alone. If you are alone, you may be an easy target for a bully, so try to be around your friends or peers during the day. If you're new to a school or neighborhood, or if you feel like you don't have many friends that you can turn to, try a new activity, learn a new skill, join a club, or volunteer to help others. You will be able to make new friends while learning new skills, and helping others really boosts your self-esteem as well!

Number 9: Seek support! Make sure that you have people in your life whom you can trust and go to for encouragement and support. A parent, teacher, mentor, coach, or other adult you trust will encourage you and help boost your self-esteem during this difficult time. Asking for help does not mean that you're weak or that there's something wrong with you. Believe me. Many bullies pick on people that they are jealous of, people that have the things that they want, like popularity, good looks, good grades, etc.

Number 10: Join your school's bullying or violence prevention programs. Did you know that you may be able to work things out with a bully through peer mediation or a violence prevention program at school? If your school doesn't have these programs, start one of your own. I bet you can rally your friends around the cause, too.

Well, that wraps up the TOP 10 strategies if you are being verbally bullied.

If you are being physically bullied, things will be a little different. This type of bullying is very dangerous, and you need to tell someone immediately. Make sure you get help from your parents right away. Physical bullying tends to get worse. So, I repeat, the sooner you tell someone, the safer you will be.

The same is true for cyberbullying, which can also be very damaging. Let's go over some strategies you can use if you are being cyberbullied:

Don't respond to any messages or posts written about you, no matter what. Don't give the bully what he wants—the satisfaction of knowing he's upset you. Also, it will be tempting to reread the posts and texts over and over again, but this will just make you angrier and angrier.

1. **Don't seek revenge,** or you will actually become a cyberbully yourself. Not only will it make the problem worse, but you could also get in trouble with the law. A good rule to follow is this: if you wouldn't say it in person, don't say it online or through a text.
2. **Save the evidence.** Make sure you keep all abusive text messages or a screenshot of the text messages. Then report them to a trusted adult immediately. If you don't report it, the cyberbully will usually be more aggressive the next time.
3. **Stop all possible communication.** Block their email address, cell phone number, and delete them from all social media accounts as soon as possible.
4. **Don't ever pass along cyberbullying messages** to anyone other than the right authorities for reporting. This could make the situation much worse.

Common Questions

These are some of the most common questions we get from kids about bullying.

1. Why am I being bullied?

There are many different reasons why bullies may be targeting you, but a few reasons could be:

- They are jealous of you.
- They want to make themselves popular.
- They want to look tough or feel powerful.
- They are being bullied themselves.
- They want to escape their own problems.

Another reason may be that you're a bit different from them. Maybe you act differently or dress differently, maybe your race, religion, or sexual orientation sets you apart, or maybe you're just the new kid at school and an easy target.

2. What if I'm the bully?

This is a very honest question. First, some people bully to deal with their own feelings of stress, anger, or frustration. Other bullies might have been bullied and now want to show their power by bullying someone else. This happens often in families if an older sibling bullies a younger sibling, and then the younger sibling bullies a younger sibling, and so on. The youngest sibling has then been bullied and has learned how to bully and may then bully someone at school.

If you have bullied someone, first talk to your parents about why you are bullying and ask them for advice on how you can change. Next, try to put yourself in the shoes of the people whom you have bullied. How do those people feel? Probably pretty awful. How would you feel? Finally, it may be a good idea to let the people whom you have bullied know that you are sorry and that you won't do it anymore. Asking them to forgive you is another step you may take when you are ready. This may help relieve you from some shame and guilt you may feel and help you to move on with a clear conscience. Going forward, try to remember to treat everyone with respect, the way that you want to be treated.

3. I'm terrified to ask for help!

Please know that you're not alone. Did you know that over 60% of bullying incidents are not reported? These are some of the reasons why:

- Kids may want to handle it on their own to feel that they have control of the situation.
- They may fear that they will be looked down upon for being a "tattletale."
- They may fear that the bullying will get worse once the bully is on to the fact that you have notified someone.
- They may not want adults to know what is being said about them.

- They may fear that adults will judge them for being weak.
- They may feel like no one cares or could understand.
- They may fear being rejected by their peers.

These are all very REAL feelings, but it is always best to ask for a parent's help on how to handle the situation when it first starts.

 **Action Steps:**

Have your child write down three things he/she can do when one of their friends is being bullied.

Have your child write down three things he/she can do when being bullied.

Activity for a Young Child:

Wrinkled Heart

Materials:

- A large cut-out heart made from paper or construction paper (big enough for kids to see clearly).
- Markers or pens.

Instructions:

1. **Introduce the Activity**
   Start by showing the paper heart and explaining that it represents someone's feelings.
   Say: *"This heart is like a person's feelings. When we are kind to others, their heart stays smooth and happy. But when we say or do hurtful things, their heart gets wrinkled."*

2. **Share Hurtful Scenarios**

   Ask your child to think of examples of unkind words or actions they've heard or experienced (without naming names). For each example, crumple the heart a little bit. Continue until the heart is wrinkled all over.

   Example scenarios might include:
   - *"You can't play with us!"*
   - *"You're weird."*
   - *"Nobody likes you."*

3. **Talk About Apologizing**

   Now, discuss how saying "I'm sorry" or being kind afterward can help. Smooth out the heart as much as possible.
   Ask: *"Do you think we can make the heart look new again, even after we smooth it out?"*

4. **Reflect on the Wrinkles**

   Point out that even though the heart is smoother, the wrinkles are still there.
   Explain: *"Words and actions can leave scars that stick around, even if we apologize. That's why it's so important to be kind and think before we speak or act."*

5. **Discussion Questions**
   - How did it feel to see the heart being wrinkled?
   - How can we prevent wrinkling someone's heart?
   - What can we do if we see someone else being unkind?

Wrap-Up

Emphasize that kindness keeps hearts smooth and happy, while bullying causes damage that's hard to undo. Encourage kids to be mindful of their words and actions, and to be the kind of person who helps protect hearts instead of wrinkling them.

Why This Works

- **Visual Learning:** Kids see a concrete example of how bullying leaves lasting damage.
- **Emotional Connection:** Reflecting on the metaphor of a wrinkled heart makes the impact of words feel more personal and memorable.
- **Empathy-Building:** The activity fosters a deeper understanding of kindness, empathy, and the consequences of negative behavior.

Activity for a Teen:

"The Ripple Effect" Activity

Objective:
To show how words and actions—whether kind or hurtful—spread and impact others beyond the person directly involved.

Materials:
- A large bowl filled with water
- Small stones or pebbles

Instructions:

1. **Set the Stage**
   Begin with a brief discussion:
   "Everything we do and say has an impact on the people around us. Like dropping a stone in water, our actions create ripples that spread far beyond the person we interact with directly. Today, we're going to see what that looks like."

2. **Demonstrate the Ripple Effect**
   - Drop a small stone into the bowl of water. Ask everyone to watch how the ripples spread outward.

- Explain: *"This is what happens when we say kind words or do something positive. The ripple spreads, affecting others in ways we might not even realize."*
- Drop another stone, and say: *"The same thing happens with hurtful words or actions. The ripples can reach far and wide, often in negative ways."*

3. **Personal Reflection**

   Have your child share examples of small actions or words that created positive or negative ripples in his/her life. Examples might include:
   - A compliment that boosted their confidence.
   - A mean comment that stuck with them for a long time.

4. **Discussion Questions**
   - How can one person's actions create a chain reaction?
   - What kind of ripples do you want to create in your relationships and community?
   - How can we help stop the spread of negative ripples when we see hurtful behavior?

Wrap-Up

Encourage your child to think about the power he/she has to create positive ripples every day. Acknowledge that being kind and standing up for others takes courage but makes a lasting difference.

Why This Works

- **Simple Visual:** The ripple effect is easy to understand and memorable.
- **Personal Connection:** Sharing real examples helps teens relate the metaphor to their own lives.
- **Empowerment:** Teens leave with a clear understanding that small actions matter and that they have the power to make positive choices.

To wrap up, I hope you feel like you have empowered your child and have given them the confidence in knowing how they can identify bullies and how to use the right strategies to prevent a bully from trying to take away their self-esteem. Hopefully, they will also be able to help others who find themselves in the circle of bullying.

Table Talk 1:

- Almost everyone has been bullied at one time or another. Did you know that (sadly) adults bully, too? It's so important to learn how to deal with bullies at a young age.
- How have you been affected by a bully?
- How did it feel?
- Did you feel like you knew how to deal with it?

Table Talk 2:

Let's talk about the circle of bullying.
- Think about the times that you have been tempted to bully…
- Times you've been or wanted to be the assistant …
- Times you've been or wanted to be the reinforcer…
- Times you've been or wanted to be the outsider …

Table Talk 3:

- How do you feel about these bullying strategies?
- Which ones do you feel will be the most helpful for you?
- Take a photo of these with your phone so that you will have it in case you or a friend has an "emergency bullying moment"!
- Do you think these strategies will be helpful to share with your friends? Why or why not?
- And times you've been or wanted to be the defender.
- Where do you see yourself the most?
- How do you think you can help the person getting bullied the most?

CHAPTER 13

Teen Dating

 **Goal: To equip your children with the knowledge, skills, and confidence to navigate relationships in a way that's healthy, safe, and fulfilling—both now and as they grow into adulthood. It's about setting them up to thrive emotionally and socially while avoiding common pitfalls.**

While numerous books explore the topic of teen dating in depth, my approach here is to focus on highlighting a few essential points. My aim is to equip parents with practical tools to facilitate open and honest conversations with their teens about a subject that can often feel uncomfortable at that age.

Teaching teens about dating is a critical part of guiding them through adolescence and preparing them for healthy relationships in adulthood. Here's a detailed breakdown of key lessons parents should focus on, based on widely recognized principles of emotional health, communication, and safety.

1. Understanding Healthy Relationships

Guide your teen to understand that a strong relationship is built on both people genuinely caring about each other's feelings, thoughts, and limits. It's about feeling safe to be themselves without being pushed to act differently or agree to things that don't sit right with them. Parents can help by asking questions like, "Do you feel like (name) listens to you?" or "Do you ever feel like you can't say no?" to spark a conversation about what respect looks like in action.

Mutual Respect: It's important that our kids know that a healthy relationship involves both people valuing each other's feelings, opinions, and boundaries. They should never feel pressured to change who they are or do something they're uncomfortable with.

Equality: Emphasize that relationships should be partnerships, not power struggles. Both individuals should have a say and feel heard. Help your teen see that a healthy relationship is a true partnership, where neither person dominates or controls the other. It's not about one-sided decisions or power games—it's about both individuals having an equal voice and feeling valued for what they bring to the table. Teens should know it's okay to speak up and expect to be heard, just as they should listen to their partner in return. Parents can open the door to this discussion by asking, "Do you feel like your opinions matter as much as (name)?" or "How do you both decide things together?" These questions can gently guide teens to reflect on whether equality is present and encourage them to share their experiences, making an awkward topic feel more approachable.

Trust and Honesty: Stress the importance of being truthful and building trust. Teens should know it's okay to expect reliability and openness from a partner. Encourage your teen to recognize that trust and honesty are the foundation of any solid relationship. Being truthful with each other—about feelings, intentions, or even small everyday things—creates a sense of safety and reliability that both people can count on. Teens should feel confident that it's not only okay but essential to expect their partner to be open and dependable, just as they should offer the same in return. You can help kickstart this conversation by asking, "Do you feel like you can trust (name) to be straight with you?" or "How do you handle it when something feels off?" These prompts can ease teens into sharing their thoughts, helping them process what trust looks like and why it matters, even if the subject feels tricky to tackle at their age.

Red Flags: Help them recognize warning signs of unhealthy dynamics, like possessiveness, jealousy, constant criticism, or manipulation. For example, if a partner demands to check their phone or isolates them from friends, that's a problem. Guide your teen to notice warning signs that a relationship might be veering into unhealthy territory. Things like possessiveness, excessive jealousy, constant put-downs, or manipulation aren't just quirks—they're signals that something's wrong. For instance, if a partner insists on checking their phone, dictates who they can hang out with, or tries to cut them off from friends, that's not love—it's control. You can broach this by asking, "Does (name) ever make you feel like you're walking on eggshells?" or "How do you feel when (name) reacts to you spending time with others?" These questions can help teens open up about their experiences, giving them a chance to think critically about their relationship and recognize when behaviors cross a line, all while keeping the conversation natural and less awkward.

2. Setting and Respecting Boundaries

Help your teen understand that setting boundaries is a vital part of any healthy relationship—it's about knowing their own limits and feeling secure enough to share them. Boundaries aren't just rules; they're a way to protect their emotional well-being, physical comfort, and personal time. Teens should also learn to respect their partner's limits with the same care they'd want in return. Parents, you can turn this into a conversation by exploring specific areas and offering practical ways to build confidence in discussing them.

Personal Limits: Encourage your teen to think about what feels right for them in a relationship—whether it's how much time they spend with a partner, how physically close they're ready to get, or how much emotional energy they're willing to give. For example, they might decide they're not comfortable with physical intimacy yet, or that they need space for schoolwork, hobbies, or friends. Parents can help by asking, "What feels okay for you when you're with (name)?" or "How do you balance time with them and everything else you care about?" This invites your teens to reflect and articulate their needs, making it easier to communicate those boundaries clearly to a partner.

Saying No: Teach your teen that saying 'no' is not only okay but a strength, and they shouldn't feel guilty or selfish for it. A caring partner will respect their limits without making them feel bad. To build this confidence, try role-playing at home: practice simple scenarios, like declining a request to skip plans with friends or saying they're not ready for a certain step in the relationship. You might ask, "How would you feel telling (name) you're not okay with something?" or "What would you say if they pushed back?" This hands-on approach that you practice BEFORE the situation arises will give your teen great confidence once the situation does arise. It will make the idea of standing up for themselves less daunting and more natural when the moment comes.

Respecting Others' Boundaries: Flip the script! Teens need to understand that just as they deserve respect for their limits, they must honor their partner's boundaries, too. Pushing someone to go beyond what they're comfortable with or guilt-tripping them into agreement damages trust. You can spark this discussion with your teen by asking, "How do you know when your (name) is okay with something?" or "What would you do if they said no to something you wanted?" This helps teens see boundaries as a two-way street, encouraging empathy and mutual care in their relationships.

3. Communication Skills

Guide your teen to see communication as the glue that holds a relationship together—it's how they share what's on their mind, understand their partner, and work through bumps in the road. Teens often struggle to open up or handle disagreements, so building these skills early can make a big difference. Parents can help by breaking it down into manageable pieces and encouraging practice, turning an intimidating subject into something approachable and practical.

Expressing Feelings: Encourage your teen to get comfortable sharing what they feel and need instead of keeping it inside or hoping their boyfriend/girlfriend will magically figure it out. We all know that bottling up emotions can lead to misunderstandings, while clear words build connection. For instance, instead of pouting when plans fall through, they could say, "I feel disappointed when plans change at the last second because I was looking forward to it." Parents can ease into this by asking, "What's one thing you'd want (name) to know about how you feel?" or "How could you tell (name) if something's bothering you?" These prompts help teens practice putting emotions into words, making it less awkward over time.

Here are some strategies for your teen when upset. These strategies are useful for us as well!

- **Take a Pause:**
  When you feel like you're about to lose your temper, try counting to ten in your head or taking three slow, deep breaths. It might sound too simple, but it gives your brain a moment to catch up to your emotions before you say or do something you regret. Have you ever heard that it's extremely difficult to do math and be angry at the same time?

- **Channel the Energy:**
  Sometimes, your body has all this built-up energy, and you need to let it out in a healthy way. Go for a run, do some push-ups, or even punch a pillow. Moving your body can help you release that frustration without hurting yourself or others.

- **Talk It Out:**
  It's okay to tell someone you trust how you're feeling. It could be a parent, a coach, or a close friend. Saying, "I'm so frustrated right now, and I need to talk about it," can really help you work through those feelings.

Set an example. Kids learn by watching us. You could say, "There are times when even I feel so frustrated I don't know what to do. What helps me is stepping away from the situation, taking some deep breaths, and coming back to it when I'm calmer. I'm still working on it, too—it's a lifelong skill." Showing them that it's okay to struggle but also to keep trying makes a big impact.

Handling your emotions with maturity isn't just about helping yourself—it's also about showing respect for others. When you stay calm, even when you're upset, you're showing the people around you that you value them. And that's a big part of being the kind of person others look up to and respect. By using this approach, you're not only teaching them tools to manage their emotions but also modeling the kind of thoughtful, respectful communication you want them to develop.

Listening: Teach your teen that listening is just as important as talking—really hearing and listening without cutting them off or gearing up to argue back. It is so tempting to start preparing your rebuttal once you feel you're being verbally attacked, right? Our defenses go up, and we are ready for battle! But we all know that's not the best reaction, and we need to tone it down. As parents, our kiddos are watching every move we make in conflict, so it's important that we model what we preach. Active listening means paying attention, maybe nodding or asking a follow-up question, to show they care about what's being said. Try asking, "How do you know when (name) feels heard?" or "What do you do when they're upset—do you listen first or jump in?" Parents can even model this at home—say, "Let me make sure I get this right, you're saying..."—to show how it works. This helps teens build a habit of listening that strengthens trust with a partner.

Conflict Resolution: Show your teen how to tackle disagreements without letting things spiral into a fight. The trick is staying calm and focusing on fixing the problem, not pointing fingers. A simple approach could be: name what's wrong ("You didn't text me back all day"), share how it feels ("It made me feel ignored"), and offer a solution ("Could you let me know if you're busy?"). Parents can help by asking, "What's one thing you and (name) argue about—how could you bring it up without blaming them?" or "What would make you both feel better about it?" Role-playing a small conflict at home can also take the edge off, giving teens a low-stakes way to practice sorting things out.

4. Emotional Self-Awareness

Help your teen tune into their own emotions and build a strong sense of self as they navigate dating. Teens can easily get tangled in big feelings or outside pressures, so guiding them to understand what's going on inside—and why—sets them up for healthier relationships. Parents can make this feel less daunting by tying it to everyday moments and sharing relatable insights.

Managing Expectations: Teens often soak up dreamy, unrealistic ideas about love from movies, TikTok, or Instagram, where everything's perfect and effortless. We have to help them see that real relationships aren't always fireworks and grand gestures; they take patience, compromise, and effort. For example, a boyfriend/girlfriend might not text back instantly, and that's normal—it's not a crisis! Parents can ask, "What do you think a relationship should feel like every day?" or "How do you handle it when things don't go like you planned?" These questions nudge teens to rethink those glossy ideals and talk about what's realistic, easing them into a more grounded, realistic view of dating. If we can help them manage their expectations, our teens will be less likely to feel disappointed.

Handling Rejection: Prepare your teen for the sting of rejection—it's part of life, not a personal failure. Not every crush will like them back, and that's fine; it doesn't mean they're less worthy or unlovable. Sharing a light story of your own—like a middle-school crush who didn't notice you—can make it less heavy. Try asking, "What would you tell a friend if someone didn't like them back?" or "How do you feel about yourself when something doesn't work out?" This helps them process rejection as a normal bump, not a defining moment, and opens the door to talk about resilience. I've always explained to my kids that during their teens and 20s, they might go out with many different people, but in the end, only one will be the person they choose to marry. That means breakups are part of the journey. Knowing how to deal with those breakups—whether they're the one ending it or the one getting hurt—is a key skill to learn.

Self-Worth: Reinforce that your teen's value isn't tied to having a boyfriend or girlfriend—they're enough just as they are. Dating should be a choice, not a must-do to prove something or fit in. Help them see that being single isn't a flaw, and they don't need a partner to feel complete. Parents can spark this by asking, "What do you like most about yourself, with or without someone else?" or "Why do you think people date—do you feel that pressure?" These prompts encourage teens to reflect on their own worth, building confidence that stands strong whether they're in a relationship or not.

5. Safety First

Make sure your teen knows that staying safe is non-negotiable when they start dating, whether it's in person or online. Teens can feel invincible or unsure how to spot risks, so talking openly about practical steps and instincts helps them feel prepared, not scared. Parents can frame this as empowerment, giving teens the tools to protect themselves while encouraging them to share any worries, turning a tough subject into a manageable conversation.

Physical Safety: Talk to your teen about keeping themselves safe when they're out with someone new. Stick to public spots like coffee shops or parks for early dates and always let a friend or family member know where they'll be and who they're with—just a quick text can do it, or even better, they can share their location. Teach them to trust their instincts: if a date feels pushy, creepy, or just off—like insisting they go somewhere alone—they should feel confident walking away, no explanation needed. Parents can ask, "What would you do if someone made you uncomfortable on a date?" or "How do you decide if a situation feels safe?" These questions help teens think it through and build the habit of prioritizing their well-being. It is critical to have these conversations BEFORE dating.

Online Dating Risks: If your teen's dipping into dating apps or connecting through social media, highlight the pitfalls—like people pretending to be someone they're not (catfishing), or digging for too much personal info too fast. Suggest they keep early chats on the app instead of handing out their phone number or address, and caution them against meeting up without vetting the person first. For example, they could video chat before an in-person meetup and always pick a public place with a friend in the loop. Try asking, "What do you know about someone before you'd meet them?" or "How would you spot if something online seemed fishy?" This gets them thinking critically about digital safety without feeling judged.

Consent: Drive home that consent is everything—it's a clear, eager "yes" that keeps going as long as both people are into it, and anyone can change their mind anytime. Silence, hesitation, or "maybe" isn't a green light; it's a stop sign. Teens need to know it's just as important to hear a yes from their partner as it is to give one themselves—mutual agreement isn't optional. Parents can open this up by asking, "What do you think consent looks like with (name)?" or "How would you tell someone you're not okay with something?" Even a casual chat about a movie scene can spark this—"Did that seem like consent to you?"—making it less awkward and more relatable.

6. Peer Influence and Social Media

Teens are surrounded by voices—friends, followers, influencers—telling them how to act or who to be, especially when it comes to dating. Help them cut through the noise to focus on what feels right for them, not what looks good to everyone else. Parents can make this less awkward by tying it to stuff teens already know—like group chats or Instagram—and turning it into a casual, two-way talk about standing strong in a world that's always watching.

Peer Pressure: Teens often feel the heat to date, hook up, or play it cool just to keep up with the crowd—maybe their friends are all paired off, or they're teased for being single. Help them see that their worth isn't tied to fitting someone else's script; their choices should match what they value, not what gets them likes on Instagram or nods at lunch. For example, if everyone's dating and they're not ready, that's their call—no shame in it. Parents can ask, "Do your friends ever push you to do stuff you're not into?" or "What matters more to you—what you want or what they think?" These questions let teens unpack the pressure and figure out where they stand, with you as their sounding board.

Social Media Traps: Talk about how social media can twist their view of relationships—those flawless couple pics and #RelationshipGoals posts are edited highlights, not the full story. Real life has messier moments, and that's normal. Also, caution them about airing their own relationship stuff online—posting every fight or breakup can invite drama, judgment, or even creepers sliding into their DMs. Suggest keeping private things private. Try asking, "What do you think relationships are really like behind those perfect posts?" or "Have you seen someone overshare online—how'd that turn out?" This keeps it chill and relevant, sparking a chat about what's real versus what's for show.

7. Spiritual and Family Values

Teens need to know how your family's beliefs, religion, and rules fit into their dating world—it's not just about laying down the law, but helping them see where it all comes from and the purpose behind it. Whether it's household expectations or cultural roots, these values can shape their choices in a way that feels meaningful, not forced. Parents can ease into this by explaining the reasoning and inviting teens to share their thoughts, making it a conversation instead of a rulebook they might push against.

Your Household Rules: If your family has specific guidelines—like no dating until 16, or wanting to meet anyone they're seeing—don't just state them; unpack the "why." Maybe it's about safety or maturity—whatever it is, teens are more likely to buy in if they get the logic, not just "because I said so." For example, you might say, "We'd like to meet them so we know who's in your life—it's about trust, not checking up on you." Ask, "What do you think about our rule on this?" or "How would you feel if you were us?" This shows it's not about control, and gives them room to open up about how it lands with them.

Values: If your teens hold religious views on dating—such as waiting until marriage—that differ from what their peers or society embrace, help support your teen in finding their voice. They will likely feel caught between staying true to their beliefs and navigating a world where "anything goes" is the norm. Guiding your teen who's chosen to wait until marriage for sex—especially when their friends are teasing them—means building their confidence, validating their choice, and giving them practical ways to handle the pressure. Here's how you might approach it, keeping it supportive and conversational to fit your goal of opening communication:

Step 1: Affirm Their Choice

Start by letting your teen know their decision is theirs to make and worth respecting. Say something like, "I'm proud of you for knowing what you want—it takes guts to stick to your values, especially when it's not the popular take." This sets the tone that their stance isn't weird or weak—it's a strength. Ask, "What made you decide to wait?" to let them unpack their reasons—maybe it's faith, personal comfort, or a vision for their future. Hearing themselves explain it can solidify their resolve.

Step 2: Normalize the Pushback

Explain that friends teasing them doesn't mean something's wrong with their choice—it's often just people reacting to what's different. You could say, "Not everyone's going to get it, and some might poke fun because it's easier than asking questions. That's on them, not you." Share a story if you've got one—like a time you stood out and got flak for it—to show they're not alone. Ask, "How do you feel when they tease you?" to give them space to vent and process.

Step 3: Equip Them to Respond

Give them tools to push back without feeling cornered. They don't need to preach—just own it. Suggest simple lines like, "It's my call, and I'm good with it," or "You do you, I'll do me." If the teasing gets mean, they could flip it: "Why's it bug you so much what I do?" Role-play a bit—say, "Pretend I'm your friend giving you a hard time, what'd you say?" This keeps it light but builds their confidence to stand firm. Ask, "What's the toughest part of dealing with them?" to pinpoint where they need support.

Step 4: Build Their Backup

Remind them they don't need everyone's approval—focus on finding their crew. Say, "You've got people who'll respect you for this—us, maybe others who think like you. That's what counts." If faith's a factor, suggest connecting with a youth group or community that shares their values. Ask, "Who's got your back on this—friends, family, anyone else?" to help them see their support net.

Step 5: Keep the Door Open

Check in without hovering—teens can clam up if it feels like a lecture. Try, "How's it going with your friends lately?" or "Anything bugging you about this?" Let them lead the talk. If they're doubting themselves, ask, "What's making you second-guess?" to dig into it without pushing. The goal is to keep them talking, so they know you're a safe spot, not a judge.

This approach mixes encouragement with real-world tactics, helping your teen feel secure in their choice while handling the social flak. It's less about fixing the friends and more about arming your teen to stand tall—awkwardness and all.

As a closing thought, these five steps can help your teen navigate any situation where they feel pressured by friends, no matter the topic.

 **Parent/Daughter Dialogue Example: A Jealous Rage Incident**

Daughter: "Mom, can I talk to you about something?"

Parent: "Of course, sweetie. What's going on?"

Daughter: "It's about Garrett. We were hanging out with my friends yesterday, and he kind of... lost it. Like, he got really jealous because one of the guys was joking around with me, and he started yelling at me—in front of everyone."

Parent: "Wow, that sounds like a lot to deal with. I'm really sorry that happened. How did you feel when he did that?"

Daughter: "I felt so embarrassed. My friends were just staring at me, and I didn't even know what to say. But then he texted me later and said he was sorry, that he just loves me so much and didn't want anyone else flirting with me."

Parent: "I can imagine that was really uncomfortable, and it sounds like his apology left you feeling conflicted. On one hand, he said sorry, but on the other hand, his reaction wasn't okay. Is that right?"

Daughter: "Yeah. I don't know... Maybe I should've been more careful about how I acted."

Parent: "Wait. Hold on a second. It's not your fault that he got upset. Being in a relationship doesn't mean you're responsible for managing someone else's jealousy or anger. You were just hanging out with your friends, and he chose to act the way he did. That's on him."

Daughter: "Yeah... But he said it's because he cares so much about me..."

Parent: "I get that he cares a lot about you, but real care and love should make you feel safe, not embarrassed or scared. Getting jealous is normal sometimes, but how we *handle* those feelings is what matters. Do you feel like this is something that happens a lot with him?"

Daughter: "He does get jealous a lot, but this was the first time he yelled at me in front of my friends."

Parent: "Thanks for telling me. It's not easy to talk about stuff like this. What do you think you want to do about it?"

Daughter: "I don't know. I don't want to break up with him, but I also don't want it to happen again."

Parent: "That makes sense. This is your relationship, and you get to decide what feels right for you. But if you want my advice, I'd say it's important to set a boundary here. Let him know that you care about him, but yelling at you—especially in front of others—is not okay and can't happen again. If it does, that's a huge red flag. What do you think?"

Daughter: "Yeah... I guess I could try saying that. But what if he gets mad again?"

Parent: "If he reacts badly to you standing up for yourself, that's a sign he may not be ready for a healthy relationship. You don't deserve to walk on eggshells around anyone. And I want you to know—if you ever feel uncomfortable or unsafe, I'm here for you, no matter what. Okay?"

Daughter: "Okay. Thanks for listening, Mom."

Parent: "I'll always be here for you, no matter what. You're never alone in this."

Key Takeaways from the Dialogue

As the parent, you are acknowledging your daughter's feelings without minimizing or overreacting. You are also helping your daughter recognize that her boyfriend's behavior isn't her fault. You are offering advice but also leaving room for your daughter to make her own decisions. And finally, you are emphasizing boundaries and reinforcing that her well-being is the priority.

Parent/Son Dialogue Example: Navigating an Unhealthy Behavior

Parent: "Hey, I noticed you've been spending a lot of time with Catherine lately. How's that going?"

Son: "It's good... But sometimes she gets upset if I don't text back right away. It's not a big deal, though. She just cares a lot."

Parent: "I get that—it's nice to feel cared for. But can I ask, how does it make *you* feel when she gets upset like that?"

Son: "I don't know... I guess it feels a little stressful. Like, I can't always be on my phone, but I don't want her to think I don't care."

Parent: "That makes sense. It sounds like you're feeling caught between trying to keep her happy and doing what works for you. Have you talked to her about it?"

Son: "Not really. I don't want to hurt her feelings."

Parent: "I get that—it's hard to bring stuff like this up. But the thing about healthy relationships is that both people should feel free to say what they need. Like, if you're feeling stressed, it's okay to set some boundaries. You could try saying something like, 'Hey, I really care about you a lot, but I can't always text back right away. It's not about you—I just have a lot going on.' How do you think she'd respond?"

Son: "I think she'd get upset. She has said before that she needs me to be there for her."

Parent: "Hmm. It's okay for her to want support, but it's not okay for her to make you feel guilty for having your own space. If that keeps happening, it's something to pay attention to—because in a healthy relationship, both people respect each other's boundaries. What do you think?"

Son: "Yeah, thanks for helping me see that."

Parent: "It always feels good when someone supports you and makes you feel good—not stressed. I'm always here if you want to talk through things or figure out what to say. Sound good?"

Son: "Okay. Thanks so much, Dad."

Key Takeaways from the Dialogue

As parents, it's important that we avoid jumping to conclusions and instead ask our kids how they feel. We are able to validate our kids' feelings while gently highlighting unhealthy behaviors. We can offer a specific example of how to set a boundary, making it easier for our kids to imagine doing it themselves. And, instead of dictating what to do, we can encourage our kids to reflect on what they want and deserve.

Activity

Healthy Dating & Boundaries Journal

Objective: This activity helps teens reflect on the concept of healthy dating, understand boundaries, and recognize behaviors that are acceptable or harmful in relationships. It's also a way for parents and teens to have open, guided discussions.

Materials Needed:
- Journal or notebook
- Pen or pencil

Instructions:

1. **Reflection Prompt:** Have the teen write a journal entry about what they think a "healthy relationship" looks like. Encourage them to consider things like mutual respect, communication, trust, and shared values. This can also be done with a parent and teen discussing the question aloud, with the parent guiding the conversation.
   Example Prompts:
   - What do you think a healthy relationship looks like?
   - What qualities do you think are important in a boyfriend/girlfriend?

- What behaviors would make you feel respected and valued?

2. **Identify Boundaries:** The next section of the journal activity focuses on boundaries. Ask the teen to list examples of physical, emotional, and digital boundaries they think are important in relationships. If doing this as a parent-child activity, the parent can help the teen explore how boundaries look in real situations.

   Examples of Boundaries:
   - "I feel comfortable when my boyfriend/girlfriend respects my need for space."
   - "I don't want to be pressured into doing anything I'm not ready for."
   - "I believe my boyfriend/girlfriend should listen when I express that I'm not comfortable with something."

Table Talk:

- If your teen is willing, have him/her share what he/she wrote in the journal activity.
- Ask "What are the things that matter most to you in a relationship with a friend, and also someone that you would consider dating?"
- Ask "What are your deal-breakers?"
- Ask "If I see a 'big red flag' with someone you've chosen to date, would you want me to tell you or just let you figure it out in your own time?
- Share the values that are most important to you when choosing a friend or mate.

CHAPTER 14

Substance Abuse

 **Goal:** Empower your kids to understand the triggers behind drug and alcohol use while equipping them with effective strategies to confidently say NO in the face of peer pressure. This chapter also provides insight into the physical, emotional, and mental harm these substances can cause, highlighting how their choices not only impact their own well-being but also the lives of those who care about them.

How to Teach Your Kids About the Risks and Dangers of Drugs and Alcohol

Raising children in today's world comes with a unique set of challenges, especially when it comes to navigating the topic of drugs and alcohol. It's crucial for parents to have open, honest, and ongoing conversations with their kids about the risks and dangers of substance use. The goal is not just to tell them what to do but to equip them with the knowledge, tools, and confidence to make safe and healthy choices. Here are some strategies to help you address this important topic in a way that resonates with your children. I will provide summaries first before sharing detailed content (facts and statistics) that will make it easy for you to share with your children.

1. Start the Conversation Early and Keep It Ongoing

Don't wait until your kids are teenagers to talk about drugs and alcohol. Start when they're young by introducing age-appropriate discussions about healthy choices with their nutrition and the importance of taking care of their bodies. As they grow, gradually introduce more detailed conversations about the risks of substance use. Make these conversations a regular part of your relationship rather than a one-time talk. Use teachable moments from news stories, movies, or real-life situations to bring up the topic naturally. Let them know they can always come to you with questions or concerns without fear of judgment or punishment. That early "connection" with your kids will pay off!

2. Educate Them About the Risks

Kids are more likely to avoid drugs and alcohol when they fully understand the risks involved. Explain how substances can harm their physical and mental health, hinder their academic and athletic performance, and negatively impact their relationships and future goals. Share real-world examples of how drug and alcohol use has led to addiction, legal trouble, or even tragic consequences. Be honest and specific about how drugs and alcohol affect the brain and body. For example, explain that alcohol can impair judgment, making it more likely for someone to get hurt or make regrettable decisions. Discuss how drugs alter brain chemistry, leading to addiction and long-term damage to their ability to experience joy and motivation naturally.

3. Teach Them to Handle Peer Pressure

Peer pressure is one of the most common reasons young people try drugs or alcohol. Help your kids develop strategies to say no confidently and assertively. Role-play scenarios where they might be offered substances, and practice how they can respond. For example, they can say:

- "No thanks, I'm not into that."
- "I've got an important game/test tomorrow, so I'm staying sharp."
- "I don't need that to have fun."

Empower them to make decisions based on their values and not just go along with the crowd. Reinforce that true friends will respect their choices and won't pressure them into doing something they're uncomfortable with.

4. Help Them Build Confidence and Healthy Coping Skills

Kids who feel confident and capable are less likely to turn to drugs or alcohol to escape stress or fit in. Encourage your children to pursue hobbies, sports, or activities that boost their self-esteem and give them a sense of purpose. Celebrate their achievements and help them develop a positive self-image. Teach them healthy ways to cope with stress, anxiety, or strong emotions. Whether it's exercising, journaling, meditating, or talking to a trusted adult, having positive outlets can reduce the temptation to use substances as an escape.

5. Set Clear Expectations and Be a Role Model

Be clear about your family's rules and expectations regarding drugs and alcohol. Let your kids know that you expect them to avoid these substances and explain the reasons why. Discuss the consequences of breaking the rules, but also balance this with understanding and support. Make it clear that they can come to you for help if they ever find themselves in a difficult situation. Your actions speak louder than words, so be mindful of the example you're setting. If you drink, model responsible behavior by drinking in moderation and never driving under the influence. Avoid glamorizing substance use, even in casual conversation, and emphasize healthy habits in your own life.

6. Encourage Open Communication!

Create an environment where your kids feel safe sharing anything with you, including sensitive topics like drugs and alcohol. Prioritize listening to their thoughts and concerns without interrupting or passing judgment. Show empathy and understanding, even if they've made a mistake. The goal is to maintain open lines of communication, ensuring they feel supported and valued.

In our house, one of the most effective ways we kept those lines of communication open was through "hot tub time." At the end of the day, I'd hop in the hot tub, and the kids would often join me (or vice versa). It became a relaxing space where conversations naturally flowed. Another idea to foster connection is to set up a "puzzle table." It's a simple spot where your kids know they can find you engaged in an activity, creating an easy and low-pressure opportunity for meaningful conversations.

Ask open-ended questions to encourage discussion, such as:

- "What have you heard about drugs at school?"
- "How do you think drinking or using drugs could affect someone's future?"
- "What would you do if a friend offered you something?"

7. Provide Real-Life Examples

Sometimes, real-life examples can have a powerful impact. Share stories about individuals who faced the consequences of drug or alcohol use, whether it's someone in your community or a public figure. Be honest about the outcomes and how these choices affected their lives, families, and futures. Highlight the dangers of addiction and how it can take hold before someone even realizes it. Encourage your kids to research the stories of people like Kurt Cobain, Amy Winehouse, or Heath Ledger—individuals whose lives were tragically cut short due to substance abuse. Understanding the real-world consequences can help them see the seriousness of the issue.

8. Foster a Strong Support System

A strong support system can make all the difference. Encourage your kids to surround themselves with positive influences, including friends who share their values and make healthy choices. Stay actively involved in their lives, whether it's attending their games, helping with schoolwork, or simply spending quality time together. Let them know that they are never alone and that you're always there to help and guide them. Building a strong, trusting relationship with your kids makes them more likely to turn to you for support instead of seeking unhealthy coping mechanisms.

Conclusion

Teaching your kids about the risks and dangers of drugs and alcohol is one of the most important lessons you can impart as a parent. By starting early, maintaining open communication, and equipping them with the tools to make healthy choices, you can help them navigate these challenges with confidence. Remember, your guidance and support play a crucial role in shaping their decisions and ensuring they have the knowledge and strength to say no. Together, you can help them build a future full of health, happiness, and success.

Before moving on to some important information about drugs and alcohol, let's look at a few dialogues.

 **Parent/Teen Dialogue Example: Peer Pressure to Drink**

Teen: "Ugh, I don't even know if I want to go to this party tomorrow."

Parent: "Oh no, what's up? You were really excited about going yesterday."

Teen: "It's just... Everyone's been talking about drinking at the party, and I know they're all going to try to get me to drink."

Parent: "Hmm, I can see why that would feel stressful. That's a tough situation to be in, but not impossible."

Teen: "Yeah. Like, I don't want to be the only one saying no, but I also don't want to drink."

Parent: "I get you. That's a tough spot. But, I'm really proud of you for knowing what you want AND for thinking about this ahead of time."

Teen: "I just feel like they're going to think I'm lame or something."

Parent: "I get that. Nobody wants to feel left out or judged, especially by friends. But here's the thing—being true to yourself and what you're comfortable with takes a lot of self-control and strength. You really don't have to explain yourself to anyone, but if it helps, I have an idea. Do you want to brainstorm some ways you could handle it?"

Teen: "Like what?"

Parent: "Well, one option is to have a short response ready, like, 'Nah, I'm good, but thanks.' You could even hold a soda or something in your hand. People are less likely to ask if you already have a drink."

Teen: "Yeah, maybe."

Parent: "You could also use humor and say, 'My football season is starting, so I'll only be drinking water and Gatorade.'"

Teen: "Yeah... I like that!"

Parent: "And you know you can always blame me if you want. Say something like, 'My parents will kill me if they smell alcohol anywhere near me! It's not worth it.' I'm totally okay being the bad guy in this scenario."

Teen: "That may work, too!"

Parent: "And remember, you always have the option to leave if things get uncomfortable. I'm happy to pick you up, no questions asked. Let's come up with a code that you can text your mom or me if things get dicey."

Teen: "Thanks! I'm just so happy that we could talk about this openly and honestly."

Parent: "Anytime. I'm really proud of you for sticking to what feels right for you. You've got a good head on your shoulders, and I really admire you."

Teen: "Thanks so much, Dad. I really value your opinion!"

Parent: "You've got this. And I'm here if you need me."

This dialogue shows a supportive and open exchange where the teen feels comfortable sharing his concerns about a party involving drinking. The parent listens empathetically, validates the teen's feelings, and praises their self-awareness without being judgmental. Together, they brainstorm practical strategies—like using humor, holding a non-alcoholic drink, or blaming the parents as an excuse—to help the teen navigate the situation while staying true to his boundaries. The parent also offers a safety net (a pickup option with a text code) and reinforces trust and admiration, strengthening their bond. The key points are:

- **Open Communication:** The teen feels safe discussing a tough topic with the parent.
- **Empathy and Support:** The parent acknowledges the challenge without lecturing.
- **Problem-Solving:** They collaborate on actionable ways to handle peer pressure.
- **Trust and Respect:** The parent empowers the teen while being a reliable backup.

It's a solid example of how parents and teens can tackle peer pressure together, balancing independence with guidance.

 ### Parent/Teen Dialogue Example: Confessing to Giving In to Peer Pressure

Teen: "Hey, Mom. Can I talk to you about something?"

Parent: "Of course. What's up?"

Teen: "I messed up."

Parent: "Okay, tell me what happened."

Teen: "Remember the party I went to Friday night? I told myself I wasn't going to drink. I really meant it... But then everyone was handing out drinks, and they kept saying, 'Come on, it's no big deal.' I just gave in."

Parent: "Thank you for telling me. I can see this is really weighing on you."

Teen: "It is. I feel so stupid. I didn't even enjoy it, and now I just feel so disappointed in myself."

Parent: "I hear you. It sounds like you're really upset about it."

Teen: "Well, yeah. I knew better! I don't even know why I let it happen."

Parent: "We all know that peer pressure can be tough, especially when everyone around you is doing the same thing. It doesn't make you a bad person or a failure. It makes you human. We all have temptations in life."

Teen: "I know, but I still feel like I let myself down."

Parent: "I get that. And it's okay to feel disappointed—it shows that you care about making good choices. What matters most now is what you do next."

Teen: "Like what?"

Parent: "Well, first, take this as a learning experience. Think about what you'd do differently next time you're in a similar situation. Maybe it's leaving the party earlier, sticking with a friend who isn't drinking, or having a plan for how to say no."

Teen: "Yeah... I guess I didn't really have a plan."

Parent: "That's okay. It's something we can work on together. Let's come up with a plan ahead of time. And just so you know, of course I'm here to help you figure things out—no judgment, no lectures."

Teen: "Thanks, Mom. I was so scared you'd be mad at me."

Parent: "I'm not mad. I'm proud of you for being honest with me. That takes a lot of courage."

Teen: "Thanks. I promise I'll do better next time."

Parent: "And I know you will. I'll always be here to talk, no matter what. I love you."

Teen: "That means a lot. Thanks, Mom."

Parent: "Anytime. We all make mistakes—it's how we grow."

This exchange highlights a teen's vulnerability and guilt after succumbing to peer pressure to drink at a party, despite their initial resolve. The parent responds with empathy, gratitude for the teen's honesty, and reassurance rather than criticism, creating a safe space for reflection. They frame the mistake as a human moment, not a defining failure, and shift focus to growth by encouraging the teen to learn from it and plan for the future. Together, they agree to strategize for next time, reinforcing teamwork and trust. Key points include:

- **Honesty and Courage:** The teen bravely admits their mistake, and the parent praises this openness.

- **Non-Judgmental Support:** The parent avoids anger or lectures, prioritizing understanding over punishment.
- **Learning Opportunity:** They treat the incident as a chance to grow, not a permanent setback.
- **Collaborative Solutions:** The parent offers to help the teen prepare for future challenges, strengthening their bond.

It's a strong example of how a parent can guide a teen through a misstep with compassion and practical support, fostering resilience and accountability without shame.

* * *

Let's move on to this next section, where you may feel bombarded (in a good way) with loads of content that you can share with your kids.

Did you know that 90% of addictions start in the teen years? And did you know that every 19 minutes, someone is dying of a drug overdose? Yikes... These stats are scary.

People start using drugs and alcohol to try to change something in their lives. They think that using these substances is a solution to a problem or at least a temporary escape from a problem. So, let's take a closer look at why young people start down the path to addiction and what the alternative plan can be.

1. The first reason is to relieve boredom. Many youth today may think that life gets boring and they need an outlet. They may think that experimenting with drugs and alcohol will offer some excitement and something new to explore. They may have way too much free time on their hands. Many kids today are just bored and have no other interests, and see drugs and alcohol as a pastime to be explored.

2. Another reason kids turn to drugs and alcohol is anxiety. Life throws countless challenges our way, especially for kids who face the mounting pressures of school, sports, maintaining good grades, getting into college—or keeping up once they're there—navigating social life, managing social media, and still trying to find time for family and friends. That's a lot to handle! First and foremost, it's important to understand that anxiety has *nothing* to do with a lack of strength, character, or courage. In fact, those who experience anxiety are often some of the strongest people you'll meet because they keep showing up and pushing forward despite the struggle. Did you know that 1 in 5 young people experience anxiety? Now, imagine if all those individuals turned to alcohol or drugs to cope. The world would be in chaos.

So, what's a healthier, more effective alternative for our children to manage anxiety? Let's dive into some strategies and solutions.

1. Mindfulness: Because anxiety is caused by your "what if" thoughts, meaning, "what if I fail this class," or "what if I get cut from the team," or "what if I don't get chosen for America's Got Talent!" Practicing mindfulness will teach your brain to stay in the present. Not only can mindfulness help with stress and depression, but it can also improve concentration, academic performance, and the ability to focus. Great added benefits!

2. Exercise: Now, you don't have to run a marathon for it to be effective; actually, a brisk 20-minute walk will do!

3. Breathwork: Take slow, deep breaths, breathing in for 3, holding for 1, and then exhaling for 3.

4. Sleeping and Eating: Get the right amount of sleep, not too little or too much. And eat the right food! Believe it or not, if you are eating too much processed food or too much sugar, it can knock out the good bacteria in your gut. This can send funky messages to your brain and heavily influence your mood. The healthier your gut, the healthier your mental state. Gut bacteria are the mental rock stars of the world.

5. Positive People: If you feel worried or nervous about something, talking about it with someone who listens and cares can help you feel more understood and better able to cope. You'll be reminded that everyone has these feelings sometimes. You're not alone.

I hope that once you share some specific strategies for managing anxiety, your kids will feel more confident and prepared.

3. Now, let's move on to the third reason people often start experimenting with drugs and alcohol: curiosity. Many young people try substances simply because they want to know what it feels like. Young people, in particular, often feel invincible and assume that nothing bad will happen to them. They think they can try it once and stop whenever they want. But if you talk to someone who's used drugs, they'll tell you it usually starts with an amazing high—one so intense that they keep chasing it. The reality is that you'll never fully satisfy that feeling.

Drugs create a high that's far beyond anything ordinary life offers because they flood the brain's pleasure centers. Over time, this distorts the brain, pulling you into a harmful cycle of seeking that high while trying to escape the crash that follows. This is how addiction takes hold.

One way to address their curiosity is to encourage research.

4. A 4th common reason is peer pressure and wanting to fit in. If they are with people who are drinking and doing drugs, it's very easy to fall into the trap of giving in to peer pressure.

A few great strategies for dealing with peer pressure:

- Choose good friends. Hang out with the right people who share your values.
- Learn how to say no. Imagine yourself in different scenarios BEFORE they happen so that you can be armed with a response once someone approaches you. You won't have to think of an excuse because you already have a "bank of answers" for every possible situation.
- The following responses were taken from a survey of high school kids that I did a few years ago.

Let's take a look at their responses:

1. "What, are you crazy? That stuff will kill you."
2. "I'm taking some medicine that I can't mix with drugs."
3. "My body is a temple. I'm an athlete. I can't use."
4. "I'm the designated driver. I'm not going to let my friends down."
5. A simple, confident "No thanks." Then change the subject.
6. Say with humor: "No thanks! No drink in the world could have enough alcohol in it to solve all of my problems right now!"

7.   "That stuff killed my cousin. I'm not going there."
8.   "I really don't want to disappoint my parents/mentor/teammates, etc."
9.   "I'm an athlete. I only drink water and Gatorade. No sodas. Nothing else."
10. "I have a big test to study for tomorrow, and I can't be hungover."
11. Have an escape plan. Have a code word for a friend that you need to leave ASAP.
12. Find something to do at the party so that you look busy. (Dance, play cornhole, etc.)
13. Keep a bottle of water or a red solo cup with a non-alcoholic drink with you. People will be less likely to offer you something if they see that you already have a drink in your hand.
14. "No, I'm saving all my money to buy a car."
15. "No, I'm really not into that stuff."
16. "No thanks, I tried it once, hated it, and threw up all over the couch."
17. "No thanks, I need all the brains I've got."
18. "No thanks, doing illegal stuff just doesn't turn me on."
19. "My life's difficult enough without having to deal with this added hassle."
20. "No, I have an addictive personality, and I don't want to get hooked on that stuff!"

Have your kids take a look at this list and choose one that suits them! Or even better, they can add their own unique responses.

5. A fifth and final reason many young people turn to drugs is to relax.
The teen years and early twenties can be incredibly challenging, filled with highs, lows, and intense emotions. In an effort to cope, some may turn to drugs as a way to unwind and manage their feelings. However, while it might seem like a quick fix, the truth is that using drugs only creates a bigger problem. Instead of helping, it makes dealing with tough emotions even harder and often leads to physical, emotional, and even legal consequences.

Helpful strategies for our kids:

- Talk about your feelings regularly, don't let them build up.
- Find healthy ways to relax and have fun: art, music, exercise, etc.
- Avoid the drama: hang out with people who are low stress and low drama.

The good news is this: If you set your kids up with the tools they need NOW, these tools should hopefully last a lifetime!

Effects on the Mind and Body

As we know, alcohol is one of the many substances considered a drug, like amphetamines, cocaine, marijuana, and other drugs. Drugs are essentially poisons, and the amount of drugs taken determines the effect on the body. Drugs affect both the mind and the body. They distort your view of what is happening, and they can result in inappropriate, irrational, or destructive behavior. They have a direct impact on your kidneys, liver, brain, heart, muscles, etc., and can even have lasting effects on your brain and body.

Let's look at these stats from the American Academy of Child & Adolescent Psychiatry:

- An estimated 208 million people internationally consume illegal drugs.
- 19.9 million Americans aged 12 and older used drugs in the month prior to a recent survey.
- The most commonly used illegal drug in the U.S. is marijuana—it's been legalized in just a few states.
- The most commonly abused drug in the U.S. is alcohol.
- Alcohol related motor accidents are the 2nd leading cause of teen death in the U.S.

Wow. So, let's take a look at the bad effects of alcohol and then some of the drugs that they may have been exposed to or will be exposed to, and the effects that they can have on you as well. Sit down with your kids and explain in detail each of the following drugs and their negative effects.

1. Alcohol:

Alcohol acts as a depressant, slowing down important body functions. That's why people slur their speech and have unsteady movements and slower reaction times when drunk. It also affects the brain, making it harder for a person to think rationally and have good judgment. Alcohol overdose happens when the effects are so severe that it becomes toxic (poisonous) for the body and results in a coma or death.

Drinking is more harmful to a younger person because a teenager's brain is still developing throughout adolescence and into adulthood. Drinking during the teen years can lead to lifelong damage to brain functioning, especially for memory, motor skills, and coordination.

Here are some facts:

- People who begin drinking before the age of 15 are about **four times more likely to develop alcohol dependence** than those who start at age 21 (NIAAA 2004).
- High school students drive after drinking approximately **2.4 million times each month**, and young drivers ages 16–20 are **17 times more likely to die in a crash** when their blood alcohol concentration is .08% or higher than when sober (CDC 2012a; CDC 2012b).
- Alcohol is a significant factor in the leading causes of death among young people under 21—including motor vehicle crashes, homicides, and suicides (CDC 2023; NIAAA 2023).
- Some prevention organizations report that teens who drink are **7.5 times more likely to use other illegal drugs and 50 times more likely to use cocaine**, but these statistics are less well-documented in primary research sources (Utah Legislature 2008).

Before we move on to other drugs, I want to spend a minute talking about *binge drinking*.

Binge drinking is defined as "drinking lots of alcohol in a short space of time or drinking to get drunk." So, how much is "lots of alcohol"? For guys, it's having over 8 units in a single session, and for girls, it's about 6 units. Five to seven units are equal to 2–3 pints of beer. Risks include: accidents, injuries, losing self-control, or using bad judgment in risky situations.

What are other dangers? Your body can only process one unit of alcohol per hour.

2. Marijuana:

It is one of the Top 5 substances that lead to people being admitted to drug treatment facilities. In the U.S., marijuana is stronger today than ever. As a result, there are more ER visits than ever by young smokers. Long-term effects include lower resistance to illness, reduction in male sex hormones, study difficulties, lack of motivation, and growth disorders.

3. Ecstasy:

Ecstasy smothers the natural distress signals given by the body, so that people on ecstasy are more likely to take risks. Long-term use can lead to long-lasting permanent damage to parts of the brain responsible for thought, memory, learning, sleep, and emotion. It can cause depression and anxiety, and can lead to kidney failure.

4. Cocaine:

Cocaine is one of the most psychologically addictive drugs because it artificially stimulates the pleasure centers of the brain and causes temporary euphoria, which means an intensely happy feeling. Plus, a tolerance develops very quickly, meaning the user needs to use more and more over time to achieve the same effect. In the short term, cocaine can cause increased heart rate, muscle spasms, and convulsions, and make people anxious, hostile, and paranoid. Because cocaine initially makes people feel euphoric, coming down from cocaine causes severe depression, which becomes more intense after each use. The depression and the desire to escape it can become so severe that the person will do anything to get the drug or escape the pain, including murder and suicide.

5. Heroin:

Even a single dose of heroin can start a person on the road to addiction. Heroin is more popular than ever among young people. It's no longer the drug of the dark alleys. In fact, between 1995 and 2002, the number of teens in the U.S. between the ages of 12 and 17 who tried heroin increased by 300%. A person who would never put a needle in his arm may think it's okay to smoke or sniff the drug, thinking it's less risky. The truth is that heroin is just as addictive and dangerous in any form. People can't just try it once or twice because it's so highly addictive. The rush that a person feels after taking heroin fades as the person becomes sleepy, and body functions, such as breathing and heartbeat, slow down. However, as soon as the initial effects wear off, the user's body begins to crave more, and the body goes into withdrawal. Withdrawal symptoms are so severe that the body has aches and pains, diarrhea, vomiting, restlessness, etc., that the user needs more drugs just to feel normal again. The mortality rate for heroin users is very high, estimated to be 20 times greater than the population!

6.   Inhalants:

Inhalants are chemicals found in household products such as aerosol sprays, cleaning fluids, glues, paint, etc. They can be sniffed or "huffed." People may tell you that "huffing" is not dangerous, but the fact is, inhalants affect the brain. They can cause permanent physical and mental damage. People who use inhalants may lose their sense of smell, develop liver, lung, and kidney problems, and continued use can cause reduced muscle mass and strength. People who use inhalants are unable to walk, talk, and think clearly because the brain tissue is destroyed by the toxic fumes of the inhalants.

Think of this... Would you ever consider drinking a tiny drop of bleach? A tiny drop may or may not cause serious damage. But would you take that chance? Probably not. You know this is poison, and even a little bit could burn your mouth, stomach, and throat and possibly cause death. Drugs are poisonous just like bleach, and it's unclear how much could cause long-lasting and permanent damage. Also, everyone's body is different and reacts to things differently. There's no set "universal tolerance effect." So, think of drugs like that drop of bleach. It's not worth it even to take the chance!

Let's move on to prescription drug abuse.

Prescription Drug Abuse

The use of prescription drugs is really becoming a serious problem. National studies show that a young person is more likely to have abused a prescription drug than an illegal street drug. This may be because people think that a prescription drug is safe because a doctor prescribed it. FALSE. Taking these kinds of drugs for nonmedical use can be just as dangerous as taking a street drug. People can have different reactions to the same drug, and a drug that is safely used by one person can be deadly for another. BEWARE!

The abuse of prescription drugs is a slippery slope. Here's how. You feel a little behind in your studies. Someone suggests a Ritalin or Adderall to give you the extra energy you need. You figure, why not? One pill for an entire night of studying? Seems okay. But the fact is that amphetamines like Ritalin or Adderall can be just as destructive as cocaine. Really. The "up" feeling is always followed by a "crash," which causes fatigue and depression. The depression can only be cured by another fix. And so it goes. You become addicted. In some tragic cases, people have died due to heart attacks caused by the damage linked to these types of drugs.

OPIOIDS:

The opioid crisis has received much attention in the United States. More people than ever are dying from opioid overdose. This is a very popular drug among young people, especially those who have had an injury, as opioids are painkillers. OxyContin, Vicodin, and Percocet are as powerful as heroin! These are highly addictive drugs that are meant to be used only in the short term for pain relief following an injury. These drugs have similar withdrawal effects to those of heroin. Tolerance builds, and the person must take higher and higher doses to get the same effect and to ward off the withdrawal.

Most often, the problem starts with an injury and the desire, especially for an athlete, to play through the pain, as this is often possible with the use of painkillers. Sadly, many people keep taking painkillers in order to keep performing, despite the pain. But if anyone tells you to play through the pain with the use of painkillers, they do not have your best interest at heart. Pain is a signal telling your body to stop and rest. Listen to your body. Rest and resume activity when your body has healed, when you no longer need painkillers, and when the doctor gives you the OK.

So, one more thing I want to add is taking pills. Have any of your kids been invited to a Pill Party? If you're not sure what a pill party is... It's a party in which people bring all kinds of over-the-counter and prescription medications. It usually involves mixing all these pills together and placing them into shot glasses or other cups and taking them at once. It can lead to a high or altered fantasy state depending on the drug interactions and the body's response, or it can lead to liver failure, heart and lung issues, and death if you are very unlucky in the pill mix you ingest. Hard-core people also mix designer drugs.

Vaping: The Teen Craze That's a Total Nightmare

Picture this: 3.6 million middle and high school kids in the U.S. are hooked on vaping. That's right—those sleek little gadgets called e-cigarettes are everywhere, puffing out clouds of trouble. Vaping's just inhaling and exhaling vapor from devices like e-cigs, vape pens, or tricked-out MODS. No tobacco smoke here, just a sneaky aerosol packed with toxic chemicals linked to cancer, lung issues, and heart disease. Yikes!

The king of the vaping world? JUUL. This USB-lookalike is small, slick, and easy to stash—perfect for dodging teachers or parents. It's got flavors like mango and crème brûlée, and get this: one JUUL pod has as much nicotine as a *whole pack of cigarettes*. That's a brain-buzzing wallop! It's no wonder JUUL owns 72% of the vape market.

But here's the juicy part—vaping's not just a trend; it's a ticking time bomb. Health experts are sounding the alarm: the risks, especially for teens, are wild. Nicotine in these things messes with your brain (it's still growing, folks!), jacks up your heart rate, and can lead to lung disease, chronic coughs, even type 2 diabetes. Too much? Think nausea, seizures, or hacking up phlegm like a chain-smoking grandpa. Gross.

Vaping Horror Stories That'll Make You Gasp

- **Lung Burn Blunder:** A guy in England ditched cigarettes for vaping to "get healthy." One day, his device backfired, shooting scorching nicotine juice down his throat and blasting a hole in his lung. Talk about a plot twist!
- **Family Fire Fiasco:** A 15-year-old's e-cig charger sparked a blaze that torched his bed—and then his whole house. His family of four lost everything. Can you say guilt trip from hell?
- **Face-Bomb Nightmare:** In New York, a dude's vape battery exploded mid-puff, smashing his teeth and tearing his tongue. "It was like an M80 bomb in my mouth," he said. Ouch doesn't even cover it.

Ditch the Vape: 5 Epic Ways to Quit

1. **Make a Quit Plan:** Write down why vaping sucks—cash drain, health scare, whatever. Peek at it when cravings hit.
2. **Dodge Triggers:** Love vaping after breakfast? Swap it for a jog or a coffee jolt instead.
3. **Rally the Crew:** Tell your squad you're quitting. Warn them you might be a grump while nicotine's clawing at you. Bonus: get a vape buddy to quit with you!
4. **Doctor's Orders:** Can't hack it solo? Hit up your doc for meds like Chantix or grab some nicotine gum—no prescription needed.
5. **Cold Turkey or Slow Fade:** Pick your poison. Weaning off nicotine takes time, but eases the pain. Cold turkey's fast but brutal—toss that vape and brace yourself!

Quitting Hacks

- **Weaning:** Drop from 16 mg to 11 mg, then 8 mg, over weeks. Chill with zero-nicotine juice 'til you're free.
- **Cold Turkey:** Set a quit date, trash your gear, and stay busy—think gym, hobbies, anything but puffing.
- **Withdrawal Survival:** Cravings hit hard for a month. Chew gum, slap on a patch, or reward yourself with candy for resisting.

Vaping's a sneaky beast—cool until it's not. With exploding batteries, lung holes, and nicotine's chokehold, it's a gamble not worth taking. Ready to kick it? You've got the firepower now. Go crush it!

Top 10 Reasons NOT to Use

Number 10: It will affect your academic performance—there is a clear link between substance abuse and academic difficulties, and not completing high school. There is also evidence that when teens stop using drugs, their academic performance improves.

Number 9: It destroys family relationships—The American Association for Marriage and Family Therapy reports that even small degrees of drug use can have extreme negative consequences for a person's family life.

Number 8: It will ruin your reputation—Junkie, Crackhead, Smacker, Stoner, Pothead, Speedfreak, Banger. Is this how you want to be known? Is this YOUR brand?

Number 7: It destroys your health. In addition to harming your brain tissue and affecting your bones, liver, and kidneys, drug abuse is linked to health problems such as HIV/AIDS, cancer, and heart disease. Some health problems happen when drugs are used at high doses or over long periods of time, but some health problems can occur after JUST ONE USE!

Number 6: It will affect your income. Research shows that young people who use drugs are not as able to become self-supporting. Think about the drug users you know—are they financially independent? Do they have good, reliable jobs? Several studies have linked marijuana use to lower income, greater welfare dependence, unemployment, and criminal behavior.

Number 5: It causes or increases emotional problems. People who abuse drugs are at higher risk than nonusers for mental health issues like depression, anxiety, behavioral problems, and suicide attempts.

Number 4: It can lead to other delinquent behaviors. There is a very strong link between crimes committed by teens and their use of alcohol and other drugs. See the table below for some statistics.

Number 3: It will become your new best friend and your worst enemy. People who use drugs are often alienated from their peers as they become more involved and dependent on their new "best friend"—their drug of choice. Once your body gets used to the drug, you have to keep taking it just to feel normal. That's when you become trapped in a dependent relationship with your drug of choice. And the drug becomes a needy, possessive, and demanding "friend" you just can't get rid of.

Number 2: It will take control of your life. People on drugs do things they wouldn't ordinarily do if they had a clear head. Drugs influence judgment and behavior. People on drugs may drive impaired, hurt another person, take unnecessary risks, have unprotected sex, take a more lethal drug, or other impulsive actions. The mistakes you may make while taking drugs can impact and control the rest of your life...

Number 1: It CAN KILL YOU. 105 people in the U.S. die EVERY DAY from drug overdoses. And this does not even count the number of people who die due to violent crimes related to drugs, car accidents related to drugs, or suicides related to drugs. The good news is that drug addiction is treatable. The sad news is that it is the most untreated disease in the US. Most drug abusers never receive treatment.

ACTIVITY 1:

Have your teen print or take a photo of Top 10 Reasons NOT to Use to remember the reasons why it's never the right choice to start down the path to drug abuse!

ACTIVITY 2:

Have your kids look up stories about people like Kurt Cobain, Amy Winehouse, Chris Kelly, Derek Boogaard, Michael Jackson, Andy Irons, Whitney Houston, Chris Farley, Heath Ledger, Elvis Presley—the list goes on.

These examples show the devastating consequences of drug use. Knowledge is power, and being informed is the best way to stay ahead of temptation.

Life Lessons

Let's look at just a few stories of the many famous people who have abused drugs and have seriously affected their careers and lives.

Here are three stories of celebrities whose lives were significantly impacted or ended due to struggles with drugs or alcohol, based on widely known accounts:

1. **Whitney Houston:** Whitney Houston was a global superstar, celebrated for her powerful voice and hits like "I Will Always Love You." However, her life unraveled due to a long battle with drug and alcohol addiction, reportedly exacerbated by her tumultuous marriage to Bobby Brown. Her substance use began overshadowing her career in the late 1990s and early 2000s, leading to erratic public behavior, canceled performances, and a decline in her vocal ability. On February 11, 2012, she was found dead in a hotel bathtub at age 48. The coroner's report listed drowning and the effects of atherosclerotic heart disease and cocaine use as the cause, with evidence of chronic drug abuse—including cocaine, marijuana, and prescription pills—contributing to her tragic end. Her death marked the loss of an extraordinary talent to addiction's grip.

2. **Heath Ledger:** Heath Ledger, an Australian actor known for roles in *Brokeback Mountain* and *The Dark Knight*, died at 28 on January 22, 2008. His death was ruled an accidental overdose from a toxic combination of prescription medications, including oxycodone, hydrocodone, diazepam, and others. Ledger had spoken about struggles with insomnia and the pressures of fame, particularly while preparing for his intense role as the Joker. While not a stereotypical "party drug" case, his reliance on prescription pills to cope with anxiety and sleep issues spiraled into a lethal mix. His passing left behind a legacy of brilliance cut short, with his posthumous Oscar win underscoring the potential lost to substance misuse.

3. **Amy Winehouse:** Amy Winehouse, the British soul singer with a voice that captivated millions, succumbed to her demons at 27 on July 23, 2011. Known for songs like "Rehab," where she defiantly sang about resisting treatment, Winehouse's life was plagued by alcohol and drug addiction, including heroin and crack cocaine. Her public decline was painfully visible—missed concerts, incoherent performances, and tabloid coverage of her chaotic personal life. Her death was officially attributed to alcohol poisoning, with a blood alcohol level over five times the legal limit. Winehouse joined the infamous "27 Club," a group of artists who died at that age, often due to substance abuse, leaving a haunting reminder of addiction's toll on even the most gifted.

These stories reflect how addiction can devastate lives, regardless of talent or success, often fueled by personal struggles, pressure, or a lack of effective support.

Action Steps:

Have your child choose a few responses on why he/she will say NO to drugs and alcohol when offered.

Table Talk 1:

- Which drugs do you think are the most common?
- The most addictive?
- The most deadly?
- What are some other drugs that are commonly used?
- Are prescription drugs safe for all because a doctor has prescribed them?

Table Talk 2:

- Discuss vaping with your child.
- Do you think people your age know how dangerous vaping can be?
- What can you do to let them know the real dangers of vaping?

PART 4

PLAYING IT RIGHT

CHAPTER 15

Social Media

 Goal: Teach your children the "Dos and Don'ts" of reputation management in the digital world. While addressing the dangers of social media, you will also guide your children in understanding how it can be a powerful tool for capturing college and career opportunities. You will be able to guide your kids to use their devices to build a positive online presence, inspire and encourage others, and amplify their voice to support causes and values that matter to them.

Is Your Social Media Working for You, or Is It Working Against You?

This is the big question we all wish we could ask our kids. In today's world, it's almost inevitable that someone will Google them at some point. Whether it's a potential employer, college, coach, or scholarship provider, people will want to know more about them. They're not looking for gossip or dirt but rather trying to understand if they'd be a good fit for a team, college, or job. So, how are our kids presenting themselves online—their "personal brand"—for the world to see? This brings up another important question: How do your kids feel about you following them on social media? Many parents report that their teens don't allow it. It's a delicate balance, but allowing parents to follow their teens on social media helps ensure their safety, offer guidance, and keep the lines of communication open—all while maintaining respect and not being overly intrusive.

Here are a few key reasons why this approach can be beneficial:

1. **Safety and Oversight:** Teens are still developing their ability to navigate online spaces responsibly. Parents being able to follow them gives them a chance to monitor what their kids are posting and who they're interacting with. It provides a safety net, particularly when it comes to issues like cyberbullying, inappropriate content, or online predators.

2. **Guidance in Social Media Etiquette:** Social media isn't just about fun; it's also about reputation, privacy, and communication skills. Parents can help guide teens in navigating these areas by modeling positive behaviors, such as thoughtful sharing, respecting others' boundaries, and understanding digital footprints.

3. **Building Trust:** When parents follow their kids on social media, it can open up a natural space for conversations about online life. It helps teens feel that their parents are involved in their digital world, without being too intrusive. In turn, this fosters trust and makes it easier to have more meaningful discussions when things go wrong online.

4. **Setting Boundaries and Expectations:** Having the ability to monitor a child's social media allows parents to set clear expectations for behavior. Parents can communicate their values around digital interactions and help teens understand the importance of responsible social media use, which can reduce risky behaviors like oversharing or engaging with inappropriate content.

5. **Teaching Self-Reflection:** The more parents are involved, the more teens will learn to be intentional about what they post. This opens the door for conversations about their online image and personal brand. It's a good chance for parents to teach their kids how to curate content that reflects their values, aspirations, and personal identity.

It's also important that parents approach this issue with respect, acknowledging their child's desire for privacy while balancing it with the need for guidance. Involving teens in the conversation about why they should follow them on social media—and being transparent about what they will and won't monitor—can help maintain that important trust.

The following dialogue is a good example of a teen needing some parental guidance.

 **Parent/Teen Dialogue Example: Social Media Rant Consequences**

Son: "Ugh! This is so unfair. Mr. Jackson called me into his office and said I may lose my spot on the student council because of my post. That's ridiculous!"

Parent: "Whoa. Slow down. What post are you talking about?"

Son: "The one about how some of the school's rules are ridiculous and how the administration is out of touch. Everyone was agreeing with me!"

Parent: "I know you're frustrated, and I get that it felt good to speak your mind. I just wonder how it might've come across to the people who are trying to run the school. Do you think there's a better way to express your opinion without putting people on the defensive?"

Son: "Well... yeah. But I was just venting! It's my opinion, and I should be able to say what I want."

Parent: "You *can* say what you want. But free speech doesn't mean free from consequences. Think about it from their perspective. The student council is supposed to work *with* the administration, not trash them online."

Son: "But that's not fair! I was just speaking up for everyone and expressing how frustrated everyone is."

Parent: "I get that. And you *should* speak up about things that matter to you. But there's a difference between constructive criticism and an emotional rant. One gets heard, and the other just hurts feelings and burns bridges."

Son: "So, what am I supposed to do now? Just delete the post and pretend it didn't happen?"

> **Parent:** "Deleting it is a start, but damage control is more than that. If you care about your reputation and your spot on the student council, you need to take responsibility. Go meet with Mr. Jackson, acknowledge that your post wasn't the best way to handle things, apologize, and ask if you can start over and talk about real solutions instead."
>
> **Son:** "Ugh, this is going to be awful. I really messed up. I hope I won't get kicked off the student council. I worked so hard to get elected."
>
> **Parent:** "Yes, you made a mistake. We all make mistakes, but what you do next is really the most important part. Take ownership, apologize, and move on. Learn from this."
>
> **Son:** "Thanks so much, Mom. You always know the right thing to say."
>
> **Parent:** "Well, you know I love you. Thank you for sharing this situation with me and being honest and willing to ask me for advice. I'm always here for you."

You can tell from this dialogue that Mother and Son seem to have a mutually respectful and trusting relationship with each other, where they can connect. Mission accomplished!

Some Guidelines for Posting

Number 1: Don't ever post anything that you wouldn't want EVERYONE to see. I'm sure you've heard this at least a million times from people who care about you, and guess what? They are right! When you are posting, *never* assume that only SOME of your friends will have access to it. Regardless of your privacy settings, accounts ARE hacked and leaks DO happen. I'll say that again... regardless of your privacy settings, accounts ARE hacked and leaks DO happen! So, don't post negative comments, inappropriate photos of yourself OR others, offensive jokes, or highly emotional content, like rants about personal situations or relationships.

Number 2: Avoid VENTING. Venting never belongs on social networks. Of course, we all need to vent at times, but there are many better ways to vent and confront others AWAY from social media. Remember, once you post something online, it's there forever.

Nothing is ever lost. Even if you delete items, it's pretty scary how they actually stay on other people's servers and accounts. There's just no way to be absolutely certain that what you post will remain private. And on a little sidenote here, I hope that none of you ever get into trouble with the law, but please know that everything you have ever posted, even things you've taken down from your account, can be recovered and used against you. Scary. Yikes!

Trust me on this. Your identity and posts can always be discovered. Even if you create a post or share something online "anonymously," it's actually a lot easier than you may think to track it back to you. Your number one rule should be this:

If you don't want someone to be able to see something, don't post it at all.

Number 3: Don't bully or intentionally aim to hurt someone. As you know, a bully may see a social media page go up and have everyone post their hateful messages about you, a friend, or a classmate. Don't ever be a part of this. In fact, be a GOOD influence on your friends, NOT to take part in this either. Speak up!

Number 4: Avoid online drama. Run as fast as you can! The attention it attracts can be very hurtful. For instance, let's say a girl's picture gets posted with a horrible caption. As tempting as it may be to comment, don't engage. Take the high road. Think about how you would feel if the focus were on YOU.

This goes for the powerful subtweet as well. So, what exactly is a subtweet? Well, Urban Dictionary says: "It's a tweet that is directly referring to a particular person without mentioning their name or directly mentioning them."

For example, you may see something like this: "I hate it when people on my team always show up late to practice." Now, if you had just shown up late to practice, you would likely know that this post was about you. However, because the post did not "tag" you, include your name, or call you out, the person who posted it can deny it if they are confronted.

Subtweeting is a bad way to deal with issues or problems that you have with other people. These issues should be kept off of social media and be kept completely private. Remember what I said earlier about potential employers, colleges, and recruiters? Don't put negative vibes out there for them to see. It never solves problems. In fact, it can do just the opposite... create more problems! You know, we all encounter problems and difficult situations at times, and the best way to handle them is to speak PRIVATELY with the person you are having the problem with rather than broadcasting it for the whole world to see! So, to wrap this topic up, don't use social media to vent. This will only hurt your reputation. Remember: Be intentional about branding yourself in a positive way.

Number 5: Avoid complaining! This goes along the same lines as venting. Don't use social media to complain! We all know that nobody likes a complainer! There are a lot of people out there who just use social media to complain about everything! I have yet to see that complaining actually works— how about you? It never seems to fix problems! On the other hand, it drags people down. It gets old. AND HONESTLY, NO ONE WANTS TO BE AROUND A CHRONIC COMPLAINER! I can't be more straightforward than that!

Number 6: Don't ever impersonate. Impersonation happens mainly in two ways: either by hacking into someone's profile and producing fake posts "as them" or by creating new fake profiles using their information. Not only is this extremely dishonest, but it will come back to bite you and give you a bad reputation, which will negatively affect the great brand you're trying to create for yourself.

Number 7: Avoid shaming. Shaming is a form of bullying and can be very hurtful. For example, a Facebook group called "100 reasons why we hate Jamie Johnson" is intended to hurt Jamie Johnson. I hope this never happens to you, but there is something you can do about it. You can officially report pages, groups, or sites to the social media platform (like Facebook) and request that the page be taken down.

Another type of shaming is posting a picture of a certain friend group together while intentionally trying to make someone feel excluded who was not included in the activity.

FACTS:

Harvard recently rescinded admission offers for some incoming freshmen who participated in a private Facebook group sharing offensive memes. College admissions staff, future employers, and even potential dates are more and more likely to check your profile and make decisions or judgments about you.

1. College Admissions:

- **Prevalence of Social Media Checks:** A 2023 Kaplan survey found that 28% of college admissions officers review applicants' social media profiles during the evaluation process (Kaplan, 2023).
- **Perception of Fairness:** The same survey revealed that 67% of admissions officers consider examining applicants' social media posts as "fair game" for making admissions decisions (Kaplan, 2023).
- **Employer Practices:** According to a 2018 CareerBuilder survey, 70% of employers use social networking sites to research job candidates, and 54% have decided not to hire a candidate based on their social media content (CareerBuilder, 2018, as cited in *Backstage Country*).

These findings underscore the importance of maintaining a responsible and professional online presence, as both educational institutions and employers increasingly consider social media activity in their decision-making processes.

2. What Are Recruiters Watching Out For?

So, what are the potential hazards to avoid? These are some of the types of posts that leave a bad impression:

- References to illegal drugs, sexual posts
- Incriminating or embarrassing photos or videos

- Profanity, defamatory, or racist comments
- Politically charged attacks
- Spelling and grammar issues
- Complaining or bad-mouthing. What's to say you wouldn't do the same to a new school, company, boss, or peer?

If your child asks: "How can I clean up my social media accounts?"

The answer is: research. Both the college of your dreams and your future employer could Google you, so you should do the same thing. Also, check all of your social media profiles—even the ones you haven't used for a while—and get rid of anything that could send the wrong message. Remember, things can't be unseen.

Bottom line: Would you want a future boss, admissions officer, or blind date to read or see it? If not, don't post it. If you already have, delete it.

A Filtered View

It's important to help your kids understand that what they see on social media is often a carefully filtered version of reality—not the whole picture. Think about it: How often do you see posts that only highlight the fun with friends, amazing vacations, or perfect meals? These "highlight reels" can make it seem like everyone else is living an ideal, picture-perfect life—even when that's far from the truth.

As adults, we know how easy it is to fall into the trap of comparing ourselves to others online. For kids and teens, who are still figuring out who they are, this pressure is amplified. Social media makes it possible to measure popularity by something as simple as the number of likes or comments a post receives. It's tempting for kids to chase that validation, but constantly comparing themselves to others' curated posts can fuel anxiety, lower self-esteem, and even lead to symptoms of depression.

Encourage your kids to step back and recognize that no one's life is as perfect as it looks online. Remind them to focus on who they are, what makes them unique, and the things they're grateful for. Gratitude is one of the best ways to combat the false narratives of social media and stay grounded in what truly matters.

Social Media Literacy

So, what does that mean? I'll give you a hint. I'm sure you've heard the term financial literacy, which means the ability to understand and effectively use financial skills. So, social media literacy means the ability to understand and effectively use social media.

To be even more specific, social media literacy means the ability to **access, analyze, evaluate, create, and act** using all forms of communication.

This checklist can be a great tool for your kids to use to assess whether their posts are responsible and meaningful. Now, let's break it down.

1. To ACCESS means this: What kind of social media content are you accessing? Is it healthy? Is it meaningful? Does it go along with your values?
2. To ANALYZE means: What message is being sent? Is it clear and easy to understand? Is it true?
3. To EVALUATE means: Did you know that each message is created by someone with their own goals and opinions? Are they similar to yours? Is this someone you want to follow? Is this someone you want to follow you?
4. To CREATE means: When you create a post, are you thinking about what YOUR responsibility is to those who are viewing it? What result do you want?
5. Are you following the guidelines that you learned earlier?
6. To ACT means: What are you going to do with all of the info you are receiving? Are you going to comment, share, retweet, or block?

Hopefully, you can show your kids how important it is to think about all of these things before they post. Just like we strive to be financially literate to have financial success, we should also strive to be "social media literate" to be able to manage and have successful, responsible communication with the world.

There's been quite a bit of content on what NOT to post on social media, but now and for the rest of this chapter, the focus will be on how to use social media in a **positive** way. As you know, there are great ways to make social media work FOR you to uplift, inspire, and encourage. Let's take a look.

Once again, this section has been written for your teens directly for them to read. No edits necessary.

Teach Young People To Use Social Media in a POSITIVE way

1. You can brand yourself in a positive way!

Many haters may say, "Stay away from social media! It is really bad for you!" But the truth is, in today's world, social media is just like the air we breathe! It is everywhere. We can't stay away from it. In fact, it's a GREAT form of communication that we all need to learn how to use responsibly. Let's look at it in a different way and take advantage of having a positive outlet!

Since people will be searching for you, give them something to find that will be a positive reflection of your character. This is your opportunity to be intentional about branding yourself. What's unique about you? Who inspires you? What things are you passionate about? What kind of difference do you want to make in this world? Social media can be your unique platform for all the world to see.

2. You can use social media for inspiration and support ... to actually DO GOOD in this world. For example, you can set up a crowdfunding page like GoFundMe to help a friend or an organization in need. You can also set up a page of encouraging quotes that will help others who may be feeling anxious or depressed. Through these large social networks, you can now learn about important issues and people from all over the world and then use your voice to speak up, to support each other, and to talk about bigger issues than only your personal lives. Super cool!

3. You can expand your worldview. This means that through social media, you are exposed to people outside the sphere of your own community or circle of friends, and you can make new friends from different backgrounds. It can expose you to different viewpoints, news, and people from all around the world. It can be beneficial for you to start learning about what's happening outside of your own world and start understanding big issues. Remember, knowledge is POWER, so learn as much as you can!

4. You can lend a voice! Sometimes, we may feel like we're not listened to, or we may be shy or unsure about speaking up in person. However, social media can give you a way to express yourself in a different manner. You can choose to express yourself in a less direct way, such as writing, creating photos, using images, or recording videos, without having to have an audience or a large group of people watching you in person. In fact, social media can allow you to have a voice and give you the confidence you need to speak out more offline. This can be a big confidence booster for you!

5. Social media has many educational benefits! You can learn new things through articles shared on social media or by watching videos. The educational info is endless! You have access to such a wide variety of resources that can help you with school projects, as well as your personal interests, like sports, music, etc. Hey, you can even start to develop great thinking and writing skills along the way as you are posting blogs! Also, if you're trying to find a solution to a problem, you can find opinions and suggestions from professionals and experts who have great experience.

6. You can increase your creativity! With sites like Pinterest, you can get 1000s of ideas regarding cooking, fashion, art projects, and so much more. Plus, it's a great place to showcase your own awesome creative ideas. There are many ways for you to engage and show off your creativity. For example, if you like taking photos or videos, these sites and apps can help you perfect your skills and show off what you're doing. For you guys that like to write or create graphics and digital designs, social media is an ideal place to share your work and get encouragement and instant feedback.

7. Did you know that social media can actually become a source of income for you? Yes! It's true. Social media is a direct source of income for many people. With some guidance, you can actually run a huge business!

Making fun apps and games, selling online products, and making informative pages regarding popular topics, can be a good source of income for you.

You can also make money being an influencer. Influencers are basically people who have a large following on social media platforms and can influence their followers to buy the products that they promote by sharing links on their social media accounts. They'll basically give a promotion of a product or a service to their followers, and then they are paid for it as a result. In order to do this, they have to have a large social media following. Once they do, they need to get links, share those links, and try to get as many people as possible to click on the link. There are specific strategies to get followers. This is something that would be fun to check out in your free time.

Young People Are Changing the World Through Social Media

Did you know that there are hundreds of young people who are engaging in social media to create excitement for a cause or change the world in some way? Here are four examples:

1. Julia Warren uses her blog to get volunteers and donations for her nonprofit, called Celebrate RVA, which she started in high school. The nonprofit's mission is to provide birthday celebrations for disadvantaged children in her community.

2. Hannah Alper, just 13 years old, has over 34,000 followers on Twitter. She writes for the newspaper, the *Huffington Post*, and has a large following on her blog. Her aim is to inspire others to change the world in their own way. Hannah advocates for animals' rights, anti-bullying efforts, and environmental causes.

3. 14-year-old Joshua Williams is determined to end hunger around the world. The Joshua Heart Foundation has recruited over 100,000 teen volunteers and has raised over half a million dollars!!! WOW! A half million dollars! Joshua makes use of social media channels, such as Facebook, Twitter, Instagram, and others, to spread the news about his cause.

4. One day, Jah'Kiyla Atwaters was cheerleading, and a group of other girls stood at the gate watching. Jah'Kiyla has the opportunity to

afford to participate in cheerleading. Yet, when she approached the girls at the gate, they told her that they couldn't afford to cheerlead and that their mom had passed away. Jah'Kiyla realized that there are girls who probably would love to cheerlead but who don't have the resources to do so. In response, Jah'Kiyla started a charity to help raise the funds for those who want to play sports but who can't afford it.

These stories should be inspiring to both parent and child. What do you think all of these young people had in common? Well, a few things.

1. They saw a need.
2. They had a passion for helping others.
3. They took the initiative to act on their passion.
4. They had the discipline to follow through.

As you can see from the examples above, there are so many positive ways to use social media. Teens are building charities, advocating for a cause, and staying positive for their peers. In fact, when an issue gets posted on social media, there's more attention drawn to it, and in turn, there are more teens focused on doing good in the world than creating harm.

 **Action Steps**

What NOT to do.
- Don't post anything that you wouldn't want EVERYONE to see
- Avoid venting
- Don't bully
- Don't get involved in online drama
- Don't complain
- Don't impersonate
- Don't shame

Now, the Dos.
1. Brand yourself in a POSITIVE way
2. Use social media for inspiration and support
3. Expand your worldview

4. Lend a voice
5. Learn as much as you can
6. Get creative
7. Create a source of income

Activity:

Together with your child, look for friends or influencers on social media who share positive, encouraging, and uplifting content that would be great to emulate.

Table Talk:

- When you have the urge to vent on social media, what should you do instead?
- If you have already made the mistake with an inappropriate post, what should you do?
- How do you feel about subtweeting? Have you ever subtweeted about someone, or has someone ever subtweeted about you? How did this make you feel?
- Does being on social media ever make you feel depressed? Anxious? Why or why not?
- Does being on social media make you happy?
- If you could change something about social media, what would it be?

CHAPTER 16

Teen Internet Safety

 Goal: Equip your children to spot and steer clear of the web's hidden dangers while embracing smart safety habits.

If you're raising teens, odds are they're glued to their screens—scrolling social media, gaming, or exploring corners of the internet you might not even know exist. And that's not all bad! The online world can spark creativity, connect them with friends, and open doors to learning. But here's the catch: beneath the fun and flashy surface, there's a darker side—things like predators, scams, and content that can mess with their heads or even put them at risk. That's why it's so critical for parents to step in and guide them.

Teaching internet safety isn't about scaring them off the web. It's about arming them with the know-how to enjoy it without stumbling into trouble. Teens often think they've got it all figured out, but their brains are still wiring up impulse control and judgment—stuff science backs up, like studies showing the prefrontal cortex doesn't fully mature until their 20s. They might not see the red flags: a "friend" asking for pictures, a too-good-to-be-true deal, or a sketchy link that could swipe their info. Without your input, they're more likely to overshare, trust the wrong people, or wade into spaces that could leave lasting scars—emotionally, financially, or worse.

Plus, the stakes are higher than ever. The web's a 24/7 playground, and bad actors don't clock out—think cyberbullies, catfishers, or creeps lurking in DMs. Stats from places like the National Center for Missing & Exploited

Children show millions of kids face online enticement yearly, often because they didn't know the signs. Teaching them to follow safety guidelines—like keeping personal stuff private, sticking to public meetups if they connect in real life, or pausing before clicking—can cut those risks big-time. It's not just about dodging danger; it's about building habits that let them thrive online with confidence.

So, your job? Show them the ropes. Help them spot what's shady, set boundaries that stick, and feel okay coming to you if something goes sideways. Ask, "What's the wildest thing you've seen online lately?" or "How do you decide who's legit to talk to?" to get them chatting. This chapter's here to break it down—because a teen who's web-savvy isn't just safer, they're freer to enjoy the good stuff without the shadows creeping in.

 **Parent/Teen Dialogue Example: The Online Scam**

Teen: "Mom, this is so annoying. Some random person messaged me about a giveaway I won, but I don't even remember entering. They said I just have to click this link and confirm my info."

Parent: "Hmm... that sounds suspicious. What kind of giveaway was it?"

Teen: "It was for free AirPods. I commented on a post the other day, and I guess they picked me. The account looks legit—there's a little lock emoji in their bio that says 'verified giveaway.'"

Parent: "Okay, let's slow down for a second. Did you check if the account is actually verified? And what kind of info are they asking for?"

Teen: "Just basic stuff—name, email, and they need my card info to 'verify my identity.' But they said they won't charge anything."

Parent: "That's a huge red flag. No real giveaway would ask for your credit card just to claim a prize. Scammers use this trick to steal your information or even drain your bank account."

Teen: "Seriously? I was excited for nothing?"

Parent: "I get it—it's frustrating. But this is exactly how scammers operate. They make it seem real, so you don't think twice. Have you shared any other personal info with them?"

Teen: "No, I was about to, but then I showed you first."

Parent: "That's really smart. Always check before sharing anything. Let's block and report the account, and if you ever feel unsure about something online, just ask me. No judgment—I just want to keep you safe."

Teen: "Yeah, I guess I need to be more careful. I'll double-check before trusting stuff like this again."

Parent: "That's smart. The internet's great, but there are people out there trying to take advantage. The more you know, the safer you'll be."

Teen: "Thanks so much, Mom. You always make it easy for me to talk to you, and you always give me the best advice."

Parent: "Of course! And I'm thankful that you want and trust my advice."

We all know that the internet is a powerful tool—it connects us to friends, knowledge, and entertainment. But for teens, it also comes with risks that can impact their privacy, well-being, and future. Here's why internet safety is crucial:

1. Protecting Personal Information

Teens often share details about their lives online without realizing how that information can be used against them. Personal data—like location, school, or even daily routines—can make them targets for scams, identity theft, or even predators. Teaching them to safeguard personal details is essential. They need to be aware of how much information they are revealing about themselves, and who they are revealing it to on their social networking pages. As their parent, make sure that they know how to apply privacy settings and that they know how to use the reporting mechanisms when something is wrong.

Do your teens know that their information can be sold to others? Every website has a "privacy policy." It will tell you how that website uses all the personal information about you, like your name. In some cases, though, some websites ignore their privacy policy and sell your email address to other companies. One way to know that this has happened is if you open your email one day and you have 150 spam emails in your inbox as a result. If a website is asking for too much information about you, take control and leave the site. Again, would you give this information to some older stranger at the mall? Probably not.

2. Never share your username and password with ANYONE, not even your best friend.

It's just that simple. What if one of their friends logs on and pretends to be them just as a joke, and then says something horrible and gets *them* in trouble? Sure, it might seem funny to the friend at the time, but this can actually get pretty serious fast! What if the post got your child in trouble with their friends, parents, or worse, got them expelled from school, or even worse, got them in trouble with the law? So, please instill in your kids to always keep their name and password private.

3. Avoiding Online Predators

The anonymity of the internet makes it easy for predators to pose as someone they're not. Grooming and manipulation happen subtly, often through friendly interactions that build trust over time. Being aware of red flags and knowing when to block and report suspicious behavior can prevent dangerous situations. They should never tell anyone their real name or where they live. *Any* information that a predator could possibly use to find them... even "small clues" like what school they attend or the sports team they play on. These small bits of info are just enough for a predator to figure out their identity. I mean, surely they wouldn't tell some random 40-year-old man or woman they met at the mall their name and where they live, would they? So, why would they tell *CoolCowboy13 or HotChick22* from the chat room?

4. Understanding the Digital Footprint

What teens post today can follow them for years. Colleges, employers, and even future relationships may come across old posts that don't reflect who they are anymore. Encouraging mindful posting helps prevent regret down the road. **The Internet has a Great Memory... it NEVER forgets!** Every search, website visit, online posting, and email is registered somewhere on the internet. Yes, the internet is awesome for sharing and getting the word out, but what happens when you are done with sharing? The internet isn't a dry erase board that you can erase what you've written at your leisure. Once something is out there on the internet, it will more or less be there forever. It won't go away.

So, say your daughter posts a very risqué picture of herself that she thinks looks great at the time, but after a while, she is mortified that she ever posted such a photo, and so she deletes it. Problem solved. However, did you know that her photo still remains on the internet even though she may not be able to see it? Just know that it can always be dug up to haunt you.

This also goes for any rude or mean comments that are posted. There's a fine line between cruelty and humor. Your kids need to be very careful and not impulsive. Have them try building an internal "pause button" to counter potential impulsive behavior. For example, if they are feeling emotional about something, it would be a good idea for them to step away from their computer or cell phone before posting or sending anything, taking a "time-out." Hate emails, online threats, or bad language in chat rooms is never acceptable. They need to watch what they allow their friends to post about you as well. Make sure that they get your permission to be in a photo or video that they want to post, tag, or pass along. There will be a time when you begin filling out college applications, and they will want to be certain that they are reflected in a positive way.

Since we are on the topic of photos and videos, it is NEVER okay to post or pressure someone to send or share nude or semi-nude photos of yourself or of someone else. If they receive a nude picture, it is considered sexual harassment/assault to distribute it without proof of consent. No matter how innocent it may seem, sexting is a crime. Sexting is sending and receiving sexually explicit messages, primarily between cell phones, the internet, or other communication devices. Anyone under the age of 18 commits the crime of sexting when they knowingly use a device to send images or videos that consist of nudity or sexual conduct to another minor, as well as when a minor receives and possesses any nude or explicit images that are sent by another minor. It is important to note, however, that if the recipient of the text message did not solicit, transmit, or distribute the photo and took reasonable steps to report the photo, they will not be in violation of a sexting crime. Minors can commit a sexting crime that results in a misdemeanor of the first degree, or a felony offense, depending on the circumstances surrounding the case.

5. Preventing Cyberbullying

Cyberbullying can be relentless and have devastating effects on mental health. Unlike traditional bullying, it doesn't stop when a teen leaves school—it follows them home through their devices. Teaching kindness, blocking bullies, and knowing when to seek help can protect their well-being.

6. Avoiding Scams and Misinformation

Not everything online is trustworthy. Scammers use fake giveaways, phishing emails, and fraudulent websites to steal personal data. Similarly, misinformation spreads quickly, influencing opinions and decisions. Helping teens develop critical thinking skills keeps them from falling into these traps.

7. Managing Screen Time and Mental Health

Too much screen time—especially on social media—can affect self-esteem, sleep, and mental health. The comparison trap is real, and constant exposure to curated, unrealistic portrayals of life can lead to anxiety or depression. Encouraging balance and offline activities helps maintain a healthy mindset.

Empowering Teens with Smart Online Habits

Internet safety isn't about avoiding the internet—it's about using it wisely. Here are some key habits to encourage:

☑ **Think before sharing**—Would you be okay with your post being public forever?

☑ **Use privacy settings**—Limit who can see personal information.

☑ **Recognize red flags**—Be cautious of strangers asking for personal details.

☑ **Fact-check information**—Not everything online is true.

☑ **Balance screen time**—Take breaks to focus on real-life connections.

"Street Smarts for the Screen"

1. Tech Talk: Everyday Conversations

Frame internet safety as an *ongoing dialogue*:

- "Just like we talk about crossing the street safely, we talk about how to scroll safely."
- Encourage weekly check-ins: "Seen anything weird or uncomfortable online lately?"
- Example dialogue:
  Parent: "If a stranger walked up and asked you personal questions, would you answer them?"
  Child: "No way."
  Parent: "That's why we don't give our full name, school, or location online, either."

2. Practical Boundaries Checklist

Use this checklist with their kids:

- Do we keep devices out of bedrooms overnight?
- Do we ever use devices behind closed doors?
- Do we only follow/accept people we know in real life?
- Do we understand how to block/report someone?
- Have we talked about what to do if we see something inappropriate?

Tip for parents: Set the boundaries before the device becomes part of everyday life. It's harder to take it back once it's been given.

3. Red Flags Game

Make it interactive:

Play a game where you both list red flags. What kind of online message would make you pause or feel weird?

- A stranger asking to keep a conversation secret
- A message with lots of flattery and pressure
- Someone asking for photos or offering gifts

4. Teach Your Kids the "Pause, Think, Act" Tool

Include this memorable tool:

- **Pause:** What just happened? Why does this feel off?
- **Think:** What would I do if this happened in real life?
- **Act:** Tell a trusted adult. Block. Report.

Tip for parents: Use a relatable story of a kid who trusted their gut and told an adult. Show that *asking for help* is strong, not weak.

5. Real-Life "What Would You Do?" Scenarios

Include short scenarios and questions for parent/kid discussion:

> **Scenario**: Someone you don't know says you're cute and wants to FaceTime.
> **Question**: "What's your first instinct? What do you do?"

> **Scenario**: A classmate keeps messaging you mean things in a group chat.
> **Question**: "How would you handle that? What do you think we should do together?"

6. Digital Reputation: The "Backpack Rule"

> "Everything you post online becomes part of the backpack you carry with you into the future. What kind of things do you want to carry?"

Use the metaphor to help kids understand that digital choices don't disappear and can either help or weigh them down.

7. Set the Standard by Modeling

- Model healthy screen habits. If we expect kids to unplug at dinner or walk away from drama, we should do the same.
- Let them hear you say, "I'm logging off—this is getting negative." That's leadership in action.

 **Action Steps**

😕 **"WHAT WOULD YOU DO?" SCENARIOS**

Discuss these with your child and talk through possible responses.

A classmate sends you a video with lots of curse words. You feel weird watching it.

What do you do? Who could you talk to?

Someone online asks for a photo and says, "Don't tell anyone."

What do you think is really going on here? What would be a smart move?

A friend is posting mean comments about another friend or another student.

What would you do? Would you screenshot it? Unfollow? Talk to an adult?

You make a mistake and post something that gets a lot of negative attention.

How could we handle it together?

Activities

Construct a Family Tech Agreement

We agree that technology should help us grow, learn, and connect safely. These are the guidelines we will follow:

Together, we agree to:

- **Use devices in open areas of the house**
- **Ask before downloading apps or games**
- **Tell a trusted adult if something online feels off, scary, or inappropriate**
- **Avoid chatting with strangers online—even if they seem nice**
- **Never share personal info like our full name, school, phone number, or address**
- **Think before posting—because what goes online stays online**
- **Take regular breaks from screens**
- **Remember: kindness online is just as important as kindness in person**

Parents agree to:

- **Stay informed and involved—not snooping, but staying connected**
- **Model healthy screen habits**
- **Keep an open-door policy for questions or uncomfortable moments**
- **Adjust rules as kids grow and show responsibility**

Signed:

Child: _____

Parent(s): _____

Date: _____

✅ TECH SAFETY CHECKLIST

Let's do a quick digital checkup together:

- Do we know how to block/report someone?
- Do we have privacy settings turned on?
- Do we keep passwords private—even from friends?
- Do we only follow/add people we know in real life?
- Do we take screen breaks throughout the day?
- Do we unplug from devices at bedtime?
- Do we talk regularly about what we're doing online?

"Would You Post That?" — A Social Media Safety Challenge

Objective: To help teens evaluate the impact and risks of their digital footprints and encourage them to think critically before posting online.

STEP 1: SCENARIO CARDS

You have a choice to make. What is your choice? Choose one of these: Rethink it. Or Delete it.

Then explain your choice in the space below.

1. You post a TikTok dancing in your room, but your home address is visible on a delivery box in the background.
   Your choice: _____
   Why? _____

2. You comment on a classmate's post using a sarcastic joke that could be misinterpreted.
   Your choice: _____
   Why? _____

3. You accept a follow request from someone you don't know because they "seem cool."
   Your choice: _____
   Why? _____

4. You repost a meme making fun of another student's appearance.
   Your choice: _____
   Why? _____

5. A friend sends you a screenshot of someone talking about you in a group chat.
   Your choice: _____
   Why? _____

STEP 2: REFLECT ON YOUR POSTS

Look at your five most recent posts or shares online. Answer honestly:

- Would I be okay with a future coach, teacher, or employer seeing this?

_____

- Does this reflect who I want to be?

_____

Is there anything I'd delete if my younger sibling saw it?

_____

STEP 3: BUILD YOUR PERSONAL POSTING GUIDELINES

Write three rules you'll use to guide what you share online:

1. _____

2. _____

3. _____

4. _____

BONUS: TALK TO YOUR PARENT OR TRUSTED ADULT

Share your three guidelines with them and ask:

"What would your rules be if you were a teen today?"

Parent/Adult Response: _____

My Reaction: _____

_____

_____

This activity helps you lead with values, not pressure. Be intentional. Be smart. Be YOU.

By making internet safety a regular conversation, we can empower teens to make smart choices, stay safe, and use the online world in ways that benefit them.

Table Talk:

- How do you decide what's safe to share online and what's not?
- What would you do if someone you didn't know tried to contact you online?
- Have you ever seen something online that made you uncomfortable? How did you handle it?
- Do you know how to create strong passwords and why it's important?

CHAPTER 17

Sportsmanship

Goal: To teach our children about playing fair, following the rules, respecting judgment, and treating others with respect, win or lose!

What It Means to Play with Heart

Picture a packed soccer field on a crisp Saturday morning—kids racing after the ball, parents cheering from the sidelines, the air buzzing with energy. One team scores, and a player from the losing side jogs over, offers a high-five, and says, "Nice shot." That's sportsmanship in action, not just a polite gesture, but a quiet strength that says, "I respect you, win or lose." Sportsmanship is the unwritten code of playing fair, showing grace under pressure, and valuing the game over the scoreboard. It's shaking hands after a tough match, owning up when you mess up, and cheering for effort, not just victory. For kids, it's less about mastering a rulebook and more about learning how to carry themselves with dignity, humility, and grit, whether they're holding the trophy or walking off empty-handed.

Now, flip that scene. Imagine little Tommy missing a goal, kicking the dirt, and yelling, "The ref's blind!" while his teammate chucks a water bottle at the bench. Or worse—there's the kid who struts like a peacock after scoring, taunting, "Can't touch me!" That's bad sportsmanship in all its glory: tantrums, blame games, and ego trips that turn a fun game into a mini soap opera. And let's not forget the sideline MVP—the classic "soccer mom," decked out in team swag, hollering, "That's my baby!" while arguing with the ref over a call she saw through her hot mocha latte steam. We've all seen her... the one who'd storm the field with a rulebook if her minivan had turf tires. It's funny until you realize: if parents don't step in, kids might think that's how the game's played—loud, proud, and a little unhinged.

But here's the thing: kids don't pop out of the womb knowing how to lose without a meltdown or win without gloating—those are learned moves. That's where parents come in—because sportsmanship isn't just a "nice-to-have" for pickup games; it's a cornerstone for life. Teaching it early sets the stage for how kids handle competition, teamwork, and setbacks, on and off the court. And in a world obsessed with likes, rankings, and being the best, where every TikTok is a highlight reel and every loss stings like a viral fail, showing them there's honor in the *how*, not just the *what*, might be one of the biggest gifts you can give. Otherwise, you're stuck with a future adult who's still chucking water bottles when the boss picks someone else's idea.

Why It's Crucial for Parents to Teach Sportsmanship Early

Kids are sponges—especially when they're young. Those early years, from toddler tantrums to grade-school rivalries, are when habits and attitudes take root. If a 6-year-old learns to say "good game" after a loss instead of stomping off, or doesn't morph into a pint-sized diva when they win, they're wiring their brain for resilience. Child development experts, like those citing studies from the American Psychological Association, point out that kids' social and emotional skills start gelling before age 10. Waiting until they're teens, when peer pressure and egos kick into overdrive, can make it harder to shift the script. By then, you're battling a kid who's mastered the eye-roll and thinks sportsmanship's for suckers, not to mention the sideline cheerleader who's swapped her latte for a megaphone.

Parents are the first coaches, even if you've never held a whistle. You model it when you clap for the other team's effort or stay cool after a ref's bad call (instead of channeling your inner soccer mom and debating the offside rule), they notice. Teaching sportsmanship early isn't just about avoiding sore losers or pint-sized braggarts; it's about building character before the stakes get higher. A kid who learns to handle a missed shot with a shrug and a "next time" is less likely to unravel when life throws bigger curveballs, like a failed test or a job rejection. Plus, sports are a safe sandbox for these lessons. The stakes are low, a trophy's not a mortgage, but the payoff is huge: they practice respect, self-control, and empathy in a setting where screwing up won't break them.

And let's be real: kids who don't learn this can turn into *those* players—the ones who trash-talk, cheat, or blame the muddy field, the coach, or the sun in their eyes. That's not just tough on teammates; it's a preview of how they might act in a classroom or office or how they'll parent their own kids, turning into the soccer mom who brings a lawyer to the peewee playoffs. Teaching sportsmanship early nips that in the bud, showing them that winning at all costs isn't winning—it's losing who you are.

How Good Sportsmanship Translates to Life

Here's the magic: sportsmanship isn't stuck on the field. It spills over everywhere. That kid who learns to lose gracefully? He's the teen who can take constructive criticism from a teacher without shutting down. The one who cheers a rival's big play? She grows into the coworker who celebrates a colleague's promotion instead of stewing in jealousy. It's like a muscle. Work it in sports, and it flexes in friendships, school, and even future careers.

Take respect. It's the backbone of sportsmanship. Shaking hands after a game teaches kids to see opponents as people, not enemies. That carries into life: they're less likely to bully, more likely to listen, and better at building bridges when opinions clash. Or think about resilience—bouncing back from a blown lead in basketball prepares them to dust off after bombing a presentation. Humility, too. Winning without rubbing it in translates to getting an A without bragging, or landing a job without acting like they're above everyone else.

Real-world stats back this up: a 2019 study from the Aspen Institute found kids in team sports who learn positive behaviors like sportsmanship score higher on leadership and empathy scales later in life. Employers love it. Surveys like those from the National Association of Colleges and Employers consistently rank teamwork and adaptability (hello, sportsmanship!) as top hires' traits. Even in relationships, it shines. Handling a breakup with grace or supporting a partner's wins mirrors that post-game handshake.

So, when you teach your kid to play fair and stay classy, you're not just raising a good athlete—you're raising a good human. It's a ripple effect: one lesson on the field can shape how they navigate the messy, unpredictable game of life. Start early, keep it simple—say, "We play hard, but we play kind"—and watch it grow into something they carry forever.

 **Parent/Child Dialogue Example:**

Scenario: *Your child, Alex, just finished a soccer game. After losing, he threw his water bottle, refused to shake hands with the other team, and stormed off the field.*

Parent: "Hey Alex, my little field warrior! Caught that Oscar-worthy tantrum after the game—what's going on here?"

Alex: "Ugh, no! We were *robbed*! That ref was basically blind—missed every call! And their team? Total goons—kicking shins like it's a martial arts movie. It's straight-up injustice!"

Parent: "Oh, I feel you—losing stinks, especially when it's a circus out there. But let's rewind: chucking your water bottle and ditching the handshake line—what's the vibe you're going for there, champ?"

Alex: "That I was mad! Because I was!"

Parent: "Yeah, I could tell. And it's okay to feel mad. But do you think that's how the best athletes handle losing?"

Alex: "I don't know... maybe not."

Parent: "Let's think about your favorite players. Messi... Ronaldo... What would you say if you saw them do what you did today?"

Alex: "I guess I'd think they were being a really poor sport."

Parent: "Exactly. And being a good sport doesn't mean pretending to be happy when you lose. It just means showing respect—for the game, for your teammates, for your opponents, and for the officials (even if you think they are making bad calls). Because how you act when things don't go your way says a lot about who you are."

Alex: "But why should I shake hands if they played dirty?"

Parent: "Because sportsmanship isn't about them—it's about you. You get to decide the kind of player and the kind of person you want to be. And great players? They keep their cool, win or lose. They show respect, even when it's hard. That's what makes them great."

Alex: "So... even if I think the other team was unfair, I should still shake hands?"

Parent: "Yep. Not for them—for you. Because at the end of the day, your character matters more than the scoreboard."

Alex: "Okay... next time, I'll really try."

Parent: "That's important. And hey, I know it's tough—so if you ever need to vent after a game, I'm here for that, too. Just maybe... without the water bottle toss? Haha!"

Alex: "Yeah, okay. That was kinda bad. Thanks, Dad!"

This parent nails it by being relatable (using humor), respectful (validating feelings), and strategic (guiding Alex to his own conclusions). They turn a potential showdown into a bonding moment, teaching sportsmanship without losing the kid's buy-in. It's entertaining enough to keep Alex hooked and wise enough to plant seeds for growth—textbook win!

Why Sportsmanship Matters

Sportsmanship is a tradition in competition that dates back thousands of years. It's a concept we hear all the time—"be a good sport"—but it applies far beyond just the sports field. Whether your child is on a team, part of a school club, or working with others on a group project, learning good sportsmanship is key.

So, what is sportsmanship? It's treating both teammates and opponents with the same respect and fairness they'd want for themselves. It means playing fair, following rules, respecting referees and officials, and treating everyone with dignity, win or lose.

Teaching Good Sportsmanship

Good sportsmanship isn't something kids learn in the heat of the moment—it's a mindset they develop over time. As parents, it's important to talk about it before competitive situations arise. Helping your child understand sportsmanship early on will set them up for success, not only in athletics but in life.

What Does Poor Sportsmanship Look Like?

Unsportsmanlike conduct can be a game-changer! Many, many games are lost by the unsportsmanlike conduct of just one player. And people will always remember that player in a way that he or she would NOT like to be remembered. Unsportsmanlike behavior can take many forms, and it's important for kids to recognize these negative actions. This includes taunting, trash-talking, using profanity, berating referees, bragging excessively, or intentionally breaking rules. It can also extend beyond sports—to school, friendships, and family life—when kids engage in gossip, exclusion, or retaliation.

A lack of sportsmanship doesn't just impact the game—it impacts reputations. In fact, many professional athletes have been fined or suspended for poor conduct. Encourage your child to think about how they want to be remembered: as someone who respects the game or someone who lets emotions get the best of them?

Teaching Through History: The Ancient Greek Perspective

The idea of sportsmanship isn't new. Ancient Greek philosophers, including Plato, emphasized that sports were meant to build human excellence. Plato identified three key objectives for athletes that remain relevant today:

- **Piety:** Show respect to others and the game itself.
- **Courage:** Stay strong and in control, even in the face of challenges.
- **Justice:** Play fair and respect the rules.

Notice that none of these objectives include winning? Winning is great, but it's not the most important part of competition—character is.

Encouraging Your Child to Be a Good Sport

Your child's actions shape how they are perceived by others and how they "brand" themselves. Are they branding themselves as a good sport? Good sportsmanship, like honesty and trustworthiness, is a mental mindset, a habit built over time. It's about deciding to behave honorably, regardless of how others act. It just can't be turned on at a moment's notice during a time of stress or anger. Chances are that if you are a good sport "on the field," you will be a good sport off the field in everyday life... and vice versa. Being a good sport should be a lifetime goal because it goes way beyond athletic years. People who are bad sports will not be asked to join others for games, such as cards, golf, tennis, etc., which add to the joys of one's social life.

Here are ways you can encourage good sportsmanship in your child:

What Does Good Sportsmanship Look Like When You Win?

- Being gracious and humble.
- Acknowledging victory without humiliating opponents.
- Letting success speak for itself.
- Complimenting opponents, even when winning by a large margin.

What Does Good Sportsmanship Look Like When You Lose?

- Congratulating winners promptly and willingly.
- Accepting the outcome without excuses or blaming.
- Showing maturity and courage in defeat.
- Using losses as learning opportunities for future improvement.

Helping Your Child Understand Retaliation

One of the biggest threats to good sportsmanship is retaliation—the urge to "get even." In sports, retaliating often results in penalties for the second offense rather than the first. The same happens in life—responding negatively to a slight can cause more trouble than the original issue. Teach your child that self-control is key. Keeping their cool in difficult situations will serve them well, whether on the field, at school, or later in their careers. Encourage them to think before they react and focus on rising above negativity rather than sinking to its level.

Here are some examples of retaliation in sports:

- A baseball pitcher getting angry and intentionally firing a 100 mph ball at a batter
- A soccer player strategically throwing an elbow or a knee or tripping up an opponent
- A basketball player slamming an opponent to the ground in return for rough treatment
- A football player "chop blocking" on a following play in return for a late hit from the previous play

Now, here are some examples of retaliation outside of sports:

- Gossiping about a friend who snubbed you
- Lashing out at a waiter or server after poor service at a restaurant
- Engaging in social media rants
- Fighting back over a girlfriend/boyfriend

It is inevitable that people will do bad things to you at home, at school, in a sports environment, at work, etc. It's just a part of life, and many times you cannot control how others treat you, but what you CAN control is how you treat others in return.

Seeking revenge cannot only backfire, but fuming over what the person did to you and how you want to retaliate can certainly take up so much of your time and energy, and create great anxiety. There is a much better option!

It's called forgiveness.

The Power of Forgiveness

Retaliation isn't the answer—choosing forgiveness is a more powerful and constructive response. Holding onto anger and resentment wastes energy. Teaching kids to let go, move forward, and focus on their own actions rather than others' mistakes is a valuable life lesson. A great example of this was Dodgers pitcher Yu Darvish, who was the target of a racial insult during the World Series. Instead of retaliating, he accepted an apology and encouraged fans to move forward with positivity. His ability to take the high road earned him widespread respect.

The STAR Code for Sportsmanship

To help your child remember the key elements of sportsmanship, introduce them to the **STAR Code:**

1. **Show What You Can Do.** Let actions speak louder than words. In the last few years, taunting, trash-talking, and bragging have all become too common in sports. You've probably seen athletes who do more talking about how great they are than actually demonstrate it "on the field." **ACTIONS SPEAK LOUDER THAN WORDS**. If you are really that good, you don't need to say anything. (This type of talk is easier than ever because of social media. You can reach whomever you want whenever you want in just a second's time.)

   Example: Avoid bragging or trash-talking. Instead, demonstrate skill through effort and performance.

2. **Treat Everyone with Fairness,** not only your opponents, but also your officials, coaches, teammates, and fans from both sides. Sportsmanship is not only reserved for those on the field, but also for everyone involved in the sporting event.

   Example: Play fair even when tempted to bend the rules to win.

3. **Avoid Retaliation at All Costs!** Just know and accept that THERE WILL BE BAD CALLS and UNFAIR PLAY in sports. No one is right all of the time; that's one thing that you can count on. However, retaliating is just as bad as the initial offense. Remember, the one who retaliates is the one who actually ends up getting the penalty. It happens more times than not, and not just on the field, but also in life. Don't react negatively when things don't go your way.

   Example: Ignore trash talk instead of engaging in it.

4. **Respect Athleticism.** Remember to acknowledge and applaud good plays and efforts by both your own teammates and your opponents. You are all out there because you have the same common interest. Respect it. Remember, becoming a good sport doesn't just happen overnight. The time to begin is NOW.

   Example: Help an opponent up after a tough play and never boo teammates.

Applying Sportsmanship Beyond Sports

Good sportsmanship extends far beyond athletics. Encourage your child to use the same mindset in school, friendships, and eventually the workplace. Learning to win and lose with grace, work as part of a team, and show respect for others will serve them well throughout life.

Wrap-Up

Bad sportsmanship doesn't just ruin the game—it damages reputations and relationships. By teaching your child to embrace sportsmanship, you're helping them develop character traits that will benefit them in every aspect of life. Use the STAR Code as a foundation and encourage your child to think about how they want to be remembered—both on and off the field.

Action Steps:

1. **Win or lose, show respect:** Shake hands, avoid trash talk, and handle losses without excuses.
2. **Keep your cool:** Control emotions, don't argue with refs, and stay positive no matter what.
3. **Lift others up:** Encourage teammates, respect opponents, and play fair.

Activity:

The TUF Sportsmanship "STAR" code is a general set of four objectives, much like the ones Plato created for the ancient Greeks (Piety, Courage, and Justice). Within the STAR code, there is room to create your own individual code or set of objectives you can live by both on and off the field. For each of the areas outlined by the STAR code, create two personal actions you will try to use in that category. Remember, they don't all have to be sports-related.

1. Show What You Can Do. Don't Talk About It.

Examples might be:

- I will not brag about my big plays at last night's game.
- I will do chores around the house without my mom asking, and I won't point out every little thing I've done.

1) _____

2) _____

2. Treat Everyone with Fairness

Examples might be:

- I will play fair, even when I am tempted to cheat when I am behind.
- I will not give my friends in another class period the test questions and answers after I've taken the test.

1) _____

2) _____

3. Avoid Retaliation

Examples might be:

- I will force myself to ignore a player when he is "trash-talking."
- When someone spreads a bad rumor about me, I will not start bad rumors about that person.

1) _____

2) _____

4. Respect Athleticism

Examples might be:

- I will help the other team's players up off the ground even if they just beat me out on a play.
- I will not boo or criticize a teammate when he messes up.

_____

_____

Table Talk:

- What is your biggest challenge when trying to practice good sportsmanship when your opponents are practicing bad sportsmanship?
- How do you practice good sportsmanship when you win? When you lose?
- How can you practice good sportsmanship when you get a bad call or something happens that's unfair?
- How can you help your teammates practice good sportsmanship when they get a bad call or something happens that's unfair?

CHAPTER 18

Citizenship

 Goal: Teach our children the definition of citizenship and how to responsibly serve others and their communities.

Raising a good citizen is about more than teaching rules—it's about shaping character. By reinforcing these values daily, you equip your child with the tools to become a responsible, compassionate, and engaged member of their community.

We typically don't see citizenship as one of the topics in a parenting book, per se, but it is an extremely important topic that often gets overlooked because, in a world where academic achievement and career success are highly emphasized, there's often more focus on skills that directly lead to those outcomes. As parents, we sometimes forget that good citizenship isn't just about following laws or rules—it's about fostering empathy, responsibility, and community involvement. Also, with all the distractions and pressures in our society, it can be easy to forget that teaching kids to care for others, the environment, and their community can be just as important for their overall development as academic knowledge.

Another factor is that it can be tricky to teach citizenship in a way that resonates with kids, especially in today's world of fast-paced change, social media, and global issues. But in reality, teaching kids to be engaged, compassionate citizens will help them navigate the world more thoughtfully, intentionally, and responsibly.

Let's look at this scenario:

Parent/Teen Dialogue Example:

Teen: "Ugh, I can't believe I have to go to that volunteer thing this weekend. It's not even like it's going to make a difference."

Parent: "I get that it might feel like a drag, but you know, sometimes it's easy to think that small actions don't matter. But every act of kindness, every bit of help, adds up."

Teen: "Yeah, but one day of cleaning up trash or helping out isn't going to solve anything. People still litter, people still don't care."

Parent: "It can feel like a lot of people don't care, but that's where good citizenship comes in. It's not about fixing everything in one go—it's about setting an example and creating momentum. When we choose to act, even if it seems small, we show others that it's important to care for the world and others around us."

Teen: "So, you think picking up trash makes me a good citizen?"

Parent: "Well, it's not just about picking up trash. It's about being part of something bigger than yourself. Good citizenship means caring about the community, making sure it's better for the next person, and doing what's right, whether people are watching or not."

Teen: "I mean, yeah, but there are so many bigger issues out there."

Parent: "Absolutely. And those bigger issues need people who are committed to acting, even in the smaller ways. If everyone waits for someone else to take the first step, nothing gets done. Good citizenship starts with us. You never know who's watching or who might get inspired by what you do."

Teen: "So, you're saying even if I don't think it's a big deal, my actions could influence others?"

Parent: "Exactly. It's the ripple effect. You do your part, and someone else might decide to step up, too. Imagine if everyone did just a little bit—how much better our communities would be. It's not about perfection, just about showing up and doing your part."

Teen: "Alright, I guess I can see how it could make a difference. I'll go."

Parent: "I'm proud of you. Even when it doesn't seem like it matters, I promise—it really does. You're part of making the world a better place. Feel good about that."

This dialogue is a good example of teaching our kids to think about others and that all of us are a part of something so much bigger—bigger than ourselves.

Teaching Your Kids About Citizenship

As parents, one of the greatest gifts we can give our children is the understanding of what it means to be a good citizen. Citizenship isn't just about where we live—it's about how we contribute to our communities, treat others, and uphold values like honesty, respect, and responsibility. So, why is it important to teach your kids about good citizenship? Because it shapes them into responsible, engaged, and ethical members of their communities. Here's why it's so important:

- **It Helps Kids Understand Their Role in Society**
  Teaching kids what it means to be a good citizen helps them see how their actions impact others, whether at home, school, or in their country.
- **It Builds Strong Character and Values**
  Good citizenship is rooted in core values like honesty, respect, responsibility, and kindness. When parents teach these values early, kids grow up with a strong moral foundation that guides their decisions.
- **It Prepares Kids to Be Future Leaders**
  Every great leader—whether in government, business, or community service—understands the importance of civic responsibility. By teaching kids about their rights and duties as citizens, parents equip them to be thoughtful and active participants in democracy.

- **It Strengthens Communities**
  A society thrives when its members care about each other. Kids who learn about citizenship are more likely to:
  - Follow rules and laws
  - Respect different opinions
  - Help those in need
  - Take pride in keeping their community safe and clean
- **It Encourages Critical Thinking and Awareness**
  Teaching citizenship means teaching kids to think for themselves. They learn how to:
  - Evaluate information (especially important in today's digital world).
  - Stand up for what is right.
  - Make informed decisions about voting and social issues as they grow older.
- **It Promotes Patriotism and Appreciation for Freedom**
  When kids understand the sacrifices made for their rights and freedoms, they develop a deeper appreciation for their country. Teaching them about history, democracy, and civic duties helps them respect the privileges they enjoy.
- **It Helps Kids Develop a Sense of Purpose**
  Being an active, responsible citizen gives kids a sense of belonging and purpose. It shows them that they have the power to make a difference—whether by volunteering, speaking up for a cause, or simply treating others with respect. By teaching kids about citizenship, parents are shaping the next generation of responsible, kind, and engaged individuals. It's not just about being a good citizen—it's about being a good human.

* * *

So now that you know why it's so important, you may be wondering HOW. How you can teach your child the importance of good citizenship:

1. Model Good Citizenship Yourself

Kids learn more from what they see than what they're told. Show them what it means to be a good citizen by living it—vote in elections and talk about why it matters, pick up litter even if it's not yours, or thank a veteran for their service. When they see you contributing to the community with kindness and responsibility, they'll naturally want to follow suit.

2. Start with Small, Age-Appropriate Responsibilities

Citizenship begins at home. Give your kids tasks that teach accountability—like feeding a pet, helping with chores, or keeping their room tidy—and explain how these little acts help the "family community." As they get older, expand it to school or neighborhood responsibilities, like helping a classmate or joining a cleanup day.

3. Teach Empathy Through Stories and Discussion

Read books or watch movies together that highlight citizenship, like stories about historical figures who stood up for justice or everyday people making a difference. Afterward, chat about it: "What would you do in that situation?" or "Why do you think they helped others?" It sparks their imagination and connects the dots to real life.

4. Get Them Involved in the Community

Hands-on experience is key. Take them to volunteer at a food bank, plant trees, or donate old toys to a shelter. Even simple acts, show them how their efforts ripple outward. Let them feel the pride of pitching in—it sticks with them.

5. Explain Rules and Why They Matter

Kids often see rules as annoying, but frame them as the backbone of a happy community. Say, "We stop at red lights so everyone stays safe," or "We take turns talking so everyone gets heard." Tie it to their world—like taking turns on the playground—and they'll start to see how rules keep things fair and smooth for everybody.

6. Encourage Respect for Differences

Good citizens value diverse perspectives. When you're out in the world, point out how people live differently—maybe a neighbor celebrates a unique holiday or speaks another language. Ask, "What do you think that's like for them?" It builds empathy and teaches them to respect others, even when they don't agree.

7. Talk About Rights and Responsibilities

Kids love hearing about their rights—like freedom to speak or play—but balance it with the flip side. Explain, "You get to share your ideas, but you also have to listen to others," or "We're free to go to school, so we should make the most of it." Keep it simple, but show how the two go hand in hand.

8. Make History and Democracy Relatable

Tell them stories about how their country came to be—focus on heroes they'd admire, like brave kids in history or everyday people who changed things. Play a game where they "vote" on family decisions (pizza or tacos for dinner?) to show how voices shape outcomes. It's a fun way to plant the seeds of civic duty.

9. Celebrate Their Efforts

When your kid does something "citizen-like"—say, helping a friend or picking up trash—praise them for it. "That was so kind! You made our space better." Positive reinforcement makes them feel like their actions count, which they do.

10. Keep the Conversation Going

Citizenship isn't a one-time lesson—it's a lifelong mindset. Ask open-ended questions over dinner: "What's one way you helped someone today?" or "What would you change in our town?" Listen to their ideas, and they'll feel like active players in the world around them.

* * *

By weaving these habits into daily life, you're not just teaching citizenship—you're raising kids who *feel* it in their bones. They'll grow up knowing they're part of something bigger, with the tools to make it better.

1. Define Citizenship in Simple Terms

Start by explaining that a citizen is simply a person who is part of a community—whether that's a country, a state, a town, a school, or even a sports team. Next, expand on the idea that citizenship is about the duties, rights, and privileges of being part of that community. Ask your child: "What kind of citizen do you want to be?"

2. Teach Key Values of Good Citizenship

Here are essential principles to discuss with your child:

- **Be Honest and Trustworthy:** Encourage your child to keep their promises and tell the truth. Trust is the foundation of a strong community.
- **Respect Others' Rights and Property:** Teach them to treat people fairly and kindly, even when they disagree. Respect also means taking care of things and returning borrowed items in good condition.
- **Show Compassion:** Help your child recognize when someone is struggling and encourage them to take action, whether by offering kind words, helping a friend, or participating in community service.
- **Demonstrate Courage:** Talk about the importance of standing up for what's right, even when it's hard. Share stories of courageous historical figures to inspire them.
- **Be Responsible:** Teach your child to follow through on commitments, whether it's turning in homework on time, doing chores, or picking up after their pet.
- **Follow Rules and Obey the Law:** Explain that laws and rules help keep communities safe and fair. Reinforce that making good choices now will help them avoid trouble later.

- **Be Loyal to Your Country:** Discuss the importance of voting, honoring national holidays, and using one's voice to improve their community.
- **Get Involved in the Community:** Encourage them to participate in local events, volunteer work, and help neighbors. Small acts of kindness can have a big impact.
- **Protect the Environment:** Instill habits like recycling, saving energy, and not littering to help preserve the planet for future generations.
- **Practice Digital Citizenship:** Teach responsible online behavior, including thinking before posting, respecting privacy, and avoiding harmful digital interactions.

3. Lead by Example

The best way to teach our children citizenship is to model it ourselves. Show honesty in your interactions, demonstrate kindness, volunteer together, and discuss current events to help them understand their role in the bigger picture. We can have a large impact on them by being intentional about giving back to our community.

4. Make It Interactive

Give your child opportunities to practice citizenship through activities like:

- Listing ways they can be honest and trustworthy at home and in school.
- Discussing examples of respectful behavior and how to handle disagreements.
- Finding ways to show compassion in their community.
- Exploring inspiring stories of courageous leaders.
- Identifying simple ways to be responsible, such as turning off lights and finishing homework on time.
- Participating in a local clean-up day or community event.
- Brainstorming positive ways to engage on social media.
- Learning more about our country and how we gained our freedom.

5. Empower Them to Make a Difference

Let your child know that their actions matter! Whether it's being kind to a classmate, writing a letter to a local leader, or helping a neighbor, they have the power to create positive change. Small actions can lead to big results!

* * *

By weaving these lessons into daily life, parents can help raise responsible, engaged citizens who appreciate and protect the freedoms they enjoy.

It's so important to teach our kids the link between freedom and responsibility. I have an excellent book recommendation for you to read with your child!

If You Can Keep It: The Forgotten Promise of American Liberty by Eric Metaxas

Our children (as well as some adults) may take our freedom for granted as they may not realize what it took to gain our freedom from British rule and what it actually takes to KEEP our freedom.

A short summary...

If You Can Keep It: The Forgotten Promise of American Liberty by Eric Metaxas is a passionate wake-up call about the fragility and brilliance of American freedom. Drawing from history, faith, and a famous response from Benjamin Franklin when asked what kind of government the Founding Fathers had created—"A republic, if you can keep it"—Metaxas argues that liberty isn't a given; it's a gift that demands active care. He dives into what he calls the "Golden Triangle of Freedom": the interplay of virtue, faith, and liberty, insisting that a free society only thrives when its people are morally grounded and engaged. The book traces America's roots to show how a shared sense of purpose once held the nation together. Metaxas warns that this unity's fading—blaming cultural drift, apathy, and a shrugging-off of civic duty. He stresses the importance of "heroic citizenship," urging readers to step up, vote, teach kids about America's ideals, and live with integrity, or risk losing it all. With his knack for storytelling (think *Bonhoeffer* vibes), Metaxas mixes reverence for the past with a nudge—well, actually, more like a shove—to get off the couch and keep America's promise alive. It's a bold take on why freedom is worth the fight. If we don't actively keep it, we will lose it. Key themes in the book include:

- **The Role of Moral Virtue:** Metaxas stresses that liberty cannot exist without a foundation of morality, echoing the Founders' belief that self-governance requires a virtuous people.
- **The Importance of Civic Engagement:** He calls on modern Americans to take an active role in preserving democracy, from voting to understanding the nation's history.
- **The Fragility of Freedom:** Using historical examples, he warns that when people take their freedoms for granted, they risk losing them.
- **America's Unique Calling:** Metaxas argues that the U.S. has a special role in promoting liberty and justice worldwide.

If You Can Keep It serves as both a history lesson and a call to action, urging Americans to rekindle their commitment to the ideals that made the nation great and our duty to take action to keep it great.

Let's look at some activities that will help kids of all ages learn about freedom, responsibility, and good citizenship in fun and meaningful ways.

Activities:

Elementary School-Aged Kids (Ages 5–11)

At this stage, kids learn best through hands-on activities, storytelling, and simple discussions.

1. "Freedom & Responsibility" Chart

- **Activity:** Create a chart with two columns: *Freedoms I Have* and *Responsibilities I Have*.

- **Example:**
    - *Freedom*: I can play outside.
    - *Responsibility*: I have to clean up my toys.
- **Lesson:** Helps kids understand that with every freedom comes responsibility.

2. Storytime with American Heroes

- **Activity:** Read books or tell stories about historical figures like George Washington, Harriet Tubman, or Martin Luther King Jr.
- **Example Books:**
    - *I Am George Washington* by Brad Meltzer
    - *Martin's Big Words* by Doreen Rappaport
- **Lesson:** Show how people used their freedoms to help others and make a difference.

3. "Citizen of the Day" Recognition

- **Activity:** Every day, recognize a child who shows good citizenship (e.g., sharing, helping, following rules).
- **Lesson:** Reinforces positive behavior and the idea that small actions make a big difference.

4. "My Community, My Responsibility" Scavenger Hunt

- **Activity:** Take a walk and look for examples of good citizenship (e.g., a stop sign, a recycling bin, a library). Make a checklist and discuss how each contributes to a strong community.
- **Lesson:** Helps kids recognize how rules, responsibilities, and shared spaces keep a community working well.

5. Patriotic Art & Songs

- **Activity:** Teach kids the meaning of the Pledge of Allegiance and national songs like "America the Beautiful." Have them draw a picture of what freedom means to them.
- **Lesson:** Encourages appreciation for national values in a fun and creative way.

Teens (Ages 12–18)

Teens benefit from discussions, real-world applications, and opportunities to take action.

1. "What Would You Do?" Debate Game

- **Activity:** Present scenarios related to citizenship (e.g., "You see someone littering—do you say something?" or "A friend shares false information online—how do you handle it?"). Discuss possible responses.
- **Lesson:** Encourages critical thinking and moral decision-making.

2. "Write to a Leader" Project

- **Activity:** Have teens write a letter or email to their mayor, governor, or representative about an issue they care about.
- **Lesson:** Shows them that their voice matters in a democracy.

3. Digital Citizenship Pledge

- **Activity:** Have teens create a personal "digital citizenship" pledge that includes:
    - o Only posting respectful comments.
    - o Thinking before sharing information.
    - o Avoiding online bullying.
- **Lesson:** Helps them understand that good citizenship applies online, too.

4. Volunteer Challenge

- **Activity:** Challenge teens to complete **four acts of service** in a month (e.g., volunteering at an animal shelter, helping a neighbor, donating clothes).
- **Lesson:** Reinforces the value of civic engagement and personal responsibility.

 **Action Steps:**

Here are **daily ways** parents can reinforce good citizenship at home in simple, natural ways:

1. Model Good Citizenship

Kids learn best by watching you! Show them what it means to be a responsible, engaged citizen through your actions:

- Follow rules and laws (e.g., wear a seatbelt, obey traffic signs).
- Treat others with respect and kindness.
- Vote and talk about why it's important.
- Stay informed about current events and explain them in an age-appropriate way.

2. Encourage Responsibility at Home

- Give kids **age-appropriate chores** and explain how contributing to the household is like being a good citizen in a community.
- Teach accountability (e.g., if they forget their homework, they take responsibility instead of making excuses).
- Emphasize keeping shared spaces clean—just like they would in their town or school.

3. Talk About Rights & Responsibilities

- Discuss **why rules exist** (e.g., traffic lights prevent accidents, school rules create fairness).
- Explain the **balance of freedom and responsibility** (e.g., you have the right to play, but you also have the responsibility to clean up).
- When kids complain about rules, ask them, **"What would happen if no one followed this rule?"**

4. Get Involved in the Community

- Take them to community events like **parades, clean-up days, or local charity drives**.

- Volunteer together (e.g., help at a food bank, donate clothes, or visit a nursing home).
- If they're old enough, encourage them to **write a letter to a local leader** about an issue they care about.

5. Teach Respect for Others

- Encourage **respectful conversations** at the dinner table, even when people disagree.
- Discuss different cultures, backgrounds, and perspectives.
- Teach **how to handle conflict peacefully** (e.g., using "I" statements, listening before responding).

6. Promote Digital Citizenship

- Set screen time and online behavior expectations.
- Talk about **kindness and responsibility online** (e.g., "Would you say this to someone's face?").
- Encourage **posting positive things** and avoiding gossip or negativity.

7. Discuss Real-World Examples

- Watch the news together (kid-friendly versions like *TIME for Kids* or *Scholastic News*).
- Ask, **"What do you think about this?"** and encourage critical thinking.
- Share stories of people who stood up for what's right.

8. Celebrate Citizenship Together

- Acknowledge national holidays like **Veterans Day, Independence Day, and MLK Day** by talking about their significance.
- Teach kids the **Pledge of Allegiance** and what it means.
- Find small ways to **show appreciation for service members, teachers, and community helpers** (e.g., writing thank-you notes).

9. Encourage Problem-Solving

- When kids see a problem, ask, **"How can you help fix it?"**
- Encourage **small acts of service**, like picking up trash, helping a neighbor, or being kind to a new student at school.

10. Reinforce the Power of Their Voice

- Let kids make small choices at home to practice decision-making.
- Encourage them to **speak up** when they see something unfair.
- Show them how voting works by taking them with you to the polls or letting them "vote" on family decisions.

By incorporating these habits into daily life, kids will naturally develop the mindset of a good citizen—one who is responsible, respectful, and ready to make a difference!

Table Talk 1:

- How do you feel when someone is being disrespectful to someone you know? How should you handle that?
- How do you feel about being respectful to those in authority over you when you don't agree with them? Why is this the right thing to do?

Table Talk 2:

- Talk about times when you have shown compassion and courage. Then, ask your child to discuss ways that they have shown compassion and courage, and ways that they can show both in the future.
- You have just heard about many ways to be loyal to your community. Is there something that you are passionate about, something you would like to see changed or improved in your school or community? How would you use "your voice" to try to create change? Who or

what would you be helping? What will that plan look like? Who would help you? Have your child choose one area of responsibility from each: community, home, and school that they would like to improve upon. Set goals to accomplish. (E.g., complete my homework without being reminded, spend more time helping my neighbors, help my parents out with the dishes, etc.)

CHAPTER 19

Raising Strong Leaders

🎯 **Goal: Equip your children with the skills to become strong, confident leaders by teaching essential character traits and providing them with a clear, actionable roadmap for success.**

In our fast-paced and ever-changing world, leadership is a crucial skill that our kids need to learn early that can set them up for lifelong success. Leadership is a quality that empowers kids to make good decisions, take responsibility, and positively influence those around them. Teaching leadership at a young age will help our kids build confidence, resilience, and strong communication skills, preparing them to navigate challenges and create opportunities. If we instill these values early, we can help shape future leaders who will thrive in their personal and professional lives.

Why Parents Should Teach Leadership to Kids Early: Building Tomorrow's Trailblazers

Leadership isn't just for CEOs or presidents. It's a life skill that shapes how kids tackle challenges, connect with others, and carve their path in the real world. When parents introduce leadership to their children at a young age, they're not just prepping them to run a boardroom someday; they're equipping them to navigate schoolyard squabbles, stand up for what's right, and grow into adults who don't just follow the crowd... They steer it. Here's why starting early matters, and why it's on parents to light that spark. Leadership lessons at a young age ripple into every corner of life. Take teamwork on a soccer field. It teaches kids how to listen, delegate, and cheer others on. These skills can be used in classrooms, friendships, and future jobs. Or resilience: a little league captain who loses a game but rallies the team for the next one learns to bounce back—a trait that's linked to long-term success. Even empathy grows. Leading means seeing others' strengths and struggles, like when a kid figures out how to include the shy one sitting by himself at lunch into his lunch group. Parents who teach this aren't just raising leaders; they're raising humans who can handle conflict, build community, and keep going when the going gets tough.

Early Habits Stick

Kids are wired to learn fast, especially when they're young. Neuroscientists, like those cited in studies from the National Institutes of Health, point out that the brain's plasticity peaks before adolescence, making it a golden window for planting big ideas like leadership. A 5-year-old who learns to take initiative—like organizing a game with friends—starts building neural pathways for confidence and decision-making. Wait until they're a sullen teen glued to their phone, and you're fighting an uphill battle against hormones and TikTok. Teaching leadership early turns it into second nature, not a chore tacked on later when they're less moldable. Parents who miss this opportunity when their kids are young risk raising kids who just coast through life waiting for someone else to call the shots.

Have a Plan: Confidence Grows from Doing, Not Dreaming

Leadership isn't about bossing people around—it's about stepping up, solving problems, and owning your choices. Kids don't get that from wishful thinking; they need practice. Parents who encourage a 7-year-old to lead a cleanup after a playdate or speak up when a sibling's hogging the Xbox are handing them real-world reps. Research from the Search Institute shows that kids who take on small responsibilities early (like leading a group project) score higher in self-esteem and problem-solving by their teens. That confidence snowballs: a kid who can rally their pals for a lemonade stand today might pitch a bold idea at work tomorrow. Without that early nudge, they might shrink back, letting others take the wheel. Encourage your kids to be intentional and carry out their ideas.

Countering the "Follower Culture"

Let's face it: today's world doesn't always scream "lead." Social media pumps out trends to chase, not ideas to shape. Teens feel more pressure to conform than ever—likes and retweets can drown out original thought. Parents who teach leadership early push back against that tide. A kid who learns to stand firm—say, pitching a new club at school despite eye-rolls—won't just blend into the scroll. They'll question, create, and take risks. Without that grounding, they might grow up outsourcing their decisions to influencers or algorithms, missing out on their own voice.

We Are Their First Mentors

No one's closer to our kids than we are, right? We see the meltdowns, the wins, the quiet moments where lessons sink in. Schools might toss in a leadership workshop, but it's Mom or Dad saying, "You figure out how we're splitting these chores," that sticks. Parents can model it, too. Leading a family meeting with fairness shows kids how it's done. If parents don't step up, who will? Coaches and teachers help, but home is where the foundation is set.

Teaching leadership early isn't just about the kid—it's about the ripple. A child who learns to lead with kindness might inspire their friends, then their coworkers, then a whole community. Parents who plant that seed aren't just raising a leader—they're launching a chain reaction. Blow it off, and you might get a capable kid who never realizes they could've been exceptional.

Teaching them early on isn't a luxury—it's a must. It's how parents turn curious, messy little humans into confident, capable big ones. From wiring their brains for boldness to arming them against a conformist world, these early lessons pay off in ways that stretch far beyond childhood. It's not about forcing them to be president—it's about showing them they can lead their own life, and maybe others', with purpose. Parents who take this on aren't just guiding their kids; they're shaping the kind of world those kids will inherit—and that's worth starting before the training wheels come off.

Let's Look at Key Leadership Traits

1. **Confidence:** Leaders have a strong sense of who they are and a healthy sense of self-worth. They believe in themselves, stand up for what they believe in, and take initiative. Encouraging our kids to believe in their abilities fosters resilience and self-trust.

2. **Honesty & Integrity:** In order to establish and maintain trust, a true leader is honest and stands by their values. Teaching our kids accountability and doing the right thing, even when no one is watching, strengthens their moral compass.

3. **Resourcefulness:** Leaders find solutions, adapt to challenges, and use available resources wisely. Encouraging our kids to think creatively and problem-solve helps them develop resilience and confidence in their abilities.

4. **Respect:** Effective leaders show respect for others, valuing diverse perspectives and treating people with kindness. Teaching our kids to listen, acknowledge others, and express appreciation fosters strong relationships.

5. **Decision-Making:** Leadership involves making good, informed choices. Guiding kids to think critically, weigh options, and consider long-term consequences builds their confidence in decision-making.

6. **Communication:** A good leader listens actively and expresses ideas clearly. Teaching effective speaking, listening, and acknowledging others' contributions helps our children become strong communicators who inspire and motivate others.

7. **Responsibility:** Taking ownership of actions and commitments is key to leadership. Instilling a strong work ethic and a sense of accountability helps our kids develop discipline and reliability.

8. **Humility:** Encouraging kids to recognize their strengths while remaining open to learning from others fosters teamwork and self-improvement. Great leaders seek growth and acknowledge they don't have all the answers.

9. **Sharing a Vision:** A leader is able to articulate a goal or a vision with clarity, passion, and strength. They inspire a group by guiding them toward a shared goal and helping them see the bigger picture.

10. **Tenacity, Grit, and Determination:** Leaders overcome obstacles and challenges by believing in themselves, working effectively with others, and maintaining a positive attitude. Encouraging our kids to persevere through setbacks builds resilience.

11. **Organization:** A leader moves forward with intention. Whether through setting clear goals or following intuition, leaders must have a structured approach to achieving their vision. Teaching our kids to plan and prioritize helps develop these skills.

Real-Life Example: The Story of Max

Max, a 14-year-old, was nervous about running for student government. He doubted whether his friends thought that he had the leadership skills to make an impact. His parents encouraged him to step outside his comfort zone, helped him practice speeches, brainstormed campaign ideas, and helped him build self-confidence. Unfortunately, Max lost the election, but the good news was that he learned resilience and perseverance. His parents encouraged him to run again the following year. Well, he ran again and won! He learned so many valuable lessons through this experience and learned that leadership is about tenacity, grit, and determination.

Let's look at this parent/teen dialogue.

 **Parent (Dad)/Teen Dialogue Example:**

Teen: "I don't think I can be a leader. I'm not the funniest or the smartest guy in my class."

Parent: "Leadership isn't about being the funniest. It's about setting a good example, making good decisions, and helping others. Can you think of a time when you helped someone?"

Teen: "Yeah, last week I helped a friend who was struggling with math."

Parent: "That's leadership! You saw a need and stepped up. What if leadership isn't about being perfect but about making a difference, one small action at a time?"

Teen: "I never thought of it that way. Maybe I can lead in my own way."

Parent: "Exactly. Think about people you admire—whether in your school, community, or even famous leaders. Many of them lead in different ways. Some lead by example, some by speaking up, and others by working hard behind the scenes."

Teen: "I guess I do admire my friend Cooper. He always helps out when someone needs something, and people respect him. But he doesn't have to be the funniest guy, either."

Parent: "That's a great observation. Leadership is about influence, not volume. What are some ways you think you can practice leadership in your daily life?"

Teen: "Maybe by helping out more and speaking up when I have good ideas instead of keeping quiet. I could also support my friends when they need it."

Parent: "Those are all great ideas! Leadership starts with small choices that build confidence over time. The more you practice, the more natural it will feel. And remember, mistakes are part of the process. Leaders learn and grow from them."

Teen: "Yeah, I think I can do that. I'll start looking for small ways to step up. Thanks Dad!"

Parent: "Yep! I believe in you. You have so many great leadership qualities already!"

This Dad did an excellent job helping his son in this scenario. Let's break it down.

1. **Reframing Leadership:** The teen initially equates leadership with being "the funniest or the smartest," which reflects a narrow, possibly stereotypical view. The parent gently corrects this by redefining

leadership as "setting a good example, making good decisions, and helping others." This shift broadens the teen's perspective and makes leadership feel more attainable.

2. **Encouraging Reflection:** By asking, "Can you think of a time when you helped someone?" the parent prompts the teen to recognize their own strengths and past actions. This builds self-awareness and confidence, as the teen recalls a concrete example (helping a friend with math).

3. **Positive Reinforcement:** The parent immediately validates the teen's example with "That's leadership!" This affirmation ties the teen's real-life experience to the concept of leadership, making it personal and relevant. The follow-up question—"What if leadership isn't about being perfect but about making a difference, one small action at a time?"—further reinforces this by emphasizing effort over perfection.

4. **Shifting Perspective:** The parent encourages the teen to "think about people you admire" and how they lead in different ways. This helps the teen see leadership as diverse and multifaceted, not a one-size-fits-all trait. The teen's mention of Alex shows they're starting to internalize this idea, noticing leadership in quieter, supportive actions.

5. **Practical Application:** By asking, "What are some ways you think you can practice leadership in your daily life?" the parent shifts the conversation from abstract to actionable. This empowers the teen to come up with their own ideas (helping out, speaking up, supporting friends), fostering ownership and initiative.

6. **Building Confidence:** The parent's encouragement—"Those are all great ideas!"—and reassurance that "leadership starts with small choices that build confidence over time" provide a roadmap for growth. Acknowledging that "mistakes are part of the process" also normalizes setbacks, reducing pressure and fear of failure.

7. **Emotional Support:** The closing lines—"I believe in you. You have so many great leadership qualities already!"—offer warmth and belief in the teen's potential. This emotional backing is crucial for motivating the teen to take risks and try leading in their own way.

Overall Assessment

The parent excelled by listening attentively, reframing the teen's misconceptions, and guiding them toward a more confident and practical understanding of leadership. They used open-ended questions to spark reflection, provided positive reinforcement, and offered a balance of encouragement and actionable advice. The teen's shift from self-doubt ("I don't think I can be a leader") to optimism ("I think I can do that") shows the parent's approach was both effective and uplifting. This dialogue models a supportive, growth-oriented parenting style that empowers the teen to see their potential. Great job, Dad!

 **Action Steps for Teens:**

1. **Take Initiative:** Look for small leadership opportunities in everyday life (helping a friend, volunteering, speaking up in class).
2. **Practice Decision-Making:** Start weighing options before making choices to build confidence.
3. **Embrace Challenges:** Step out of your comfort zone and try new experiences.
4. **Communicate Effectively:** Practice active listening and expressing your thoughts clearly.
5. **Lead by Example:** Show responsibility, integrity, and empathy in daily interactions.

Leadership isn't just about titles—it's about actions. By teaching kids these key skills, parents can help shape confident, responsible leaders who will make a difference in the world.

Leadership Activity: The Decision-Making Challenge

Objective: Teach kids how to make thoughtful and confident decisions.

Instructions:

1. Present your teen with a real or hypothetical scenario (e.g., choosing between joining a club or focusing on sports).
2. Have them list the pros and cons of each option.
3. Encourage them to think about how each choice aligns with their values and goals.
4. Let them make the decision and reflect on the process.

Lesson Learned: Leadership is about making choices with confidence and considering long-term impact.

Table Talk:

- What does being a leader mean to you, and who is someone you admire as a leader?
- Can you think of a time when you had to make a tough decision? How did you handle it?
- How do you think a good leader should treat others, especially those who may disagree with them?
- What are some ways you can show leadership at school, home, or in your community?
- How do you handle failure or setbacks, and what can you learn from them as a leader?

CHAPTER 20

Mental Health—We Have to Talk About It

This chapter wasn't originally part of the plan. But as I kept writing and reflecting on the world our kids are growing up in, it became clear: We have to talk about mental health. It's one of the most relevant and urgent topics in parenting today.

The numbers alone are hard to ignore:

- **Nearly 1 in 5 kids experience a mental health disorder each year.** About 1 in 5 children in the U.S. have a diagnosable mental, emotional, developmental, or behavioral disorder in a given year (Centers for Disease Control and Prevention [CDC], 2023).
- **Teen anxiety and depression have doubled in the last decade.** National data show sharp increases in adolescent anxiety and depression diagnoses over the past decade (National Academies of Sciences, Engineering, and Medicine, 2023).
- **Nearly 50% of high school students report feeling persistently sad or hopeless.** According to the 2023 Youth Risk Behavior Survey, almost two in five high school students reported persistent feelings of sadness or hopelessness (CDC, 2023).
- **Suicide is now the second leading cause of death for ages 10–24.** Suicide is the second leading cause of death among individuals aged 10–34, which includes the 10–24 age range (National Institute of Mental Health [NIMH], 2024).

These aren't just statistics—they're a wake-up call. Our kids are overwhelmed, anxious, disconnected, and in many cases, silently struggling.

As parents, we may not have all the answers. But we do have a powerful role to play. We can create space for open dialogue. We can model calm in the chaos. We can validate feelings, guide our kids through the hard stuff, and remind them they're not alone.

This chapter isn't about clinical diagnoses or quick fixes. It's about practical ways to connect, check in, and support your child's emotional well-being right in the middle of everyday life. Because our presence, not our perfection, can be the lifeline they need most.

So, What Can We Do?

We start by paying attention, not just to behavior, but to what's underneath it.

A child who seems defiant might actually be overwhelmed. A teen who isolates might be feeling anxious or ashamed. What looks like "attitude" is often a silent cry for help.

That's why *connection* matters so much. When kids feel emotionally safe with us—when they know they can talk without being judged or "fixed"—they're far more likely to open up.

Instead of asking, "How was your day?" (which often gets a one-word answer), try asking:

- "What part of today was the hardest?"
- "Did anything feel heavy today?"
- "On a scale from 1 to 10, how full is your stress bucket?"

And if your child says "I don't know" or shrugs you off? Don't panic. Just keep showing up. Your consistent, grounded presence is more powerful than you think.

When Your Child Shuts Down or Melts Down

What to Say When Emotions Are High:

- "I'm here. You don't have to figure this out alone."
- "Your feelings are allowed. I can handle big emotions."
- "You don't have to talk right now. But I'm ready when you are."
- "Let's take a few breaths together."
- "This feels big. Want to take a walk or sit in silence for a bit?"

What Not to Say:

✗ "You're overreacting."

✗ "Calm down!"

✗ "You're fine. There's nothing to be upset about."

✗ "If you don't stop, there will be consequences."

Tip: You don't have to "fix it." Just be the steady presence. When you stay regulated, your child begins to learn how to do the same.

Parent-Child Dialogue Examples

Example 1: Younger Child (Age 6–9)

Scenario: Your child is upset because she felt left out during recess.

Parent: "You look sad. Do you want to tell me what happened at school today?"

Child: "Nobody asked me to play at recess. I felt left out."

Parent: "That sounds really hurtful. It's okay to feel upset about that."

Child: "I just wanted to play with them."

Parent: "I understand. It's hard to feel left out. Would you like to tell me who you wanted to play with, or maybe think about ways that can help you be included, or ways you can reach out to other friends?"

Child: "Maybe."

> **Parent:** "Take some time and think about it, and whenever you're ready, I'm here to listen."
>
> **Child:** "Thanks so much, Mom."

How this helps the child:

- **Names the Emotion Safely:** The parent gently opens the door: *"You look sad..."* This validates the child's emotions instead of minimizing or rushing past them.
- **Creates Emotional Safety:** Saying *"That sounds really hurtful. It's okay to feel upset about that"* teaches the child that uncomfortable feelings are normal, accepted, and safe to share.
- **Encourages Reflection, Not Reaction:** The parent doesn't jump in to "fix it" or scold the other kids. Instead, she invites the child to explore options: *"Would you like to think of ways to be included or reach out to others?"*
- **Builds Problem-Solving Skills:** The child learns they have some agency. It's not about forcing friendships but exploring new ways to connect with guidance.
- **Models Calm and Connection:** The parent stays grounded and loving. This reinforces that the child is *not alone* in their feelings, even if the playground felt lonely.

Example 2: Teen (Age 13–17)

Scenario: Your teen feels overwhelmed with school, activities, and expectations.

Parent: "Hey, you seem really stressed lately. Want to talk about what's on your plate?"

Teen: "It's just too much—school, practice, everything. I don't know how to keep up."

Parent: "That sounds exhausting. I'm sorry you're feeling this way."

Teen: "I just want a break, but I don't think I can."

Parent: "I hear you. How about we figure out what can wait or get some help to make it easier? You don't have to do it all alone."

Teen: "Thanks, that would help me a lot!"

Parent: "I'm here for you always. Let's figure it out."

How this helps the teen:

1. **Opens the Door Without Pressure:** *"Hey, you seem really stressed lately..."* respects the teen's space while inviting conversation. It doesn't accuse or demand.

2. **Validates Feelings Without Judgment:** Saying *"That sounds exhausting"* acknowledges the weight of what the teen is carrying. Teens need to feel *seen* more than they need quick solutions.

3. **Reinforces They're Not Alone:** Offering, *"You don't have to do it all alone,"* fights the toxic pressure many teens feel to perform, please, and power through silently.

4. **Promotes Collaboration, Not Control:** Instead of taking over or minimizing, the parent offers partnership: *"Let's figure out what can wait."* This preserves the teen's autonomy while providing support.

5. **Normalizes Struggle and Support:** It models that it's okay to ask for help. It also signals that hard days don't define them, and they don't have to hide it.

Big Picture: Why These Dialogues Matter

These aren't just "nice" conversations. They're teaching tools that help children and teens:

- Feel emotionally safe
- Learn to name and express feelings
- Develop coping and problem-solving skills
- Trust that they are loved and supported even in their low moments

And most of all, they build *relational resilience*—the kind of connection that helps our kids bounce back, believe in themselves, and know they're worthy of love and support, no matter what they're going through.

Real-Life Moment: The Power of Showing Up

A mom I worked with once shared a moment with her 15-year-old son. He'd been quiet for weeks—angry, distant, refusing to engage. She had tried everything.

One night, instead of confronting or correcting him, she simply sat beside him and said: "You don't have to tell me everything. But I want you to know I see something's off, and I'm here. Always."

At first, he said nothing. Then, with tears in his eyes, he whispered: "I don't even know what's wrong. I just feel heavy all the time."

That one moment didn't solve everything. But it cracked the door open. Slowly, they talked. With the help of a therapist, things began to shift.

Sometimes, the win isn't a solution—it's a safe space.

Helping Teens Cope with Stress

Life throws plenty at our teens—from daily stressors like tests and friend drama to bigger challenges that linger in the background like a soundtrack. When teens feel unprepared or overwhelmed, stress can build up fast. And while we can't protect them from every hard thing, we can help them build the coping tools they'll need to get through it stronger.

1. Help Them Understand the Situation

One of the best ways to lower stress is by helping your teen name exactly what they're facing and how they feel about it. This gives them clarity, which builds confidence.

Try this:

Ask your teen to describe what's stressful in just a sentence or two.

→ "What's feeling hard or heavy for you right now?"

Then ask:

→ "What emotions are coming up because of this?" Encourage them to write it down or talk it out.

Example:

→ "We moved, and I started a new school. I feel lonely, sad, and mad. I miss my old friends and feel nervous about keeping up in my classes."

Next, help them gather information. What can they learn about their situation? Who else has gone through something similar? Knowledge can bring a sense of control and remind them they're not alone.

2. Encourage a Positive Mindset

A positive attitude doesn't mean pretending everything is fine—it means helping your teen stay open, hopeful, and solution-focused, even when things are hard.

What you can say:

→ "What you're feeling is totally valid—and you have what it takes to handle this."

Help them notice when they're stuck in "stinkin' thinkin'"—thoughts like "This is hopeless" or "I can't do this." Gently help them reframe with more empowering thoughts:

→ "This is hard, but I can take it one step at a time."

→ "Others have done it—and I can, too."

You can also encourage daily gratitude. Ask:

→ "What are three things you're thankful for today?"

Gratitude doesn't erase problems, but it puts them in perspective and boosts resilience.

3. Guide Them Toward Action

Stress often makes teens feel stuck or powerless. Helping them take even one small step toward change can build momentum and lower anxiety.

Questions to ask:

→ "What parts of this situation can you do something about?"

→ "What's one thing you could try this week to make it a little better?"

Example:

→ "I'm going to talk to the kid next to me in Spanish class and ask if we can study together."

Also, remind them to get support—whether from you, another trusted adult, a school counselor, a coach, or a therapist. Let them know that asking for help isn't weakness—it's wisdom.

And most importantly? Help them care for themselves. Sleep, exercise, and downtime aren't luxuries—they're tools for staying strong under stress.

Encourage things like:

- Listening to music
- Spending time with pets
- Cooking, journaling, or getting outside
- Taking breaks from screens and social pressure

Remind them:

→ "Stress is hard—but it's also something you can handle. Let's focus on what you can control, and we'll take it step by step."

When teens learn to process their feelings, shift their mindset, and take small, doable actions, they don't just survive hard moments—they grow from them. And you, as their parent, are their greatest source of steadiness and strength.

When to Get Extra Support

Sometimes, love and connection aren't enough on their own—and that's okay. Knowing when to seek help is part of parenting with wisdom and courage.

Warning signs to watch for:

- Withdrawal from friends, family, or activities
- Changes in sleep, eating, or energy
- Frequent emotional outbursts or deep sadness
- Drop in academic performance
- Talk of worthlessness or being a burden
- Self-harm or suicidal language

What to do:

1. Stay calm. Don't dismiss—but don't panic.
2. Open the door to conversation:
   "I've noticed some changes, and I want to check in. I love you, and I'm here."
3. Normalize therapy:
   "Just like we see a doctor for our body, it's okay to talk to someone about what's going on in our mind."
4. Reach out. Contact a therapist, school counselor, pediatrician, or a trusted mental health professional.

Reminder: Getting help is not a failure. It's one of the bravest things we can model for our kids.

Before We Go On: Beware the Trap of Self-Pity

Before we move into how to help our kids boost their mental health, there's one important mindset we need to talk about first: the trap of self-pity. It can sneak in quietly and feel justified when life gets hard, but if left unchecked, it can stall emotional growth, block resilience, and keep kids (and adults) stuck. It often creeps in when life feels unfair or overwhelming, and while it's natural to feel sad or frustrated, staying stuck in those emotions can lead to a victim mindset. Self-pity says, "Nothing ever goes my way," and convinces us we're powerless. Over time, it can block growth, steal motivation, and create a negative lens through which we see the world. One of the best things we can do as parents is help our kids name this mindset when it shows up, remind them that hard things happen to everyone, and guide them toward action instead of blame. Empowerment begins when we shift the focus from *what happened to me* to *how I choose to respond*. That's when real resilience starts to take root.

Let's be real: almost *everyone* goes through hard things, especially in the teen years. Maybe you've experienced being bullied, growing up in poverty, dealing with an unstable home life, going through a painful breakup, being cut from a team, getting rejected from something you really wanted, losing a job, or being left out by friends. These moments hurt. And they're real. You're not wrong for feeling upset about them.

But what happens next is important. When we stay stuck in self-pity—thinking life isn't fair or hoping others will join us in our misery—it can spiral quickly. We start seeing ourselves as victims with no control, and sometimes, we even want others to feel the same pain we do. Left unchecked, self-pity can lead to bitterness, resentment, and even destructive behavior. At its worst, it turns inward into depression or outward into anger at the world.

Think about it this way: some people respond to suffering by blaming others or becoming angry at society. This approach only deepens the pain and isolates them further. Sadly, history gives us extreme examples—like Adolf Hitler—who allowed his bitterness to grow into something horrific. While that may seem like an extreme comparison, it shows how unchecked pain and self-pity can turn toxic.

But there's another way—the *right* way.

The healthy response to suffering is to turn our focus outward. Instead of getting stuck in our pain, we look for ways to help others through theirs. This might sound strange, but it's actually one of the most healing things we can do. When we stop dwelling on what we've lost and start lifting others, something shifts. Helping others helps *us*, too.

Ronald Reagan, one of America's greatest presidents, grew up in poverty with an alcoholic father who abandoned their family. But instead of wallowing in what they didn't have, his mother made it a mission to serve others. She made soup daily for the homeless who arrived by train. Reagan said he never realized they were poor because their home was filled with purpose and compassion. That mindset shaped him into a leader.

The truth is: **self-pity drains your power. Helping others restores it.**

People who only think about themselves are rarely happy. But people who choose kindness, gratitude, and generosity tend to be strong, joyful, and mentally resilient.

Even suffering can be productive—if you choose to face it with a good attitude and use it as fuel to do good. You'll come out stronger, wiser, and more compassionate.

So, here's the question:
How do *you* handle suffering?
Which path do you want to take—the one that leads to bitterness, or the one that builds character and strength? It's important for us as parents to be role models for our children.

How to Help Your Teen Boost Their Own Mental Health

One of the most powerful gifts we can give our teens is the ability to care for their own mental well-being. This section is designed to help you guide your teen toward habits that nurture positivity, resilience, and emotional strength so they can live a happy and healthy life from the inside out.

1. Cultivate Positive Emotions

Positive emotions don't just feel good—they're essential for mental health. Studies show that people thrive when they experience at least three positive emotions for every negative one.

Help your teen build positive habits by encouraging them to:

- Celebrate small wins each day
- Notice what's going well
- Watch or listen to something uplifting
- Practice smiling or laughing more (yes, really—it helps!)

2. Focus on Others, Not Just Themselves

Teens who regularly think about how they can encourage, compliment, or support others tend to feel more fulfilled and confident. Seeing others succeed in what they do is often threatening to mentally unhealthy people, but a part of having a mentally healthy mind is to congratulate others for their good grades, success in sports, music, or other endeavors. "It is more blessed to give than to receive," and the truth in it is that when we give compliments, encouragement, or help someone who is in trouble, a feeling of contentment and joy grows in us.

What you can encourage:

- Give honest compliments to friends
- Congratulate classmates on their successes
- Help someone who looks lonely or left out
- Volunteer or do something kind anonymously

3. Practice Gratitude

Grateful teens are happier teens. When we look for the good, our brain starts to rewire itself to notice more of it.

What you can try together:

- Start a shared gratitude journal
- Name three things you're thankful for at dinner each night
- Send a quick thank-you text to someone who made your day

4. Stay Busy With Purpose

Being engaged in meaningful activities helps reduce anxiety and boredom, and it gives teens a sense of identity and community.

Encourage your teen to:

- Join a club or team at school
- Try a new hobby or creative outlet
- Get a part-time job or do community service

5. Be Inclusive and Kind

Mental wellness grows in connection. Encourage your teen to look out for others who feel left out or disconnected and take the initiative to include them.

Try asking:

- "Did you notice anyone sitting alone today?"
- "Is there someone you could invite to join your group this week?"

6. Choose Attitude Over Circumstance

There are things in life we can't control, like family situations or physical appearance, but we can choose our attitude. Help your teen see that how they respond matters more than what happens to them.

Say this:

- "We can't change everything, but we can choose how we think about it."
- "Your mindset is your superpower."

7. Forgive to Feel Free

Finally, one of the biggest areas that brings on misery and mental distress is the inability to forgive. Hating others and refusing to forgive is like drinking poison and hoping your enemy dies. Forgiveness is freedom! Anger and unforgiveness are two of the major causes that lead people down the road to mental and physical problems. Too many people's lives have been ruined by hanging on to the ways they have been hurt instead of forgiving and moving on. This is one of the greatest secrets of achieving a happy life and being mentally healthy. One of the greatest blocks to happiness is holding on to anger. Help your teen understand that forgiveness isn't about saying something was okay; it's about setting yourself free.

What to say:

- "Forgiveness doesn't excuse what they did. It just means you're not carrying it anymore."
- "Letting go of resentment gives you peace."

Final Reminder

Happiness and mental strength aren't about having a perfect life—they're about choosing to take positive, consistent steps every day. When teens choose kindness, gratitude, purpose, and forgiveness, they don't just improve their mental health—they build a life they can feel proud of.

 **Action Steps**

1. Shift the Focus: Help Someone Else

When you're feeling overwhelmed, lonely, or discouraged, the fastest way to feel better is to get your eyes off yourself. Help someone else. This doesn't have to be a grand gesture—sometimes it's as simple as holding a door, helping a classmate, or sending a kind message. When we serve others, it lifts our mood, gives us purpose, and reminds us that we are needed. Helping others helps you, too.

2. Replace "Why Me?" with "What Now?"

Life will throw challenges your way. Instead of getting stuck asking, "Why is this happening to me?", practice shifting your mindset to "What can I do now?" or "How can I grow from this?" This small change rewires your brain to look for solutions and growth rather than staying in frustration. It's a mindset that builds resilience, strength, and confidence.

3. Practice Daily Gratitude and Purposeful Action

Mental health grows with consistency. Each day, take two minutes to write or say out loud one thing you're thankful for and one small thing you'll do to move forward. Gratitude trains your brain to look for the good, and purposeful action gives you momentum. These little moments add up to big emotional wins over time.

Activities:

Go over the top stressors with your kids. Ask them which ones bring them the most stress. They can also add to the list. Next, ask them some specific ways they can manage their stress.

TOP STRESSORS for adolescents and teenagers:

→ **School**
- Exams, grades, papers, projects
- Different routines, procedures, teachers
- Transitions
- Parental expectations

→ **Homelife**
- Parental expectations
- Abuse
- Separation/Divorce
- Alcohol
- Financial problems
- Unemployment
- Sibling with special needs
- Health issue of self or family member; death in the family

- → **Social stress**
  - Peer pressure: alcohol, drugs, sex, risky behaviors
  - Toxic friendships
  - Romantic relationships
  - Bullying

- → **Self-esteem**
  - Body image
  - Negative thoughts about self
  - Changing body

- → **Lack of safety**
  - Neighborhood
  - Home

- → **Sexuality (LGBTQ)**
- → **Sports/Activities**
- → **Social Media**
  - Cyberbullying
  - Likes=Popularity
  - Inappropriate content
  - Less face-to-face, fewer close relationships

- → **Time Management**
- → **Moving/Changing schools**
- → **Future**

Table Talk:

- **What are some things that help you feel calm or happy when you're having a tough day?**
  (This helps identify healthy coping strategies.)

- **Do you ever feel pressure to act like everything's okay, even when it's not? Why do you think that is?**

  (This opens the door to discussing emotional honesty and normalizing vulnerability.)

- **Who is someone you feel safe talking to when you're feeling overwhelmed or stressed?**

  (This encourages kids to recognize their support system and use it.)

- **What would you do if you knew someone was having mental health issues?**

  (This encourages kids to recognize symptoms and know how to help.)

Let's Wrap It Up

I hope you've found the insights in this book helpful as you navigate the incredible, challenging, and rewarding journey of parenting. My hope is that you've been able to use these ideas to strengthen the lines of communication with your children, fostering deeper relationships and lasting connections. Parenting isn't about perfection—it's about progress, intention, and loving them unconditionally every step of the way. If this book has encouraged even one more meaningful conversation with your child, then it's done its job.

As parents, we all want our kids to grow into respectful, responsible, resilient, and resourceful adults. But that doesn't happen by chance—it happens through thoughtful guidance, consistent communication, and the willingness to let them grow through both their successes and their struggles. In this final chapter, we'll dive deeper into why open dialogue and embracing failure are two of the most powerful tools we have as parents.

One of the most important gifts we can give our children is the freedom to talk to us about anything, without fear of judgment or punishment. Open communication builds trust, creating a safe space where kids feel comfortable sharing both their victories and their struggles. When children know that they can come to us with anything, we become their anchor through life's highs and lows.

But open communication isn't just about talking; it's about truly listening. It's about hearing what's said—and what's left unsaid—and responding with empathy and understanding. When parents consistently model this kind of connection, kids learn that their voice matters, building their confidence and emotional intelligence.

Equally essential is the willingness to let our children fail. While it's natural to want to protect them from pain and disappointment, shielding them from failure robs them of invaluable life lessons. Failure, especially in their younger years, is an opportunity for growth. It teaches resilience, problem-solving, and humility. It allows kids to see that mistakes aren't the end of the road—they're a stepping stone to success.

When we guide our children through their failures with kindness, wisdom, and unconditional love, we equip them with tools to navigate life's inevitable challenges. They learn to reflect, adapt, and persevere. More importantly, they understand that their worth isn't tied to their successes or failures, but to who they are at their core.

By fostering open dialogue and allowing space for failure, we prepare our kids not just to survive the world, but to thrive in it. We teach them to be honest, compassionate, and resilient leaders who approach life with curiosity and courage. And in doing so, we strengthen the most important connection of all: the one between parent and child.

As a parent of four children now in their mid-20s and early 30s, I've seen firsthand how different personalities come with their own unique struggles and successes. Over my 31 years of parenting, there have been highs and lows, but the one constant has been open dialogue, communication, and most importantly, unconditional love. This foundation has kept our relationships strong, and even now, my children continue to come to us for advice. Maintaining these close relationships is a testament to the power of connection and the lasting impact of open, honest communication.

One of the most effective strategies I've found is to frontload our kids with the tools, values, and skills they need before challenges arise. This proactive approach is far more powerful than reactive parenting, where guidance only comes after something has gone wrong. When we frontload our children with knowledge about empathy, boundaries, failure, and resilience, they're better prepared to navigate life's inevitable bumps. They're not scrambling for answers in a crisis—they already have a foundation of wisdom to draw from.

This preparation empowers them to make thoughtful choices and handle challenges with confidence.

Throughout my parenting journey, I've also emphasized four non-negotiable values: respect, responsibility, resourcefulness, and resilience. These pillars have guided my children through every stage of life:

- **Respect** isn't just about manners or following rules—it's about valuing themselves, others, and the world around them. It's such an important character trait to learn early on and will take them far with their parents, teachers, coaches, and future bosses.
- **Responsibility** instills accountability. It helps kids understand that their actions have consequences for themselves and others, both positive and negative. By learning to take ownership of their decisions, they become dependable and self-aware adults.
- **Resourcefulness** encourages problem-solving and adaptability. Life rarely follows a straight path, and teaching kids to think creatively, seek solutions, and persevere through challenges equips them to thrive in any situation. Give them the opportunity to be creative and to "figure it out"!
- **Resilience** builds emotional strength and perseverance. It empowers kids to bounce back from setbacks, adapt to change, and approach life's challenges with courage and determination.

These core values, combined with open dialogue and a proactive approach to parenting, will help shape your children into thoughtful, loving, resilient, and capable adults who enjoy serving others. And that, ultimately, is what parenting is all about—raising humans who can navigate the world with confidence, integrity, and heart.

Every morning, before I even set foot out of bed, I take a moment to pray for each of my four adult children. It's a habit I've practiced since day one. With four children, there's almost nothing that we haven't experienced. There is always something on my heart—whether it's an illness, a behavior challenge, a sibling rivalry, a friendship issue, a disappointment, or simply my own peace of mind! Parenting comes with its share of mountains and valleys, and these quiet moments of prayer help me stay grounded and intentional.

Remember this: We can't always control the choices our kids make—especially once they're adults. But what we *can* control is how we choose to respond to those choices.

Through it all, I've learned that one of the most powerful things we can do as parents is to pray and to reach the heart of our children. Because true, lasting change doesn't happen on the surface—it happens in the heart. And that's where the real transformation begins.

About the Author

Andria Owen is the youngest of five siblings, married to the love of her life, Dom, and proud mom of four—three boys and one girl—all born within six busy years. A competitive tennis player, former collegiate cheerleader and diver, Andria brings her boundless energy into everything she does, whether it's parenting, business, or enjoying the outdoors with her family (and their beloved dogs).

As a realtor, interior designer, and CEO of TUF Life Skills, Andria has dedicated the past decade to empowering youth through 25 life skills courses, now used in schools and youth agencies nationwide. Her passion for helping kids thrive has led her to serve on numerous boards focused on youth development.

In her book, Connection Over Perfection, Andria draws from her personal journey, her experience as a mom in a highly competitive (and fun-loving) family, and her deep belief in the power of intentional parenting. She credits her own parents for the unconditional love and wisdom they instilled in her— lessons that continue to inspire her mission of helping families connect, grow, and lead with purpose.

Take the Next Step

Turn Connection Into Real Change

Now that you've read *Connection Over Perfection*, don't stop there! **Put it into action**.

Go to www.AndriaOwen.com to purchase the TUF Workbooks

- Designed for kids ages 11 and up
- Fun, practical, and rooted in strong values
- Perfect as a stand-alone resource OR with an Instructor's Guide

Bring TUF Life Skills to Schools & Teams

Want to make an even greater impact? Bring the complete TUF Life Skills program to your child's school, sports team, or youth group.

TUF transforms school culture by:

- Positively impacting climate
- Strengthening student–teacher relationships
- Equipping kids with essential social & emotional skills

Because here's the truth: **You can't have influence without connection. Real influence starts with real connection.**

Get Involved

Visit: www.getTUF.com
Contact: info@trainupfirst.com

Let's raise up a generation of connected, confident kids together.

For the Student (ages 11 +)

"TUF Life Skills is a new current version of social, emotional curriculum for teenagers. This cutting edge platform grabs the attention of all students, including the most reluctant learner. Students are engaged in real-world content and are building their toolbox for the future. Their menu of topics allows schools to customize their approach while meeting students' needs. If you are looking to develop well rounded students, look no further."

— Shay McRae, Area Superintendent, Hillsborough County Schools

For the Student-Athlete (ages 11 +)

"TUF is a proven product to teach today's students the life skills they need to achieve success and to escape the epidemic of bad choices and bad behavior that are destroying our campuses and communities. I believe every student should take TUF to learn the skills that they'll use for the rest of their lives... Let's change the culture of today's youth."

— Tony Dungy, Super Bowl Champion, Hall of Fame NFL Coach

Available everywhere books are sold.

www.ingramcontent.com/pod-product-compliance
Lightning Source LLC
Chambersburg PA
CBHW071708120626
46550CB00001B/151